D0520426

The History of a Town

M. E. SALTYKOV-SHCHEDRIN

The History of a Town

Translated by I. P. FOOTE

WILLEM A. MEEUWS *Publisher*
Oxford 1980

Published by
WILLEM A. MEEUWS
15 North Parade Avenue, Oxford OX2 6LX

© I. P. Foote 1980

ISBN 0 902672 39 8

Printed in England by
Skelton's Press Limited
Wellingborough, Northamptonshire

CONTENTS

Introduction

THE author of *The History of a Town* is little known to the English reader. Outside his own country Saltykov's reputation rests almost entirely on his novel *The Golovlev Family*, a powerful and gloomy account of the decline of a landowning family in the mid-nineteenth century. Few English readers know Saltykov for what he was in fact – the most penetrating satirist Russia has ever produced, one of the great comic writers in Russian literature, and a commentator on his own society of such serious historical interest that Maxim Gorky could claim that 'without Saltykov it is impossible to understand the history of Russia in the second half of the nineteenth century'. This translation of *The History of a Town* has been made to introduce to the English reader a work which reveals Saltykov's qualities as a comic and satirical writer and offers also an important and instructive analysis of the political history and mentality of Russia.

Saltykov was born in 1826, the son of a landowning family, and he died in 1889. The first half of his adult life he worked in the government service (seven years of it in an 'exile' posting in Vyatka) and he occupied a number of important posts in various provincial administrations. The last twenty years of his life he was a full-time writer and journalist, for sixteen of them with the leading radical journal of the time *Otechestvennye zapiski (Notes of the Fatherland)*. Saltykov's main literary work was done in a period that roughly coincided with the reign of Alexander II (1855–81), a key period in the modern history of Russia, which began with reforms (notably the emancipation of the serfs in 1861) and ended in reaction in the face of increasing revolutionary activity. It was Alexander's reign, coming after thirty years of stagnation under Nicholas I, that released the political and social forces which were to shape the course of Russia to revolution in 1917. In his sketches and stories, written between 1856 and 1889 under the pen-name 'Shchedrin', Saltykov gave a perceptive and detailed commentary on the changing situation of these times. His analysis was fundamental. He probed to the very depths of Russian life and put his finger on truths about Russia and the Russian character which explained the evils of his own day and, at the same time, are of lasting relevance for an understanding of Russia, past and present. Certainly, much of what he wrote is now dated and remote to the modern reader, Russian or foreign ('the dusty polemics of forgotten wrongs and abandoned causes' in the phrase of an English reviewer of the 1930s), yet at the same time there are few writers who can be so profitably read by anyone wishing to come to terms with the peculiarities of the people and of the history of Russia.

At different times and with different emphasis Saltykov concerned himself in his satires with three major themes: (i) the effects of the reforms of the 1860s on Russian society (the decline of the landowning gentry, the continuing misery of the peasants, the emergence of new 'pillars' of society – capitalists, merchants, and prosperous peasant-proprietors (*kulaks*); (ii) the ineffectuality in contemporary Russian political life of moderate policies, manifest in the reforms themselves and in the feeble conforming nature of post-reform liberalism; and (iii) what is of greatest general significance – the relationship between authority and the subject in Russia. In his treatment of these themes Saltykov was first of all passing judgement on the period in which he wrote, expressing the view that despite the reforms undertaken by Alexander II there was no fundamental change in Russian life. The social miseries continued, unaffected by palliative measures; the peasants, no longer the property of the landowners, were now preyed on by upstart rural capitalists and *kulaks*, and, as ever, remained victims of their own backwardness and ignorance. In administration the attitudes and standards of post-reform officialdom were essentially the same as before, and the basic fact of Russian life was still that of the all-powerful tyranny of authority over the uncomprehending, subservient mass of the population.

It is with this question of authority and its relation to the people that *The History of a Town* is chiefly concerned, and in it we find the most striking and coherent statement of Saltykov's view of this problem in Russia.

The work was written in 1869–70 and first appeared in serial form in *Notes of the Fatherland*, the journal of which Saltykov was then joint-editor. *The History of a Town* consists of episodes from the mock-chronicle of the town of Glupov (the name is derived from the Russian word *glupy* 'stupid', hence 'Stupidtown'), a town which is symbolic of the whole Russian Empire. First, in a chapter parodying the style and content of the old Russian chronicles, Saltykov describes the early history of the 'Glupovites' and then in a series of chapters he traces the actions and policies of the town-governors who ruled the town in the period covered by the chronicle (1731–1825). Here the author makes the central point of the satire, showing that however varied over the years the policies of individual town-governors have been, there has never been any real difference between them as rulers, because they are united in their basic policy – which is the suppression of the population of Glupov. As Saltykov, in his role as 'editor' of the chronicle, points out in his *Preface: all* the town-governors flog the inhabitants, even though the principles on which they do so may differ. For the town-governors the citizens are permanent victims, fit only to be governed and to obey, with duties but no rights, always guilty of something and due for punishment. Any act of the administration is never for, but always against the inhabitants. Consequently, the inhabitants enjoy relative happiness and well-being only in times of particularly idle or incompetent governors, whose acts of administration are rare or non-existent. The inhabitants' attitude to authority perfectly complements the official attitude towards them. For them the authorities are an all-powerful, incomprehensible, extraneous force, to which they can only submit. They accept all the official premises about their own status and seek only to ease the discomforts they suffer from the governors by a ready compliance and subservience. Extreme events may occasionally cause them to protest, but when they do protest it is not from a conscious desire to enjoy the rights and dignity of free human beings, but merely from a physical urge to escape some particularly intolerable imposition of the authorities. There is a nice irony in the scene described in the chapter 'Wars of Enlightenment', when the Glupovites assemble in protest before the town-governor's residence – *on their knees.*

As far as the Russian administrative system is concerned, Saltykov's point is clearly made – that, whatever the name the system bears, it is and always has been tyrannical and oppressive. In a narrow contemporary context *The History of a Town*, written at the end of the Reform decade, was asserting that reformed Russia was no different from unreformed Russia. In a wider context the characterization of Russian official administration and its relationship to the inhabitants of Glupov-Russia has a significance valid for the whole modern period of Russia's history.

The national significance of Saltykov's Glupov is made perfectly clear by the material on which he draws for the town's history. The period covered by the chronicle is stated to be 1731–1825, and in the persons and actions of the town-governors there are many echoes of historical figures from the corresponding period of Russian history – emperors, empresses, ministers, and others. In the earlier part of the book the connection between the satire and history is mostly of a general nature and relates to the period as a whole rather than to specific events and characters. Thus the account of the six town-governesses and their struggle for power recalls the general situation of the eighteenth century when, after the death of Peter the Great, Russia was ruled almost continuously for some seventy years by empresses (Catherine I, Anne, Elizabeth, Catherine (II) the Great), whose rise to power (as in the case of the town- governesses) had involved a variety of intrigues and coups. Some personal hints might be traced in individual town-governesses – for instance, the Empress Elizabeth, daughter of Peter the Great, may be suggested by 'Klemantinka de Bourbon', herself a 'town-governor's daughter'; and there is an obvious suggestion of Catherine the Great, a former princess of Anhalt-Zerbst, in the 'fat German' Amalya Stockfisch. There are clearer echoes of particular facts of history in the careers of the town-governors Ferdyshchenko and Borodavkin: Ferdyshchenko's absurd ceremonial journey across the town common and Borodavkin's Byzantine aspirations are a reflection of the celebrated progress of Potemkin and of the aims of his belligerent policy against the Turks. In the passing figure of Negodyaev, the governor who had been formerly a 'stoker at Gatchina', there is a clearly intended allusion to the Emperor Paul, who had his residence there.

It is, though, in the final three chapters of the book that Saltykov makes most evident use of actual historical material – in the careers of the governors Benevolensky, Grustilov, and Ugryum-Burcheev. The inspiration of Benevolensky, the law-maker, can be clearly seen in Alexander I's adviser M. M. Speransky (mentioned in the book as Benevolensky's school-fellow), who was responsible for drafting legal and constitutional reforms in the early years of Alexander's reign. In the character and career of Grustilov there is a damaging parallel to Alexander I himself. In particular, the transformation of Alexander from a liberal-minded ruler into a reactionary mystic is reflected in Grustilov's turning from light-hearted pleasure-seeking to religious fanaticism and mystical orgies. Ugryum-Burcheev, the last governor described in the book, can also be readily related to an historical prototype, in this case Count Arakcheev, the minister who played a dominant part in the reactionary policies which characterized the last years of Alexander I's reign. The lunatic scheme of Ugryum-Burcheev to turn Glupov into a military camp recalls the ill-famed settlements introduced under Arakcheev's direction, in which certain areas of Russia were turned into military colonies with the peasants organized as army units.

Such are a few of the major historical references suggested by *The History of a Town*. Saltykov's purpose, however, was not to indulge in historical portrait-painting. He did not intend Benevolensky to *be* Speransky, nor Grustilov to *be* Alexander I. He was simply making use of material provided by such historical figures as ammunition in his attack on the whole state system of Russia.

We are fortunate in having Saltykov's own account of his aims in writing the satire. With few exceptions, contemporary critics saw the work merely as a parody of Russian history of the eighteenth and early nineteenth centuries and failed to see its implications for the situation of Russia in their own time. A. S. Suvorin took this line in his review of the satire in *Vestnik Evropy* (*The European Herald*). He criticized Saltykov for 'omitting' certain events of the period in question and also condemned him for his mocking denigration of the Russian people in the work. In answer to Suvorin's review Saltykov wrote two letters (to the editors of *The European Herald* and to A. N. Pypin), in which he stated the purpose of the satire. His intention, he explained, was not to write a parody of Russian history, but to point out the basic evils of the Russian state system, evils which had existed in the past and continued in his own day. It was with their contemporary manifestation that he was concerned. The past was incidental; the Glupov chronicle with its description of events in the eighteenth and early nineteenth centuries was merely a convenient form,* in which to express his view of the Russian situation in the time he

---

* 'Convenient', that is, not only for the material it offered, but chiefly as a means to avoid objections from the censors. The device succeeded very well and in publishing the work no serious difficulty from the censor was encountered. The report on the early chapters by the censor N. E. Lebedev states: 'In this satirical sketch the provincial administration is ridiculed; its failures, weaknesses, and ineptitude are exposed in rather general terms, so that it is difficult to relate it to any particular place .... The fabulous nature of the descriptions offer still less ground for taking proceedings against the author for any intention to insult authority or its representatives ....'

wrote. 'What I had in mind', he explained, 'was not an "historical" satire, but a perfectly ordinary satire aimed at those features of Russian life which make it not altogether comfortable.' At the same time he rejected Suvorin's criticism of his treatment of the Russian people, indicating that his account of their passivity was historically accurate, though little blame could be attached to them, if one took into account the unrelenting repressiveness of those who governed them (he referred to his sympathetic justification of the Glupovites at the beginning of the chapter 'The Worship of Mammon – and Repentance').

Saltykov's target then was Russia, not Russia's past, and indeed it took an insensitive and unsympathetic critic to view it narrowly as an attack on a distant period of history, for Saltykov treats the purported period of the chronicle with extravagant elasticity, incongruously mixing material from different epochs: references to the eighteenth century stand side by side with references to Saltykov's own day – revolutionary émigrés in London, the telegraph, the railway boom, restaurants and entertainers in St. Petersburg, journals and works of literary opponents, and so on – all of which, besides being part of the comic fantasy of the book, emphasize that Saltykov was seeing across the span of Russian history and presenting a distillation of the whole modern period. If in the hundred years since *The History of a Town* was written it has dated, then it has dated only in the details of its composition, not in its substance. Particularly in the culminating chapter, which describes Ugryum-Burcheev's reorganization of Glupov and his dehumanization of man for the sake of an administrative ideal, there is an all too close relation to the development of the totalitarian state in the twentieth century. In this prescient sketch of humanity being destroyed by the power of the state one can see a direct forerunner of such modern fantasies on this theme as those of Orwell and Zamyatin.

Since its publication *The History of a Town* has remained one of the most popular of Saltykov's works. Interest in his works, which were so much concerned with contemporary events, declined after his death in 1889, and it was only seriously revived with the celebration of the centenary of his birth in 1926. From the 1930s, when Saltykov was identified by Soviet literary historians as a representative of 'revolutionary democracy', he has been the object of much detailed and valuable research and his works have been frequently republished. There have been many editions of *The History of a Town*. It is highly regarded as a masterly denunciation of tsarist Russia – its twentieth-century implications have, perhaps not surprisingly, been overlooked (though not necessarily by its readers). The only serious disagreement about the work itself has centred on the ending, and a word might be said about this. In the final chapter Ugryum-Burcheev forces the inhabitants to destroy the old town of Glupov and build a new one according to his ideal of the straight line; at last, in a moment of dimly awakening consciousness, even the long-suffering Glupovites are moved to revolt – or so we are led to presume by the sketchy details of the, at this point, 'fragmentary' chronicle. A period of confusion ensues, which is finally resolved by an awesome 'storm', which descends on the town and carries off Ugryum-Burcheev before the eyes of the terrified Glupovites. Saltykov quotes the chronicler as saying that at this point 'history ceased its course'. Two interpretations of this have been put forward: one, that in the 'storm' Saltykov was presenting a symbol of revolution or some other cleansing force, which would one day end the history of the old order represented by Glupov; the other, continuing the historical parallels of the final chapters, suggests that the dread 'it', which removes the town-governor and strikes terror into the Glupovites, is a symbolic representation of Nicholas I, whose accession in 1825 (the stated period of Ugryum-Burcheev's rule) coincided with the abortive revolt of the Decembrists.* The first interpretation has been urged by the majority of Soviet commentators on the satire, but not by all, and recently support for the alternative interpretation has been more evident. No final answer to this question can be given, though in the opinion of the present writer evidence in the text points rather to the second explanation than to the first. In either case, the ending is effective – and, in its elusive ambiguity, typically Saltykovian.

Saltykov is one of the great humorous writers of Russia. Significantly, his humour, for all its exuberance, is never gratuitous, but always directed at some clear target. *The History of a Town* is full of extravagant comic effects. There are the paradoxes of the town-governors whose most brilliant successes are achieved against the town itself – Urus-Kugush-Kildibaev, who takes Glupov by storm, and Borodavkin, who wages 'wars of enlightenment'

---

* The Decembrist rising took place in St. Petersburg on 14 December 1825 in the confused situation following the death of Alexander I. The conspirators – mostly young army officers – sought to secure major constitutional and social changes and they and the troops under their command refused to take the oath of loyalty to the new tsar (Nicholas I). The conspiracy was promptly crushed, and of the conspirators five were hanged and over 100 exiled to Siberia.

(*against* the Glupovites) to bring about the introduction of mustard. The wild anachronisms that occur have been mentioned already: typically, they make a point – of the timelessness of the satire – while at the same time being funny. Instances of authorial irony and sarcasm abound. Parody figures prominently: the chronicle of Glupov imitates the Russian chronicles, Saltykov's commentary parodies the manner of learned editors, Russian legal and official documents are parodied in statutes and memoranda concerning 'the proper baking of pies', 'the agreeable outward aspect of town-governors', and so on. In particular, fantasy is used as a major device to demonstrate the absurdity and frivolity of the Russian state system: there is a governor who flies in the air, another so tall that he snaps in two during a gale, there is the automaton governor, whose head contains a music-box, and the lax governor Pryshch, whose head (stuffed with truffles) is devoured by a colleague. These and other fantastic events are not mere grotesque exaggerations. Saltykov pointed out elsewhere that life is no less fantastic than invention, and that fantasy is capable of exposing the actual nature of things, which is normally concealed beneath the semblances of everyday life: his picture of Glupov is, he would claim, no distortion of reality, but merely a revelation of its essential quality.

However engaging his humour, it cannot be denied that Saltykov is by ordinary standards a difficult writer, and though, in comparison with most of his writings, *The History of a Town* is one of his easier works, it is written in a style and idiom which may well seem heavy to modern readers. Because of the restrictions imposed by the censorship, in his satirical works Saltykov cultivated a style that was deliberately obscure in which to express his unpalatable truths. This 'aesopic' style involved the use of heavy, complex, and allusive prose and a whole system of innocent-sounding formulae used in place of words which were taboo as far as the censors were concerned. The reader of Saltykov has to break through this barrier, and the task is obviously much more difficult for a modern foreign reader than for Saltykov's Russian contemporary, who was schooled in the conventions of his style and equipped to understand the local and topical references in which his works abound. The problem of how best to present a translation of *The History of a Town* for a non-specialist foreign reader is considerable. A full commentary clarifying all the hints and allusions contained in the book, however desirable, would be so long that it would be more likely to act as a deterrent than an aid to the reader (the best Russian edition of the text, in the recent

Collected Works of Saltykov, has a commentary of sixty pages). I have followed what seems to me the most practical course in the circumstances and have provided notes explaining the more important historical and literary references and giving help where it seems most needed.

Although this is the first English translation of *The History of a Town*, the book has already in a small way an English 'past'. Soon after its publication Turgenev wrote a review of it (in English) for the London journal *The Academy* (issue of 1 March 1871). Turgenev greatly admired Saltykov and in his review paid tribute to his satirical genius and, particularly, to his profound knowledge of Russian life, declaring that 'he knows his own country better than any man living'. He strongly recommended the book to 'lovers of humour and satirical *verve*' and, significantly, to future historians of Russia. For the prospective English translator – or reader – Turgenev offered not much comfort: his view was that the book 'could not well be translated in its entirety . . . , nor . . . be understood or appreciated by a Western public'. The present translator would have little quarrel with Turgenev's statement on the difficulties of translation, and although an entire translation has been done the resulting English version is readily acknowledged as a pale shadow of the Russian. In part this paleness is the result of a deliberate attempt to ease and clarify for the modern reader the style of the original, but much more is it due to the practical difficulties of matching in English Saltykov's robust, idiomatic, and richly allusive language. As for Turgenev's claim of the work's incomprehensibility to a Western public – one can only hope that the reader will put it to the test and find Turgenev wrong.

I. P. FOOTE

The History of a Town

edited from original documents by

M. E. SALTYKOV (SHCHEDRIN)

Notes printed at the foot of the page are the author's; the translator's notes (which have number references) are printed at the end of the book.

Preface

I have long had the intention of writing the history of some town
or district in a particular period of its development, but various
circumstances have prevented me. The main difficulty has been
the lack of any material which might be regarded as at all reliable
or convincing. But recently, while browsing in the archives of the
town of Glupov, I came across a sizeable bundle of copy-books,
tied together, and entitled 'The Chronicle of Glupov'. When I
examined them, I saw that they could help me considerably in the
fulfilment of my intention. The contents of the chronicle are all
much of a sort, consisting of biographies of the town-governors
who, for the greater part of a century, ruled over the destinies of
Glupov, and of a description of their most notable actions – such
as their furious driving of the post-horses, their energy in collecting arrears of taxes, their campaigns against the town's inhabitants, the construction and destruction of roads, the exaction of
tribute from the tax-contractors,[1] and so on. Still, even from these
few facts one can obtain a picture of the town's character and
trace how its history has reflected the various changes in higher
spheres. For example, the town-governors in the time of Biron[2]
were distinguished by their recklessness, those in the time of
Potemkin[3] by their zealous efficiency, and those in the time of
Razumovsky[4] by their unknown provenance and knightly valour.
They all flogged the inhabitants, but the first flogged them pure
and simple, the second explained their zeal by referring to the
needs of civilization, and the third asked only that in all matters
the inhabitants should trust in their valour. This variety of measures could not, of course, fail to have an effect on the inhabitants
themselves. In the first instance, they trembled unconsciously; in
the second, they trembled in consciousness of the benefit they
were receiving; and in the third, they attained to a state of
trembling filled with trust. Even the town-governors' furious
driving of the post-horses had some measure of influence on the

inhabitants, since it fortified their spirits by the example of vigour and indefatigability provided by the horses.

The chronicle was written in turn by four of the town archivists and covers the period from 1731 to 1825. In the latter year literary activity evidently ceased to be permissible even for archivists.[5] The chronicle looks perfectly genuine and there can be no doubt as to its authenticity: its pages are as yellow and covered with spidery writing, as nibbled by mice and spotted by flies as any manuscript in the Pogodin Museum. One can just see some Pimen of the archives[6] sitting over it, working in the trembling flame of a tallow candle, and concealing it as best he can from the inevitable curiosity of Messrs. Shubinsky, Mordovtsev and Melnikov.[7] The chronicle is prefaced by a separate compilation or 'schedule', evidently written by the last chronicler. There are also a few school copy-books which form a supplement of supporting documents. These contain a number of original exercises on various themes relating to administrative theory. For example, there are discourses 'On the administrative unanimity of town-governors', 'On the agreeable outward aspect of town-governors', 'On the salutary quality of punitive expeditions' (illustrated), 'Thoughts on collecting arrears of taxes', 'The perverse trend of the times', and, finally, a fairly long dissertation 'On severity'. One can say with certainty that these exercises belong to the pen of the various town-governors (several of them are actually signed) and they have great value in that, first, they present a faithful picture of the state of Russian orthography at the time they were written, and, secondly, they provide a far more complete, convincing and colourful portrait of their authors than the narratives of the 'Chronicle' itself.

The contents of the 'Chronicle' are largely of a fantastic nature and in parts must strain the credulity of anyone living in our enlightened age. There is, for example, the quite unaccountable story of the town-governor who had a music-box inside him. In one place the 'Chronicle' tells of a town-governor who flew in the air, and in another of a governor whose feet pointed backwards and who nearly ran out of his own gubernatorial territory. However, the editor felt he would not be justified in suppressing these details. On the contrary, he considers the fact that such happenings were possible in the past will demonstrate to the reader even more clearly what a gulf separates us from those times. Moreover, the editor was influenced by the fact that the fantastic nature of these stories detracts nothing from their significance as an instruction in administrative principles, and that those administrators

4

of our own time who wish to avoid premature dismissal can take warning from the governor who flew in the air.

To forestall any malicious comment, the editor feels obliged to say that his only part in this matter has been to modify the heavy, old-fashioned style of the 'Chronicle' and to exercise some control over the orthography, without interfering in any way with the actual contents of the chronicle. Throughout the course of his work the editor has been conscious of the stern figure of Mikhail Petrovich Pogodin[8] standing over him, and this alone can be taken as an assurance of the trembling and awe with which he approached his task.

Address to the Reader
from the last Chronicler*

IF it was permitted to the ancient Hellenes and Romans to exalt their godless masters and to transmit their abominable deeds to posterity for its instruction, then can it be that we, who are Christians and have received the light from Byzantium, will in such matter be less fitted and less grateful than they? In all lands there will be found Neros, full of renown, and Caligulas, shining with glory,† and can it be that only in our country none such are to be found? It is folly and nonsense to think such a thing, still more to proclaim it aloud, as do some free-thinkers, who fancy their thoughts to be free because they fly freely through their heads, like flies with no place to settle.

Not only every country, but every town and smallest village has, as it must, its own Achilles, shining with glory, set in authority by the powers above. Take the first puddle you come upon. Regard it. Even there you will find one creature which in its heroic qualities excels and overshadows all its fellows. Observe a tree. There too you will see there is one branch which is bigger and stronger and thus more glorious than the others. And, finally, regard your own person. There you will first perceive your head, and then take cognizance of your belly and other parts. Which do you think more glorious: your head, which, light though its filling, none the less strives upwards? or your belly, striving downwards, fitted only for the preparation of noisome excrement? Oh, truly thoughtless is this, your free-thinking!

* This 'Address' is printed in the exact words of the chronicler. The editor has only ventured to ensure that the rules for using the letters s and ſ were not infringed with too much liberty.

† In describing the qualities of these historical personages, the chronicler was evidently unaware even of information given in school text-books. Stranger still, he was not even familiar with Derzhavin's lines:

> 'Caligula! Though gold-clad, thy steed
> On the Senate floor shone dull indeed:
> Good deeds alone shine bright!'

Such were the thoughts which prompted me, the humble archivist of the town (paid two roubles a month, but none the less inclined to sing praises), together with my three predecessors, to sing with unsullied lips the praises of those glorious Neros,* who have wondrously graced the celebrated town of Glupov, not by godlessness and the false philosophy of the Hellenes but by firmness and by such boldness as befits those in authority. Not possessing the gift of versification, we decided against the use of song, and, trusting in God's mercy, set forth these worthy deeds in language which, though unworthy, is natural to us, avoiding only profanities. Yet do I think that we shall be excused this bold undertaking in view of the special purpose we had in beginning it.

This purpose was to portray in turn the governors who have at different times been appointed to the town of Glupov by the Imperial Government of Russia. But, undertaking to treat of such important matter, more than once did I ask myself if my strength were equal to such a task. Many of these men of signal and prodigious endeavour have I seen in my time, and many too have my predecessors seen. Altogether there have been twenty-two governors, succeeding one another in stately and unbroken line, but for the disastrous seven days when there was no governor at all and the town was well nigh brought to a state of desolation. Some governors have sped like a fierce flame, purging and renewing; others have been like a babbling brook, watering the meadows and pastures, leaving fierceness and destruction to be supplied by their chief officials. But all of them, fierce and gentle alike, are gratefully remembered in the hearts of their fellow-citizens, for they have all been governors of the town. In the face of this moving relationship the chronicler is at a loss as to which he should extol the more – authority manifesting its proper measure of zeal? or this vine its proper measure of gratitude?

On the other hand, this same relationship serves in no small way to lighten the task of the chronicler. What, after all, does his task consist in? Is it to criticize and censure? No. Is it to reason? No. What then is it? It is, oh thoughtless free-thinker, simply to describe this relationship and present the facts of it for the edification of posterity.

In this form, the task we have undertaken is within the powers of the humblest of the humble, for he himself is but the earthen vessel containing the meed of praise which is to be poured forth in abundance. And the more common the clay of which the vessel is

* Again the same regrettable error.

made, the more fine and pleasing to the taste appears that sweet potion of praise which it contains. And the earthen vessel will say to itself: See, even I am fit for something, even on two copper roubles a month!

Having set forth this much in my own justification, I must add that our native town of Glupov carries on an extensive trade in *kvass*,[9] liver, and boiled eggs, it has three rivers and is built, like Rome of old, on seven hills, where in icy weather a great many carriages come to grief and countless horses are lamed. The only difference is that in Rome there flourished impiety, while in Glupov has flourished piety; Rome was infected with turbulence, Glupov – with meekness; in Rome the plebeians ran riot, in Glupov it has been the authorities.

And this more I will say: this chronicle was written in turn by four archivists: Mishka Tryapichkin, Mishka Tryapichkin (the second), Mitka Smirnomordov, and I, the humble Pavlushka Masloboinikov. In which task we have had but one fear — that our note-books might fall into the hands of Master Bartenev and be printed by him in his 'Archives'.[10] Then, glory be to God, and an end to my prating.

Concerning the Origin
of the Glupovites[11]

'NOR do I wish, as Kostomarov,[12] to scour over the earth like the grey wolf, nor, as Solovev,[13] to spread my wings under the clouds like the blue-grey eagle, nor, as Pypin,[14] to wander in fancy over the trees, but I wish to sing of the Glupovites, most cherished by me, and reveal to the world their glorious deeds, and that most excellent root from which this famous tree has sprung and spread its branches over the whole earth.'*

This is how the chronicler begins, then, after a few remarks in praise of his own modesty, he goes on:

There was in olden times a people called the Headbeaters, and they lived in the far north, in that region where the Greek and Roman historians thought the Hyperborean Sea to be. These people were called Headbeaters, because it was their habit to beat their heads against anything that came in their way. If they came to a wall, they beat their heads against it; if they wished to pray, they beat their heads against the floor. There were many independent tribes living in proximity to the Headbeaters, but the chronicler names only the most notable of them: the Walrus-eaters, the Onion-eaters, the Slop-eaters, the Cranberries, the Boobies, the Runner-beans, the Frog-folk, the Bast-shoes, the Black-mouths, the Cudgellers, the Cracked-heads, the Born-blinds, the Lip-smackers, the Lop-ears, the Pot-bellies, the Whitefish, the Corner-peepers, the Hash-eaters and the Dunder-heads. These tribes knew nothing of religion or government, and spent their whole time in warring against each other. They were constantly making alliances, declaring war, making peace and swearing eternal friendship and trust, and whenever they spoke

---

* The chronicler is here obviously imitating *The Tale of Igor's Campaign*. 'For the seer Boyan, if he wished to make a song in someone's honour, would wander in fancy over the trees, like a grey wolf over the earth, like a blue-grey eagle beneath the clouds.'[15] And further: 'Oh, Boyan! thou nightingale of old! If thou hadst sung of these hosts . . .', etc.

falsely they always added: 'Shame on me', knowing full well that 'Shame never hurt anybody'. In this way they brought desolation to their lands and ruin to their women and maidens, at the same time priding themselves on being kindly, hospitable folk. But when they came to the point of tearing off the last scrap of bark for food from the one remaining pine tree, when the women and maidens were all done for, and their race was doomed to extinction, it was the Headbeaters who first came to their senses. They realized that someone must after all be ruler, so they sent a message to their neighbours, saying: 'Let us beat our heads against yours until one of us outbeats the other'. 'And this they did cunningly,' says the chronicler, 'for they knew that they had strong heads on their shoulders.' And, indeed, no sooner did their simple-minded neighbours agree to this cunning proposal than (with God's help) the Headbeaters promptly outbeat them all. The first to yield were the Born-blinds and the Dunderheads; those who held out longest were the Slop-eaters, the Whitefish and the Pot-bellies. In order to defeat the latter the Headbeaters even had recourse to trickery. It happened like this: on the day of battle, as both sides faced each other in mass array, the Headbeaters (who were uncertain which way the battle would go) resorted to witchcraft – they set the sun on the Pot-bellies. The sun was anyway so placed that it shone in the Pot-bellies' eyes, but to make it seem that this was done by witchcraft, the Headbeaters waved their hats towards the enemy, as if to say: 'You see what we are – even the sun is on our side'. The Pot-bellies, however, were not alarmed at first. They saw what was needed – they emptied some sacks of flour and started trying to catch the sun in the sacks. But try as they might, they could not catch it; then they saw that right was on the side of the Headbeaters and submitted.

When they had united all the other tribes, the Headbeaters turned their attention to internal organization, clearly intending to achieve some sort of order. The chronicler does not give a detailed history of these attempts at organization and mentions only individual episodes. It began with an attempt to make dough by mixing flour in the River Volga, then they dragged a calf to the bath-house, then they cooked porridge over a fire in a bag and drowned a goat in malted dough; next they bought a pig in mistake for a beaver, they killed a hound in mistake for a wolf, they lost some bast-shoes and found seven for the six they had lost, then they gave welcome to a crayfish with the church bells ringing, they chased a pike off her eggs, and next they went five miles to catch a gnat and all the time the gnat was sitting on the nose of a man from Poshekhone, then they exchanged the local priest for a dog, caulked the prison walls with pancakes, put a flea in chains, sent the devil to serve in the army, and erected poles to keep up the sky. Finally, exhausted, they settled down to see what would come of their efforts.

But nothing came of them. The pike came and sat on the eggs again; the pancakes used for caulking the prison were eaten by the prisoners; the bag in which they cooked the porridge was burnt together with the porridge. And the discord and clamour was worse than before: once again they ravaged each other's lands, led the women into captivity, and violated the maidens. There was no order, and that was that. They again tried beating their heads, but all to no avail. They then had the idea of finding themselves a prince.[16]

'He'll give us everything in a twinkling', said the wise elder Dobromysl. 'He'll make soldiers for us, and build us a prison such as we need. Come on, lads!'

They searched and searched for a prince and almost got lost among the three pine-trees, but luckily met a Born-blind from Poshekhone who knew these three pines like the back of his hand. He brought them out on to the track and led them straight to a prince.

'Who are you? Why have you come to me?' the prince asked the envoys.

'We are the Headbeaters. There is no people in the world more wise and brave than us! We even defeated the Pot-bellies!' boasted the Headbeaters.

'And what else have you done?'

'Well, we went five miles to catch a gnat', they began, then, suddenly, were filled with an irresistible desire to laugh . . . . They looked at each other and burst into guffaws.

'You were the one, Peter, who went to catch the gnat!' taunted Ivashka.

'No, it wan't, it was you!'

'No, it wasn't me. It was your nose the gnat sat on!'

Then the prince, seeing that even in his presence they could not stop their wrangling, grew very angry and set about them with his staff.

'Stupid, that's what you are!' he said. 'You shouldn't be called Headbeaters – not from the way you behave – but Glupovites: "Stupid folk". I don't want to govern the likes of you. Find yourselves the stupidest prince in the whole world – and let him rule over you.'

Having said this, he gave them another dose of his staff and dismissed them with honour.

As they went, the Headbeaters fell to thinking over the prince's words.

'Why did he give us such a rating?' said some. 'We go to him in all goodness of heart, and he sends us away to find a stupid prince.'

But there were others who saw nothing insulting in what the prince had said.

'What of it?' they retorted. 'Perhaps we'd be better off with a stupid prince. We could just give him a honey-cake and say to him: "Get your teeth in that, and don't bother us!"'

'Quite right', agreed the rest.

So the brave fellows returned home. First they decided to try again to arrange affairs themselves. They kept a cock tied to a rope so that it would not run away, they ate a dead dog that they took for a hare . . . . But still nothing came of it. So after much thought they set out to find a stupid prince.

They travelled three years and three days across a level plain, without getting anywhere at all, until at last they came to a bog. They saw a Dunderhead from Chukhomle standing by the edge of it: he was looking for his mittens which he had tucked in his belt.

'Friend Dunderhead, might you know where we can find a prince more stupid than any other in the whole world?' asked the Headbeaters.

'Yes, I know just such a one', answered the Dunderhead. 'Just you go straight across the bog here.'

They all threw themselves into the bog – and more than half of them were drowned ('Many showed zeal for their native land', says the chronicler). Eventually they crawled out of the swamp and saw a prince sitting straight in front of them on the far side of the bog – and he was as stupid as could be! He sat there eating gingerbread. The Headbeaters were overjoyed: 'What a prince! Just what we wanted!'

'Who are you? Why have you come to me?' asked the prince, munching his gingerbread.

'We are the Headbeaters. There is no people more wise or brave than us. We even defeated the Slop-eaters!' boasted the Headbeaters.

'What else have you done?'

'We chased a pike off her eggs, we put flour in the Volga to make dough . . .', the Headbeaters began, but the prince would not even listen to them.

'I may be stupid', he said, 'but I'm not that stupid! Do pikes sit on eggs? Can you make dough in a river? No, it is not Headbeaters you should be called, but Glupovites: "Stupid folk". I do not wish to rule over you. Find yourselves the stupidest prince in the whole world – and let him rule over you!'

And after giving them a taste of his staff, he dismissed them with honour.

The Headbeaters fell to thinking: that villain of a Dunderhead cheated us. He said this prince was stupider than all the rest, but he was a clever one all the time!

However, they returned home and once more tried to organize things for themselves. They put cloth leggings out to dry in the rain, and climbed to the top of a pine-tree to look at Moscow. And still there was no order, and that was that. Then Peter ('the Gnat') made a suggestion.

'I've got a friend', he said, 'who's called the "Torzhok Thief"', and if he's not smart enough to find us a prince, you can judge me from your mercy-seat and chop off my luckless head.'

He spoke with such conviction that the Headbeaters took his advice and summoned the 'Torzhok Thief'. He drove a hard bargain. For finding a prince he asked three-and-a-half kopeks, while the Headbeaters offered him two kopeks and all their possessions besides. In the end they made an agreement and set out in search of a prince.

'Find us one who isn't too wise', the Headbeaters told the 'Thief'. 'What do we want with a wise prince? To the devil with wise princes!'

The 'Thief' led them first through firs and birch trees, then through deep forest, then on through glades till he brought them out into a clearing. In the middle of the clearing sat a prince.

When the Headbeaters saw him they stopped in their tracks. The prince they saw before them was as wise as could be, and every now and then he fired a gun and brandished a sabre. And every shot he fired went straight through the heart, and with every stroke of his sword off came a head. And the 'Thief', who had done this shabby deed, stood stroking his belly and grinning in his beard.

'What have you done? Have you gone mad? Is this prince likely to come to us? The others wouldn't come, and they were a hundred times stupider than this one', said the Headbeaters, turning on the 'Thief'.

'Never mind – we'll fix it', said the 'Thief'. 'Just give me a minute and I'll have a word with him.'

The Headbeaters saw that the 'Thief' had taken them in completely, but they dared not go back on their agreement.

'No, neighbour, this isn't like beating heads with the Potbellies. No, neighbour, with this one you'll have to give an account of yourself and tell him what manner of man you are, and what's your rank and title', said the Headbeaters amongst themselves.

Meanwhile, the 'Thief' had gone up to the prince, doffed his sable-skin cap and was whispering confidentially in his ear. He and the prince whispered together for a long time, but it was impossible to hear what about. The only thing the Headbeaters did hear was the 'Thief' saying: 'And don't spare the rod with them, your highness.'

At length, it was their turn to stand in the glorious presence of his highness.

'What people are you? And why have you come to me?' asked the prince.

'We are the Headbeaters! There is no people more brave . . .', they began, but were suddenly filled with confusion.

'I have heard of you, gentlemen', said the prince, smiling ('and so graciously did he smile that it was like the shining of the sun', the chronicler remarks). 'Oh, yes, I have heard all about you. And I know about the time you met the crayfish with the church bells ringing – I know you well enough. The only thing I don't know is what you want with me.'

'We have come to your highness to say this: between ourselves we have killed many men, we have caused much destruction and done many outrages to each other, but still we have no law. Come and rule over us!'

'And might I ask which of my princely brothers you have already petitioned?'

'We went to one prince who was stupid, then to another who was stupid, but they would not rule over us!'

'Very well. It is my will to rule over you', said the prince, 'but as for going to live among you – that I will not do! For you live like beasts: you skim the top from untried gold, and bring ruin on your own sons' wives! So, then, instead of myself I send you this same "Torzhok Thief". He will govern you in your homeland and I will rule over him and you from here.'

The Headbeaters hung their heads and said:

'Yes, sir.'

'And you will pay me tribute', continued the prince. 'Whoever has a sheep which lambs, he must give the sheep to me and keep the lamb for himself; and whoever has a two-kopek piece must break it into four – one piece for me, another piece for me, and a third piece for me, and the fourth he can keep for himself. When I go to war – you shall go too. As for all other matters – they are none of your business.'

'Yes, sir', replied the Headbeaters.

'Those who mind their own business I shall spare; and those who don't will be hanged.'

'Yes, sir', answered the Headbeaters.

'And since you could not live in freedom by yourselves and have stupidly wished this bondage on yourselves, you will no longer be called Headbeaters, but Glupovites: "Stupid folk".'

'Yes, sir', replied the Headbeaters.

Then the prince ordered that they should be served with vodka and given a pie and red kerchief apiece, and, after imposing on them many taxes, he dismissed them with honour.

The Headbeaters journeyed home, and as they went they sighed. 'They sighed unceasingly and cried out aloud', the chronicler records. 'So that is the law of princes!' they said. 'And we yes-sirred and yes-sirred, and yes-sirred ourselves to the devil.' One of them took his *gusli*[17] and sang:

'Be still, oh dear green leafy wood.
'Let a young man think his thoughts
'About the morrow when he goes to meet
'The dreaded judge, the Tsar himself . . .'

The longer the song continued, the lower the Headbeaters bowed their heads. 'And among them', says the chronicler, 'were old men with grey hairs, and bitterly they wept for that sweet freedom that they had heedlessly cast away; and there were young men who had scarcely yet tasted of that freedom, and they also wept. Now only did they understand the excellence of freedom.' And at the sound of the closing lines:

'And, my son, I'll give you this reward:
'A tall house in the open field –
'Two standing posts with a cross-piece . . .'[18]

they all fell on their faces and sobbed.

But fact was fact, and there was no going back. When they reached home, the Headbeaters straightway chose a swampy place and established a town, which they called Glupov, and they themselves took the name of Glupovites, after the town. 'And thus this ancient branch came to flourish', says the chronicler.

But this submissiveness did not suit the 'Thief'. What he wanted was rebellions which he could suppress – and thereby gain the prince's favour and enrich himself on extortions from the rebels. So he began to persecute the Glupovites with all manner of injustices and, indeed, before long succeeded in rousing them to revolt. The first to rise were the Corner-peepers and then the Haggis-eaters. The 'Thief' attacked them with cannon and blazed away until he had shot them all, whereupon he made peace with them – that is, he took a dish of turbot with the Corner-peepers and a dish of haggis with the Haggis-eaters. And he was highly praised by the prince. Soon, however, his villainy reached such extremes that rumours of his incorrigible behaviour reached the ears of the prince himself. The prince was greatly enraged and sent a hangman's noose for the unfaithful servant. But the 'Thief' found a way even round this difficulty: he forestalled the executioner by cutting his throat with a cucumber.

After the 'Thief' there came 'as the prince's deputy' a man from Odoev, the one who had believed that gherkins were green eggs. But he too saw that he could not exist without rebellions, so he also persecuted the people. There was a revolt of the Pot-bellies, the Bun-folk and the Porridge-eaters, who all rose in defence of their rights and the old ways. The man from Odoev attacked the rebels and he too blazed away, but evidently to no good effect, for the rebels not only refused to give in, but even got the Black-mouths and the Lip-smackers to join them. The prince heard the useless fire of the useless Odoevan and kept his patience for a long time, but in the end he could stand it no longer and attacked the rebels in person. After shooting them all to a man, he returned to his own country.

'I sent a proper thief, and a thief he turned out to be', thought the prince sadly. 'Then I sent the Odoevan and he too turned out to be a thief. Whom shall I send now?'

He considered for a long time which he should prefer: a man from Orel – on the grounds that 'men from Orel, men from Kromy, are the biggest thieves that ever there be', or a man from Shuy, but in the end chose the man from Orel, because he belonged to the old stock of the Cracked-heads. But scarcely had the man from Orel come to take up office, when the inhabitants of Staritsa rose in revolt and, instead of greeting the governor with bread and salt, they gave their welcome to a cock. The man from Orel went to Staritsa in the hope of a tasty dish of sterlets, but when he arrived found 'nought but a sufficiency of mud'. Thereupon he burnt Staritsa to the ground and took the women and maidens of the town for his own pleasure. 'And the prince, hearing this, cut out his tongue', writes the chronicler.

Then the prince tried once more, this time sending a 'thief of more common sort', and, with this in mind, he chose a man from Kalyazin, the man who had bought a pig in mistake for a beaver. But this man proved to be a greater thief than the one from Torzhok and the one from Orel. There was a rebellion of the men of Semindyaev and Zaozere, and he 'having killed them, burnt their towns'.

Then the prince, eyes bulging, cried out:
'There is no stupidity worse than stupidity!'
And he came to Glupov in person and cried in a loud voice:
'I'll flog you!'
And with these words the era of history began.

A Schedule of the Governors appointed at different times by the Imperial Government of Russia to the Town of Glupov (1731–1826)

1. KLEMENTY, AMADEY MANUILOVICH
Brought from Italy by Biron,[19] Duke of Courland, because of his skill in cooking macaroni; later suddenly promoted to the appropriate rank and sent to Glupov as town-governor. On arrival there, continued cooking macaroni and even compelled others to take it up as well, thus gaining great renown. In 1734 was flogged for treason, had his nostrils slit and was banished to Berezov.

2. FERAPONTOV, FOTY PETROVICH
Brigadier. Formerly barber to the same Duke of Courland. Conducted many campaigns against tax-defaulters and was so fond of entertainment that he allowed no floggings to take place unless he were present. In 1738 torn to pieces by dogs in the forest.

3. VELIKANOV, IVAN MATVEEVICH
On his own account imposed a tax of three kopeks per head, first drowning the director of the Church Lands Office in the river. Bloodied the noses of many chief constables. In 1740, in the reign of the gentle Elizabeth, discovered to be carrying on a liaison with Avdotya Lopukhina.[20] As a result was knouted, had his tongue cut out and was imprisoned in the gaol at Cherdyn.

4. URUS-KUGUSH-KILDIBAEV, MANUIL SAMUILOVICH
Senior Lieutenant of the Life Guards. Noted for his reckless daring, on one occasion even took Glupov by storm. Received no praise for this from the authorities; in 1745 dismissed with ignominy.

5. LAMVROKAKIS
Fugitive Greek. No Christian name or patronymic; not even a rank; captured in the market at Nezhin by Count Kirila Razumovsky.[21] Traded in soap, sponges, and nuts; was in favour of classical education. In 1756 found dead in bed, bitten to death by bed-bugs.

6. BAKLAN, IVAN MATVEICH
Brigadier. Seven feet seven inches tall; boasted he was a direct descendant of Ivan the Great (the well-known bell-tower in Moscow). Broke in half in the great gale of 1761.

7. PFEIFFER, BOGDAN BOGDANOVICH
Sergeant of the Guards. A native of Holstein. Achieved nothing; replaced for his ignorance in 1762.[22]

8. BRUDASTY, DEMENTY VARLAMOVICH
Appointed in haste; his head contained a mechanism on account of which he was called 'the Music-box'. This did not prevent him from settling the problem of tax arrears, which his predecessor had neglected. In his term occurred the seven days of ruinous anarchy, as will be recounted below.

9. DVOEKUROV, SEMEN KONSTANTINYCH
State Councillor and knight of an order. Paved the main streets, started the brewing of beer and mead, introduced the use of pepper and bay-leaf, collected the tax arrears, was a patron of learning, and petitioned for the establishment of an academy in Glupov. Wrote a treatise 'Description of the Lives of the Most Notable Monkeys'. A man of strong constitution, had eight mistresses in succession. His wife, Lukerya Terenteva, was also very obliging, thus adding much to the brilliance of his governorship. Died in 1770 of natural causes.

10. MARQUIS DE SANGLOT, ANTON PROTASEVICH
A native of France and friend of Diderot. Noted for his frivolity and fondness for ribald songs. Flew in the air in the municipal gardens and would have flown right away, but his coat-tails caught on a spire, and he was, with the utmost difficulty, got down. Dismissed for this escapade (in 1772), but the following year, nothing daunted, gave performances at Isler's Spa Restaurant.*

11. FERDYSHCHENKO, PETR PETROVICH
Brigadier. Former orderly of Prince Potemkin.[24] No great mental ability and incapable of articulate speech. Neglected the collection of tax arrears; fond of boiled pork and goose with cabbage. In his term as governor the town suffered famine and fire. Died of overeating in 1779.

---

* This is clearly a mistake.[23]

12. BORODAVKIN, BASILISK SEMENOVICH
His governorship was the longest and most brilliant. Led the campaign against tax-defaulters and burnt down thirty-three villages, by these measures exacting two and a half roubles in tax arrears. Introduced the card game 'La Mouche' and the use of olive oil; paved the market square and planted birch trees along the street leading to the government offices; presented a new petition for the establishment of an academy in Glupov. It being refused, built a gaol. Died in 1798 while attending a flogging; given the last rites by a chief constable.

13. NEGODYAEV, ONUFRY IVANOVICH
Formerly stoker in the palace at Gatchina.[25] Unpaved the streets paved by his predecessors and built monuments with the stone thus obtained. Relieved of office in 1802 on account of his disagreement with Novosiltsev, Czartoryski and Strogonov (the noted triumvirate of that time)[26] on the subject of a constitution, in which he was justified by subsequent events.

14. MIKALADZE, PRINCE KSAVERY GEORGIEVICH
A Circassian, descendant of the voluptuous Princess Tamara. Of captivating looks, possessed such a weakness for the female sex that he practically doubled the population of Glupov. Left a useful manual on the subject. Died of exhaustion 1814.

15. BENEVOLENSKY, FEOFILAKT IRINARKHOVICH
State Councillor. School-fellow of Speransky.[27] A wise man with a bent for legislation. Foretold the institution of public trials and the *zemstvo*.[28] Carried on a liaison with Raspopova, the widow of a merchant, and dined on pie in her house every Saturday. In his spare time composed sermons for the clergy of the town and translated Thomas à Kempis from the Latin. Reintroduced the use of mustard, bay-leaf and olive oil. Was the first to impose dues on tax-contractors, from which he received three thousand roubles a year. In 1811 was called to account for being favourably disposed towards Bonaparte, and exiled with imprisonment.

16. PRYSHCH, IVAN PANTELEICH
Major. His head turned out to be filled with force-meat, a discovery made by the Marshal of Nobility.

17. IVANOV, NIKODIM OSIPOVICH
State Councillor. So small that he could not take in extensive laws. Died of strain in 1819 trying to assimilate a Senate decree.

18. DU CHARIOT, VICOMTE, ANGEL DOROFEEVICH
A native of France. Liked to dress in women's clothes and fond of
eating frogs. On examination, turned out to be a woman. Deported
in 1821.

19. GRUSTILOV, ERAST ANDREEVICH
State Councillor. Friend of Karamzin.[29] Noted for his tenderness
and sensibility: fond of taking tea in the woods and always shed
tears on seeing the black grouse at mating time. Left a number of
writings on idyllic subjects, and died of melancholy in 1825.
Raised the revenue from tax-contracting to five thousand roubles
a year.

20. UGRYUM-BURCHEEV
Former regimental punishment-orderly. Destroyed the old town
and built a new one in a different place.

21. PEREKHVAT-ZALIKHVATSKY, ARKHISTRATIG STRATILOVICH
Major. Of him, as the governor now in office, I will say nothing.
Rode into Glupov on a white horse, burnt down the high school
and abolished learning.

'The Music-Box'*

IN August 1762 there was an unaccustomed flurry of activity in Glupov, on the occasion of the arrival of the new town-governor, Dementy Varlamovich Brudasty. The inhabitants were in a state of jubilation. Although they had not yet actually seen the new governor, they were already telling stories about him and saying how handsome and clever he was. They joyfully congratulated each other, kissed, and shed tears. They went into the taverns, came out, and went back in again. In a burst of ecstasy they recalled the old liberties of Glupov, and the leading citizens gathered in front of the church bell-tower to form a town-assembly, making the air ring with their cries of 'Our father and protector! Our handsome, clever governor!'

There were even some dangerous day-dreamers, who, moved less by reason than by the stirrings of a grateful heart, declared that under the new governor trade would flourish, and that with police supervision arts and sciences would spring up. They even went so far as to make comparisons. They remembered the old governor, who had just left, and found that though he too had been handsome and clever, the new governor was still to be preferred if only for the fact that he was new. In short, on this occasion, as on other occasions, full expression was given both to the enthusiasm and to the frivolity which were characteristic of the Glupovites.

Meanwhile, the new governor turned out to be taciturn and morose. He galloped into Glupov hell-for-leather (the times were such that quick action was essential), and he had no sooner arrived on the town common than he gave a whipping to a whole

* No. 8 in the 'Schedule'. The editor has found it convenient to depart from the strictly chronological order in publishing the contents of the 'Chronicle'. He also thought it best to present only the biographies of the most notable of the town-governors, since the less noteworthy are sufficiently well characterized in the 'Schedule' which precedes the present chapter.

host of stage-drivers, then and there, hardly having set foot in his territory. But even this did not cool the ardour of the Glupovites, for their minds were full of the recent victories over the Turks, and they all had hopes that their new governor might capture Khotin[30] all over again.

Soon, however, they realized that their hopes and rejoicing had been, to say the least, premature and excessive. The usual reception was held, and here, for the first time in their lives, the Glupovites discovered to what bitter trials even the most devoted love of authority can be subjected. There was something unaccountable about the whole thing. The governor walked in silence round the ranks of the official hierarchs, flashed his eyes, and said: 'I'll not have it!' – then promptly disappeared into his office. The officials were dumbfounded; the Glupovites were dumbfounded in turn.

Despite their insuperable firmness of character, the Glupovites are a spoilt and extremely coddled people. They like to see a friendly smile on the face of their superior, they like to hear from his lips an occasional witty pleasantry, and when all that these lips emit are snortings and enigmatic sounds they are simply perplexed. A superior can undertake what measures he likes, he can even undertake no measures at all, but unless he is ready to exchange a few friendly words he will never be popular. There have been truly wise governors, men, even, who could entertain the idea of founding an academy in Glupov (for example, State Councillor Dvoekurov, who appears in the 'Schedule' under No. 9), but, because they never addressed the Glupovites as 'my boys' or 'my hearties', their names have been forgotten. On the other hand, there are governors, who, without being positively stupid (such governors there have never been), still performed only average deeds – that is, flogging and collecting tax arrears – but since they always accompanied these activities with a pleasant word or two, their names have not only been preserved, but have even become the subject of a wide variety of popular legends.

So it was in the present case. However warm had been the feelings of the Glupovites on the arrival of the new governor, they were considerably cooled by this reception.

'What do you call this? All he did was snort and turn his back on us. As though we hadn't seen backs in plenty before now! He only needs to talk to us friendly. Kindness is the way to get the right side of us. He can be as hard as he likes, if only he is good to us afterwards.' So the Glupovites talked as they tearfully remembered the superiors they had known in the past, always affable and kind, – and handsome fellows too in their fine uniforms! They even recalled the runaway Greek, Lamvrokakis (No. 5 in the 'Schedule'), and they remembered how Brigadier Baklan (No. 6 in the 'Schedule') had arrived in 1756, and at his very first reception had shown what a fine fellow he was.

'Steady pressure', he had said, 'and quick action, lenience and severity; and at the same time a judicious firmness. This, gentlemen, is the object, or, to be exact, these are the five objects, which I hope, with the help of God, to achieve by certain administrative measures, which form the essence, or, I should rather say, the kernel of my plan of campaign.'

And they remembered how he had turned adroitly on one heel and added to the Chairman of the Town Council:

'And on feast-days we shall celebrate at your house!'

'There now, that's how a governor ought to receive us', sighed the Glupovites. 'But what does this one do? Snorts, and disappears!'

Alas, succeeding events not only confirmed the inhabitants in their views, but even surpassed their worst apprehensions. The new governor shut himself up in his office, ate and drank nothing, and spent the whole time scratching away with his pen. Occasionally he would march out into the main office, toss the clerk a pile of papers covered in writing, and announce: 'I'll not have it!' – and once more disappear into his office. Suddenly, there was unprecedented activity throughout the town. The police-superintendents, the police-inspectors, the court assessors all bustled about; the constables forgot what it was to have a proper meal and, ever since, have had the pernicious habit of taking pickings where they can. All the time they were arresting and seizing, flogging and birching, compiling inventories and selling up goods . . . . And still the town-governor sat and scratched out a never-ending flow of new orders. There was noise and clamour throughout the town and above all the uproar and confusion, like the cry of some bird of prey, sounded the ominous phrase: 'I'll not have it!'

The Glupovites were filled with dismay. They recalled the wholesale flogging of the stage-drivers, and it suddenly struck them – what if he should flog the whole town? They began to wonder what was meant by the phrase 'I'll not have it!', and finally turned to the history of Glupov, looking for instances of salutary severity, but though they found an astonishing variety of things, they found nothing to fit the present case.

'If he would only say straight out how much he wants from

each of us', said the bewildered inhabitants. 'But all he does is scrape away with his pen, and what can you do?'

And Glupov, carefree, kindly, cheerful Glupov fell into a state of gloom. No more lively gatherings at the gateways, no more clicking of teeth on sunflower seeds, no more knuckle-bones. The streets were deserted, wild animals appeared in the squares. People left their houses only when absolutely necessary, and after showing a glimpse of their worn, frightened faces, they disappeared again. According to the old inhabitants, it was rather like the times of the mock-Tsar of Tushino,[31] or like it had been under Biron,[32] when the wanton, Ugly Tanya, almost brought down punishment on the whole town. But even then things had been better; at least they had understood something of what was happening, now they were only afraid, ominously, unaccountably afraid.

It was particularly painful to see the town at late evening. Glupov, which was anyway never very lively at this hour, became completely dead. Hungry dogs had the streets to themselves, and even they did not bark, but indulged (in the most orderly manner) in degenerate, dissolute practices. The streets and houses were in total darkness, and only in a window of the governor's apartment did an ominous light glimmer deep into the night. An inhabitant waking at that hour could see the town-governor sitting bent over his desk, still scratching at some document with his pen .... Then suddenly he would go to the window and shout: 'I'll not have it!' and again sit at his desk and scratch away with his pen. . . .

Ugly rumours began to circulate. It was said that the new governor was not a governor at all, but a werewolf, who had been sent to Glupov through someone's folly, and at night he was said to hover over the town in the shape of an insatiable vampire and suck the blood of the sleeping inhabitants. Of course, these things were said and passed on in whispers, but there were some bold spirits who suggested that the whole population should fall on their knees and beg forgiveness. But they too had second thoughts. What if this was all according to plan? What if it had been deemed necessary that Glupov, for its sins, should have this kind of governor rather than another? These ideas seemed so reasonable that those who had been so daring disavowed their proposals and began accusing each other of mischief-making and incitement to rebellion.

Then suddenly it became known that the town-governor was paying secret visits to Baibakov, the watch-maker, who also made music-boxes. There were reliable witnesses who said that

26

on one occasion in the middle of the night they had seen Baibakov, pale and frightened, coming out of the governor's apartment and carefully carrying something wrapped in a napkin. And the odd thing was that on this memorable night not only was no one woken by the cry of 'I'll not have it!', but the governor himself appeared to have temporarily abandoned his review of the tax arrears registers* and fallen asleep.

The question arose: what need could the town-governor have of Baibakov, who, apart from the fact that he never stopped drinking, was also a notorious adulterer?

A variety of tricks and manoeuvres were employed to find out the secret, but Baibakov remained as close as an oyster, and to all their blandishments responded only by trembling all over. They tried to make him drunk, but, while not refusing the vodka, he did nothing but sweat and gave nothing away. The lads apprenticed to him were able to supply one piece of information: that one night a constable had indeed come and fetched their master, and he had returned an hour later with a bundle and locked himself in his workshop, since when he had fallen into a state of melancholy.

Nothing more could they discover. In the meantime the governor's mysterious meetings with Baibakov had become more frequent. In time Baibakov's state of melancholy passed and he even became so bold as to threaten to have the Chairman of the Town Council sent for a recruit, whether or not he was due for service, if he did not provide him with the money to buy his daily tot. He had a couple of new suits made, and boasted that he would soon be opening a new shop in Glupov which would give even Winterhalter† something to think about.

In the midst of all these rumours and gossip there suddenly came a bolt from the blue – a note inviting the most notable members of the Glupov intelligentsia to attend at such and such an hour on such and such a day to be harangued by the governor. The notables were thrown into confusion, but prepared for the occasion.

It was a fine spring day. All nature was rejoicing: the sparrows

* An evident anachronism. In 1762 there were no registers of tax arrears, and money was raised simply by exacting the due amount from each person. Consequently, there could be no review of them. However, this is not so much an anachronism as an example of the foresight which the chronicler here and there reveals in such a marked degree that the reader must find it uncanny. Thus, for instance (as we shall see below), he foretold the invention of the electric telegraph and even the institution of provincial councils.

† A fresh example of foresight. Winterhalter's did not exist in 1762.[33]

chirped, the dogs yelped and wagged their tails for joy. The inhabitants, with their straw baskets under their arms, crowded in the courtyard of the governor's residence and tremblingly awaited their fate. At last the moment for which they were waiting arrived.

He came out, and for the first time the Glupovites saw on his face that affable smile for which they had been longing. It seemed as though he too had been affected by the kindly warmth of the sun (at any rate, many declared afterwards that they had actually seen his coat-tails quiver). He went round the inhabitants in turn and, though he said nothing, graciously received all that was offered. Then he stepped back towards the porch and opened his mouth . . . and suddenly something inside him started to whirr and hum, and as it continued, the more and more his eyes rolled and flashed. 'H...h...ave it!' burst finally from his lips, and with this sound he flashed his eyes for the last time and rushed headlong through the door of his apartment.

When we read in the 'Chronicle' the account of this unprecedented occurrence, we, who are witnesses of another age and participants in other events, can easily and naturally view it with equanimity. But if we go back in our minds a hundred years and put ourselves in the position of our worthy ancestors, we can readily understand the terror which must have seized them when they saw those rolling eyes and the open mouth, which produced nothing but a whirring and some senseless noise, not even like the striking of a clock. But it was here that the sterling qualities of our ancestors were revealed: shocked as they were by the scene which has been described, they were not carried away by any of the revolutionary ideas then in fashion, nor by the temptations offered by the prospect of anarchy. No, they remained true to their love of authority, merely allowing themselves some slight feeling of pity and reproach for their very singular governor.

'How did they come to send us such a brute of a governor?' the Glupovites asked in astonishment, attaching no special significance to the word 'brute'.

'Watch out we're not called to account for him!' said some.

Then they went quietly to their homes and set about their normal occupations.

And Brudasty would have remained for many years the husbandman of this vineyard, rejoicing the hearts of his superiors by his zeal and efficiency, and the Glupovites would have been unaware of anything unusual in their lives, but for a purely fortuitous circumstance – a mere oversight – which put an end to his career at its very height.

One morning, soon after the reception mentioned above, the governor's secretary went into his office to make a report and was confronted by the following spectacle: the body of the governor, dressed in its official coat, was seated at the desk, and before it, on a pile of tax-registers, like some flamboyant paper-weight, lay the governor's head – completely empty . . . . The clerk fled, his teeth chattering with alarm.

They ran to fetch the governor's deputy and the chief inspector of police. The first reaction of the deputy town-governor was to set upon the inspector and accuse him of negligence and conniving in this bare-faced act of violence, but the inspector was able to defend himself. He maintained, not without reason, that the governor's head could not have been emptied unless the governor himself had allowed it, and, moreover, some part in the matter had been played by a craftsman of some kind, since among the material evidence on the desk were a chisel, a gimlet and a small saw. They summoned the head doctor of the town for consultation and put to him three questions: (i) Could the governor's head be removed from his body without any bleeding? (ii) Would it be possible to admit that the governor might have removed his head and emptied it himself? and (iii) Would it be possible to suppose that the governor's head, once detached, could by some unknown process grow on again at a later date? The disciple of Aesculapius thought for a bit, muttering something about 'gubernatorial matter', which was supposedly pouring from the governor's body, but then, realizing that this was nonsense, he avoided giving a straight answer by saying that the mysteries of the physical structure of town-governors had still not been fully investigated scientifically.*

Receiving this evasive reply, the deputy town-governor was at a loss what to do. There were two courses open to him: he could either immediately report what had happened to the authorities and at the same time start a local investigation, or he could say nothing for the time being and await events. Faced with such difficulties, he chose a middle course, that is, he started an investigation and at the same time ordered the strictest secrecy in the matter, so as not to disturb the people or put any fanciful notions into their heads.

But however strictly the constables kept the secret, in a few minutes the unprecedented news of the removal of the governor's

---

* It has now been proved that the bodies of *all* town-governors are subject to the same physiological laws as any other human body, but it must be remembered that in 1762 science was still in its infancy.

head was all over the town. Many of the inhabitants wept at the loss of their father and protector, afraid too that they would get it in the neck for obeying a governor who had not a head but an empty vessel on his shoulders. There were others who also wept, but claimed that they would be praised, not punished for their obedience.

At the club that evening all the members were present. They excitedly discussed the matter, recalling the various circumstances and discovering a number of rather suspicious facts. For instance, Tolkovnikov, the court assessor, told them how he had once gone unexpectedly to the governor's office on particularly urgent business and found the governor toying with his head, which he had then hastened to return to its proper place. At the time Tolkovnikov had paid no special attention to the matter and had supposed it was a mere flight of fancy, but now it was clear that the governor did occasionally remove his head when relaxing and put on a skull-cap in its place, just as the dean of a cathedral changes his headdress when at home. Another court assessor, Mladentsev, recalled that once he had passed the workshop of Baibakov, the watch-maker, and had seen the governor's head in one of the windows surrounded by tools of various kinds. But Mladentsev was not allowed to finish, for at the mention of Baibakov everyone recalled his strange behaviour and his mysterious nocturnal visits to the governor's apartment.

Still, from all these stories nothing very clear emerged. Those present were rather inclined to think that the whole business was nothing more than a story invented by idle folk, but then they remembered about the London agitators[34] and by adding one thing to another they came to the conclusion that treason had found its way into Glupov itself.* This caused a storm of noise and agitation. They summoned the local schoolteacher and asked him if there had ever been any cases in history where people had given orders, conducted wars, and made treaties, with nothing but an empty vessel on their shoulders. The teacher thought for a moment and replied that many things in history were obscure – but there had been a certain Charles the Simple who had had on his shoulders a vessel which, if not empty, had seemed to be so, and he had indeed conducted wars and concluded treaties.

While these discussions were going on, the deputy town-governor was not idle. He had also remembered about Baibakov and called him to account for himself. At first Baibakov refused to say anything and answered only: 'I don't know a thing, not a

* Even this was foreseen by the 'Chronicle'!

thing!'. But when they produced the evidence that had been found on the table, and also promised him half a rouble to buy himself some liquor, he saw reason and, being literate, himself wrote down the following deposition:

'My name is Vasily, son of Ivan, my surname is Baibakov. I am a craftsman of Glupov. I never go to confessions or mass because I am a Mason and am a false priest of that sect. I was tried for living sinfully with Matrenka and found by the court to be a flagrant adulterer, in which situation I still continue. Last winter, I do not remember the date or month, I was woken in the night, and taken by the police sergeant to our town-governor. On arrival I found him sitting and nodding his head left and right in strict time. Being struck with fright (and also under the influence of spiritous liquor), I stood by the door and said nothing. Suddenly his worship the governor beckoned me with his hand and gave me a paper on which was written: "Do not be surprised, but mend what is broken". Then his worship took off his head and gave it to me. On inspecting it I found that in one corner it contained a small music-box, which played certain simple pieces. These were two in number: "I'll break you!" and "I'll not have it!". But since the head had got damp in transit, some of the wheels had worked loose on the spindle and others had dropped out altogether. Because of this his worship the governor was unable to speak clearly, and when he did speak he missed out some of the letters and sounds. Wishing to repair this fault, with the governor's permission, I with due care wrapped the head in a napkin and went home. But there I saw that I had taken on too much, for try as I would to fix the wheels that had fallen out, I had such small success in my task that if I was the least bit careless or my fingers numbed with cold, the wheels dropped out again, and in the end all his worship could say was '. . . have it!'. In this extremity he grew angry and sought to ruin me for life, but I avoided his blow and suggested to his worship that he should send for help to Winterhalter, the maker of clocks and music-boxes in St. Petersburg, which he faithfully did. Since then I have daily inspected the governor's head and cleaned out the dirt. This I was doing on the morning when, through my carelessness, your excellency confiscated my tools. Why the new head ordered from Master Winterhalter has not arrived I do not know, but suppose that it is at present held up in transit on account of the spring floods. In answer to your excellency's enquiring, firstly, can I, in the event of the new head arriving, fix it in position, and, secondly, will the head, when fixed, work properly, I have the honour to reply as follows: I can fix it and it will work, but it cannot have any real thoughts. To this deposition the adulterer Vasily Ivanov Baibakov puts his hand.'

When the deputy governor heard Baibakov's statement, it occurred to him that if it had actually been allowed that Glupov should have a governor whose head was a mere empty casing, then it must be perfectly right and proper. He therefore decided to wait, but at the same time sent an urgent telegram to Winterhalter.* Then he locked up the room with the governor's body and devoted his attention to calming public opinion.

But all his devices were in vain. Two more days passed and at last came the day when the St. Peterburg post arrived. But it brought no head.

Anarchy set in. The government offices were deserted; such an amount of taxes went uncollected that when the local treasurer looked into the treasury cash-box, his jaw dropped in amazement and remained like that for the rest of his life; the police inspectors got quite out of hand and were unashamedly idle; the official 'days' ceased. But that was not the end of it. There were a number of murders, and the headless corpse of an unknown man was found on the town common; they could tell by the cut of his tunic that he was a lifeguardsman, but for all the efforts of the chief constable and the emergency police department the body's missing head could not be found.

At eight o'clock in the evening the deputy town-governor heard by telegraph from Winterhalter's that the head had been dispatched long since. He was utterly and completely dumbfounded.

Another day passed and still the body of the town-governor sat in his office. It was even beginning to decay. The people's love of authority which had been temporarily shaken by the strange behaviour of Brudasty now began modestly, but clearly, to manifest itself. The leading citizens went in procession to the deputy governor, and urged him to take measures. The deputy governor, seeing that the tax arrears were mounting up, that drunkenness was increasing, that justice was disappearing from the courts, and that resolutions were remaining unsigned, appealed for help to the town clerk. The latter, being an obliging man, telegraphed the authorities about what had happened, and got the reply that for reporting such balderdash he was dismissed from his post†.

* Absolutely astonishing!

†This worthy official was able to exonerate himself and, as we shall see below, took a very active part in subsequent events in Glupov.

When the deputy governor heard of this, he went into the office and wept. The court assessors came, and they also wept. The town clerk appeared, and he also was too overcome to speak.

Meanwhile, what Winterhalter had said was quite true – the head had indeed been duly made and dispatched. But the task of delivering it on the mail-coach had been rashly entrusted to a boy who knew nothing whatever about music-boxes, and this inexperienced emissary, instead of holding the parcel carefully, had tossed it into the bottom of the waggon and dozed off to sleep. He had already travelled several stages in this way, when he suddenly felt a bite in the calf of his leg. Bewildered by this sudden pain, he had quickly opened the straw basket in which the mysterious consignment was wrapped and was confronted by a strange sight. The head was opening its mouth and shifting its eyes, and not only that – loudly and quite distinctly it declared: 'I'll break you!'

The boy was terrified out of his wits. His first reaction was to throw the talking parcel on to the roadway, his second to climb down unobserved from the waggon and take refuge in the bushes.

Perhaps this strange episode would have ended like this, with the head lying for a time in the road, gradually being crushed by passing carriages and finally carted off to the fields for manure, if matters had not become complicated by a circumstance so fantastic that even the Glupovites did not know what to make of it. But let us not anticipate events, but see what was happening meanwhile in the town.

Glupov was in a state of commotion. The citizens had not seen the governor for several days and they were in revolt. They made no bones about accusing the deputy governor and the chief inspector of police of making away with this item of government property. Holy fools wandered freely about the town foretelling all manner of disasters. A certain Mishka Vozgryavy declared that he had had a vision in the night and that a man, terrible to behold and clad in a bright cloud, had appeared to him.

In the end the Glupovites' patience was exhausted. Led by the honoured citizen Puzanov, they formed themselves in a square outside the government offices and demanded that the deputy governor be handed over for trial, otherwise they would tear him and his house apart.

With terrifying suddenness anti-social elements came to the surface. There was talk of pretenders to the throne, and of a certain Stepka who with a band of outlaws had only the day before carried off two merchants' wives in full view of the public.

'What have you done with our good master?' cried the crowd furiously when the deputy governor appeared.

'My boys, my good fellows! How can I take him away from you when he is safe under lock and key?' said the terrified official, roused by events from his administrative torpor. Saying this, he gave a surreptitious wink to Baibakov, who at this signal promptly disappeared.

But the unrest continued.

'You're lying, you traitor!' answered the crowd. 'You and the police-inspector have got together to rid yourselves of our good master!'

And heaven alone knows how this turmoil would have ended if the sound of a harness-bell had not just then been heard and a cart had not driven up, in which were seated the chief constable and by his side . . . the missing town-governor!

He was dressed in lifeguard's uniform and his head was mud-stained and bruised in several places. But despite this, he jumped nimbly down from the cart and flashed his eyes at the crowd.

'I'll break you!' he cried, in a voice so deafening that all at once fell silent.

The disturbance was immediately suppressed, and the crowd, which had just been so loud and threatening, was now so quiet that you could hear the buzzing of a gnat, which had flown from a nearby bog to wonder at 'this absurd and risible confusion of the Glupovites'.

'Step forward the ring-leaders!' commanded the governor, raising his voice even higher.

They began picking ring-leaders from among those who had not paid their dues, and had chosen a dozen or so when a new and simply staggering circumstance gave a completely different turn to the situation.

While the Glupovites were sadly whispering, trying to remember which of them owed most in dues, the assembly was approached by the governor's carriage, which the inhabitants knew so well. Before they had time to look, down from the carriage jumped Baibakov, and after him, in full view of the crowd, there was a second town-governor, identical in every way to the one whom the chief constable had brought a minute before. The Glupovites stood rooted to the spot.

The head of this second governor was a perfectly new one coated with varnish. Some keen-eyed citizens thought it odd that a large birth-mark which a few days earlier had been on the governor's right cheek was now on his left cheek.

The pretenders met and looked each other up and down. The crowd slowly and silently dispersed.*

* The Editor thought it best to end the present story at this point, although the 'Chronicle' makes various explanatory additions. It says, for instance, that the head on the first town-governor was the one which Winterhalter's messenger had thrown from the waggon and that it had been attached by the chief constable to the body of the unknown lifeguardsman; on the second town-governor was the earlier head which Baibakov had repaired on the instructions of the deputy governor, and into which by mistake he had placed not a musical device, but some superseded orders. All of this is quite childish, and all that one can be sure of is that both these governors were impostors.

The Tale of the
Six Town-Governesses.
Civil Strife in Glupov

AS one might expect, the strange events in Glupov had further consequences.

Before the disastrous diarchy had time to spread its pernicious roots a messenger arrived from the provincial capital who took charge of the two pretenders and carried them off for investigation in special containers filled with spirit.

But this seemingly natural and just demonstration of administrative firmness almost created difficulties even worse than those caused by the uncanny appearance of two identical governors.

Hardly had the messenger set off with the pretenders, and hardly had the Glupovites realized that they were now left with no governor at all, than, stirred by their ardent love of authority, they promptly lapsed into anarchy.

'And the town', says the 'Chronicle', 'would have remained in this fatal abyss until this day, if it had not been delivered by the firmness and devotion of a dauntless staff-officer[35] living in the town.'

The anarchy began when the Glupovites assembled round the bell-tower and threw from the top of it two citizens, a certain Stepka and Ivashka. They then went to the establishment of the French woman, Mademoiselle de Sans Culotte (in Glupov she was known as Ustinya Trubochistikha; it was subsequently learned that she was the sister of Marat;* she died of a troubled conscience), where they smashed the windows. They then went on to the river, where they drowned two more citizens, one Porfishka and another Ivashka. Then, having achieved nothing, they went home.

In the meantime treason was not idle. There were ambitious persons who saw ways of exploiting the break-down of authority

---

* Marat was unheard of at this time. However, the mistake can be explained by the fact that these events were evidently not recorded by the chronicler at the time, but some years afterwards.

for their own purposes. And the singular thing on this occasion was that the anarchic element was represented entirely by women.

The first who contrived to seize the reins of power in Glupov was one Iraida Paleologova. She was a childless widow, inflexible in character and masculine in physique, with a dark brown face like the pictures in old prints. Nobody could remember when she came to live in Glupov, but some of the old inhabitants reckoned that it must have been at the dawn of time. She led a solitary life and lived on meagre fare, lending out money at interest and cruelly tormenting her four serf-girls. She had evidently given careful thought to her daring enterprise. Firstly, she had reckoned it would be impossible for the town to exist for a minute without someone in authority; secondly, she regarded the fact that she bore the name Paleologue as some mysterious portent;[36] and, thirdly, there was the quite promising fact that her late husband, a former controller of state liquor sales, had once in time of need acted as governor in some town or other. 'Reckoning thus', says the 'Chronicle', 'this same venomous Iraidka went into action.'

The Glupovites had still not recovered from the events of the previous day, when Paleologova, taking advantage of the fact that the deputy governor and his followers had settled down to a game of boston at the club, drew from its sheath the sword of the late controller of state liquor sales, filled with Dutch courage three members of the local irregulars' detachment, and stormed the treasury. After taking the treasurer and book-keeper prisoner and shamelessly plundering the public funds, she went home. On the way she scattered coppers among the populace, and her drunken supporters shouted: 'That's our good mother! Now, lads, we'll not go short of a drink!'

When the deputy governor woke the following day, it was all over. From his window he saw the inhabitants congratulating each other, exchanging kisses and weeping. He did make an attempt to seize the reins of government once more, but promptly dropped them again because of his shaking hands. In dejection and despair he hurried to the Town Hall to find out how many constables were still loyal to him, but on the way he was seized by the court assessor Tolkovnikov and brought before Iraidka. There he found the town clerk, tied up, also awaiting his fate.

'Do you acknowledge me as town-governess?' Iraidka cried to them.

'If you have a husband and can prove that he is the governor of this town, then I will acknowledge you as town-governess!' was the staunch reply of the deputy governor. The town clerk trembled all over, and his trembling seemed to emphasize the bravery of his colleague.

'Nobody is asking you if I'm wife or widow. I want to know if you acknowledge me as town-governess!' cried Iraidka in still greater fury.

'If you have no better proof, then I do not!' replied the deputy governor with such firmness that the town clerk's teeth chattered and he struggled in panic to escape.

'What's the good of talking? To the bell-tower with them!' howled Tolkovnikov and his followers.

There is no doubt that the fate of these officials who had remained true to their duty would have been a very lamentable one, if they had not been saved by an unforeseen circumstance. While Iraidka was unconcernedly celebrating her victory, the dauntless staff-officer had not been idle and, guided by the saying that 'It takes a wedge to shift a wedge', he had persuaded a certain adventuress by the name of Klemantinka de Bourbon to come forward and claim power for herself. This claim was based on the fact that her father, the Chevalier de Bourbon, had at one time been governor of a town, a post from which he had been dismissed for cheating at cards. Furthermore, the new pretender was tall in stature, fond of vodka, and rode on horseback like a man. She easily gained the support of four of the irregulars' detachment and, with the secret support of a Polish conspiracy, this villainous rogue of a woman at once won over the inhabitants. Once more the Glupovites rushed to the bell-tower and threw from the top of it one Timoshka and a third Ivashka. After that they went to Trubochistikha's and razed her establishment to the ground, then rushed to the river and drowned Proshka and a fourth Ivashka.

This was how things stood when Tolkovnikov and his comrades set off to take the gallant martyrs to the bell-tower. In the street they were met by the mob led by Klemantinka (with the dauntless staff-officer in the middle keeping constant watch) and the prisoners were immediately set free.

'Well, old fellows, do you acknowledge me as town-governess?' enquired the wanton Klemantinka.

'If you have a husband and can prove that he is the governor of this town, then we acknowledge you as governess!' replied the deputy governor bravely.

'Lord bless them! Give them a patch of ground apiece where

they can grow cabbages and keep a few geese', said Klemantinka mildly, and moved on to the house where Iraidka had barricaded herself in.

A battle ensued. All day and all night Iraidka defended herself, skilfully sheltering behind the captive treasurer and book-keeper.

'Surrender!' cried Klemantinka.

'Give in yourself, you brazen hussy, and call off these dogs of yours!' came Iraidka's bold reply.

However, by the following morning Iraidka had begun to weaken, though this was only because in an excess of civic valour the treasurer and the book-keeper had flatly refused to defend her stronghold. The situation of the besieged was now very doubtful. Besides having to repulse the attackers, Iraidka had to cope with treachery in her own camp. Seeing things must end badly, she decided on a hero's death and, gathering up all the money she had taken from the treasury, in full view, she blew herself sky-high – together with the treasurer and book-keeper.

Next morning, as the deputy governor was planting his cabbages, he saw that the inhabitants were once more congratulating each other, exchanging kisses, and weeping. Some of them even made so bold as to come and pat him on the back and jokingly address him as 'swineherd'. Needless to say, the deputy governor promptly noted the names of these bold spirits on a scrap of paper.

News of the Glupovites' 'absurd and risible confusion' finally came to the authorities. The order was given 'to find and deliver the wanton, Klemantinka, and her accomplices, and to give strict instructions to the Glupovites to refrain from drowning innocent citizens in the river or brutally throwing them from the bell-tower'. But still no news came concerning the appointment of a new governor.

Meanwhile, matters in Glupov were becoming more and more involved. A third pretender appeared, called Amalya Stockfisch. She was a native of Revel and based her claim simply on the fact that she had for two months been the mistress of a town-governor. Once more the Glupovites rushed to the bell-tower, threw from the top a Stepka, and were on the point of throwing over yet another Ivashka when they were restrained by the honoured citizen Sila Terentev Puzanov.

'See here, my hearties,' he said, 'If we carry on like this, we shall kill everybody and still be no further forward.'

'That's a fact!' they agreed, on second thoughts.

'Hold on, though!' cried some. 'Why does Ivashka here make

such a shindy? That's not orders, is it?'

The fifth Ivashka stood by the bell-tower, half-dead with terror, mechanically bowing in all directions.

At that moment Mistress Stockfisch came riding up on a white horse, accompanied by half a dozen drunken soldiers, who were leading captive the wanton Klemantinka. Stockfisch was a plump, blonde German with a prominent bosom, rosy cheeks and full lips, like cherries. The crowd stirred with excitement.

'There's a fat one for you! Full of dimples she is!' exclaimed several of the crowd.

But Stockfisch had evidently weighed up the hazards of her situation beforehand, and hastened to dispel them by her coolness.

'Now, my hearties!' she roared at the top of her voice, making a bold gesture towards Klemantinka, who was drunk and lost to the world. 'Here is that wanton Klemantinka, the one the order said was to be found and delivered! Do you see her?'

'Yes, we see her!' roared the crowd.

'You *do* see her? And you recognize her as the same wanton Klemantinka the order said was to be found and delivered?'

'Yes, that's her all right!'

'Then fetch them out three barrels of the best!' exclaimed the dauntless Stockfisch, turning to the soldiers, and then rode leisurely out of the crowd.

'Amalya Karlovna! She's the one for us! Our good mother! Now, lads, there'll be drink for us in plenty!' cried the brave lads as she rode off.

That day the whole of Glupov was drunk, and drunkest of all was the fifth Ivashka. The wanton Klemantinka was put in a cage and carried out on to the square; the brave lads went up to her and taunted her. Some of the better-natured ones gave her vodka, but told her to cut them a caper in return.

The ease with which Stockfisch, the fat German, had gained her victory over the wanton Klemantinka is very simply explained. No sooner had Klemantinka destroyed Iraidka than she closeted herself with her soldiers for a spell of dissipation. The Polish conspirators, Pan Kszepszyciulski and Pan Pszekszyciulski, of whom she had been the secret tool, appealed, protested, and threatened in vain, – within five minutes Klemantinka was drunk and past understanding. The Pans kept it up a little longer, but then, seeing that further insistence was useless, withdrew. The same night Klemantinka had been taken unconscious from her bed and dragged into the street in her shift.

The dauntless staff-officer was in despair. All his plots, devices, and disguises had achieved precisely nothing. The town was in a state of complete anarchy; there was no one in authority, the Marshal of Nobility had fled into the country, the chief inspector of police and the school-inspector were in hiding and trembled together in the straw in the fire-station yard. The staff-officer himself was sought throughout the town and a three-kopek reward was offered for his capture. The inhabitants were most excited, for it would have been a feather in anyone's cap to pocket those three kopeks. The staff-officer was already wondering whether it would not be as well to surrender and have the reward for himself, when an unexpected occurrence gave a completely different turn to events.

It had been easy enough for Amalya Stockfisch to deal with the wanton Klemantinka, but it was incomparably more difficult to put a stop to the Polish conspiracy, which moved in hidden, subterranean ways. After the defeat of Klemantinka Pan Kszepszyciulski and Pan Pszekszyciulski had gone sadly home, loud in their complaints about the ineptitude of the Russians, who even for such an occasion as this could not produce a single person of talent. At that moment, however, their attention was caught by a seemingly insignificant occurrence.

It was a fresh May morning and there was a heavy dew. The Glupovites, after a riotous and sleepless night, had gone to bed, and a deathly hush lay over the town. The Pans saw two youths daubing tar on the gate of an unprepossessing wooden house. The youths, evidently thrown into confusion on seeing the Poles, took to their heels, but the Poles fetched them back.

'What are you doing here?' they asked.

'We were just tarring Nelka's gate', confessed one of the youths. 'She's been running very loose of late.'

The Pans exchanged glances and whistled meaningly. They walked on, but a plan had already taken shape in their minds. They remembered that it was a compatriot of theirs, Anelja Ladochowska, who lived in this old wooden house. She kept an inn there, and although she had absolutely no right to the title of gubernatorial mistress she had on one occasion been sent for by the governor. And this was quite enough for the Poles to put forward a new pretender and weave a new Polish intrigue.

It was all the easier for them, since at that time the licence of the Glupovites had reached unprecedented heights. Not only did they in a single day throw from the bell-tower and drown in the river several dozens of favoured citizens, but they had without any authority apprehended an official travelling to the town on official business from the provincial capital.

'Who are you? What do you want here?' the Glupovites asked him, as he was about to enter the town.

'I am an official of the provincial administration', answered the traveller and gave his name. 'I have come to investigate the infamous doings of Klemantinka.'

'He's lying! That baggage Klemantinka sent him herself! Off with him to the lock-up!' cried the Glupovites.

In vain did the traveller protest and resist, in vain did he produce papers – they believed nothing and refused to let him go.

'We've seen papers like that before, friend, and it never did any good! And we'd better not talk to you, for anybody can tell from the look of you that you are one of Klemantinka's spies', shouted some.

'Why waste time talking? Into the river with him, and be done with it!' cried others.

The unfortunate official was led away to the lock-up and handed over to the gaolers.

Meanwhile Amalya Stockfisch was taking active measures. She imposed a tax of three kopeks on each household of the ordinary townsfolk, and claimed a pound of tea and a large sugar-loaf from the merchants. Then she went to the barracks and personally served each soldier with a glass of vodka and a slice of pie. On her way home she met the deputy governor and the town clerk, who were driving geese from the meadow.

'Well, old fellows, how is it? Changed your minds? Do you acknowledge me?' she asked good-humouredly.

'If you have a husband and can prove that he is our governor, then we will acknowledge you as town-governess!' replied the deputy governor firmly.

'Well, the Lord be with you, tend your geese', said Amalya and went her way.

Towards evening it rained so heavily that for hours the streets of the town were impassable. Because of this the night passed peaceably for everyone, except the unfortunate official from the provincial capital, who, for his more certain torment, had been placed in a dark and narrow cell that had always been known as 'the greater flea-pit' (as distinct from the 'lesser' one, where less dangerous criminals were put). The following morning was similarly unprofitable for the Polish conspiracy – since, always operating in the dark, it cannot stand the light of day. Amalya, the fat German, deceived by this outward calm, thought herself well established and even ventured into the street and ogled the passers-by. However, that evening, for the sake of form, she called all the most experienced constables together and held a conference. The constables made the following unanimous recommendations: firstly, that the wanton Klemantinka should be drowned forthwith to stop her rousing and provoking the populace; secondly, that the deputy governor and town clerk should be put to torture; and, thirdly, that the dauntless staff-officer should be found and delivered. But such was the blindness of this unfortunate woman that she would not heed suggestions for acting with severity and gave orders for the visiting official to be transferred from the greater flea-pit to the lesser.

Meanwhile, the Glupovites had gradually begun to come to their senses, and the forces of law and order, which had been hiding in the back yards, now took modest, but firm steps into the open. The deputy governor, after discussions with the town clerk and the dauntless staff-officer, tried to persuade the Glupovites to turn from the false and evil ways of Amalya Stockfisch and Klemantinka. He strongly condemned the order which led to the official from the provincial administration being shut up in the flea-pit and warned the Glupovites of the serious trouble this would bring on the town. Sila Terentev Puzanov shook his head so sadly, that if the brave lads had had the least bit more spirit they would certainly have torn the gaol down, board by board. As it happened, the wanton Klemantinka also did a service of some value to the party of law and order.

She was still in her cage in the square, and it was the delight of the Glupovites in their idle moments to come and bait her, since this roused her to a state of incredible fury, particularly when they touched her with the red-hot end of an iron rod.

'How's that, Klemantinka, is that nice?' asked some, roaring with laughter, as the wanton writhed in pain.

'Yes, lads, and how much of our good vodka has this baggage put inside her? Far too much!' chimed in others.

'It was yours I drank was it?' snapped back the wanton Klemantinka. 'If I'd had no taste for liquor and if those dear Poles of mine hadn't walked out on me, you would have known the sort of woman I am by now!'

'It looks as though old fatty has shown you the sort of woman *she* is first!'

'You and the fat one! Whatever I am, I'm still a governor's daughter, and you've landed yourselves with a German baggage who used to trade herself in the market.'

The Glupovites paused for a moment and thought over what Klemantinka had said. She had posed them a nice problem.

'What do you think, lads? You know, Klemantinka's right, wanton though she is', said some.

'Let's go and give it to the fat one!' cried others.

And if the constables had not just then come hurrying up, it would have been too bad for the fat one, and she too would have gone head first off the bell-tower. But the constables were strict, and the cause of law and order was delayed and the brave fellows, after a little more noise, went home.

But the triumph of the 'saucy German' was anyway coming to an end. That night, she had scarcely closed her eyes when she heard a suspicious noise in the street. She realized at once that the game was up. Wearing only her shift and with nothing on her feet, she rushed to the window, intending at least to avoid the humiliation of being put in a cage like Klemantinka. But it was too late.

The strong hand of Pan Kszepszyciulski held her firmly by the waist, and Nelka Ladochowska, 'waxing furious as never before', called her to give account of herself.

'Is it true, Mistress Stockfisch, that you have deceitfully seized power and falsely called yourself the town-governess, thus leading many souls into error?' she asked her.

'It is true', said Amalya in reply. 'Only there was nothing deceitful or false about it, for I was and still am the town-governess.'

'And how did you come to get such nonsense in your head, you baggage? Who put you up to it?' demanded Ladochowska, going on with her questions regardless of Amalya's reply.

At this Amalya took umbrage.

'There may be a baggage here', she said. 'Only it's not me!'

After that, Amalya answered no more questions and maintained a scornful silence. Try as they would to make her admit her guilt, she refused to do so. They decided to lock her in the cage with Klemantinka.

'It was a dread sight', says the 'Chronicle', 'to see these two wanton women given to consume each other by that other, still more wanton. Suffice it to say that by morning all that was left in the cage was their reeking bones!'

When they awoke, the Glupovites were surprised to learn what had happened, but even now they were not put out. Once more they came into the street and began congratulating each other, exchanging kisses, and weeping. Some of them suggested they should be allowed a drink to clear their heads.

'A plague on you!' cried the dauntless staff-officer, as he witnessed this scene. He then turned dispiritedly to the deputy governor and asked what they could do now.

'We must act', replied the deputy governor. 'I know! Why not start a rumour that this rascally Nelka had ordered Roman churches to be set up in place of our holy Orthodox ones?'

'Splendid!'

But by midday there were even more alarming rumours. Things happened with incredible swiftness. In the Soldiers' quarter on the outskirts of the town another pretender, called Dunka Tolstopyataya, had declared herself, while in the Musketeers' suburb a similar claim had been made by a certain Matrenka-Nozdrya. Both based their claims on the fact that they too had several times gone to 'solace' the governors of the town. It was necessary, therefore, to repulse not one pretender, but three at once.

Both Dunka and Matrenka went on a wild rampage. They went into the street and punched up the passers-by, they went to the taverns and single-handed smashed them to pieces, they captured young men and hid them in cellars, they ate babies, cut off women's breasts and ate them too. With their hair flying loose in the wind, wearing only the clothes they had got up in, they ran through the town like women possessed, spitting, biting and mouthing obscenities.

The Glupovites were simply terror-struck. Once more they ran to the bell-tower, and there is no telling how many citizens were dashed to death and drowned. A general day of reckoning began. Everyone recalled all manner of things about his neighbour, even things his neighbour had never as much as dreamed of, and since all proceedings were summary, nothing was to be heard in the town but a continuous Splash! Splash! Splash! Around four o'clock in the afternoon the gaol caught fire. The Glupovites rushed to the spot and saw to their horror that the official from the provincial capital had been burnt to a cinder. Once more a day of reckoning began. They asked themselves whose villainy it was that had brought about the fire and decided that it must have been caused by that arrant rogue and criminal the fifth Ivashka. They put him on the rack and told him to make a clean breast of the whole thing, but while they were doing this a fire broke out in the Cannoneers' suburb in the house known as the 'lesser beetle-den', and everyone hurried off there, leaving the fifth Ivashka stretched on the rack. The alarm-bell was rung, but the flames

45

quickly engulfed everything and every beetle perished. The Glupovites then captured Matrenka-Nozdrya and set about drowning her decently in the river, demanding to know who had encouraged her (arrant rogue and criminal that she was) in her villainy and who had abetted her. But Matrenka merely blew bubbles and betrayed none of her accomplices or followers.

In the general confusion the Glupovites had completely forgotten the villainous Nelka. Nelka, seeing her cause had failed, retired to her inn, and the Poles, Pan Kszepszyciulski and Pan Pszekszyciulski, opened a ginger-bread shop. This left only Dunka Tolstopyataya. But there was no getting the better of her.

'We must get rid of her, lads, without fail!' Sila Puzanov exhorted the Glupovites.

'All right then, you go and catch her!' they replied.

It was now the sixth day since the uprising began.

The scene that followed was a touching and unprecedented one. The Glupovites were exalted in spirit and performed of themselves a modest deed for their own salvation. They had killed and drowned a great host of people, and at last definitely decided that no trace of sedition could now be left in Glupov. Those who were left were all well-intentioned,[37] and each man now could look the others straight in the eye, knowing well that they had not been guilty of supporting Klemantinka, or Iraidka, or Matrenka. They decided on joint action and began by making contact with the outlying suburbs of the town. As might be expected, the first to step forward was the dauntless staff-officer.

'Fellow-citizens!' he began in an agitated voice – but, as what he had to say was secret, naturally none of it was heard by those present.

Still, the Glupovites were moved to tears by his speech and urged the deputy governor to take up the reins of government again. This, however, he resolutely refused to do until Dunka had been taken. There were sighs from the crowd and cries of 'Oh, great are our sins!' – but the deputy governor was not to be moved.

'Now my hearties!' came a voice from the crowd, 'If there is still treason left in any man, let him step forward!'

The crowd was silent.

'Are you all purged?' asked the same voice.

'Yes, yes!' roared the crowd.

'Cross yourselves, brothers!'

They all crossed themselves, and a general levy was declared to campaign against Dunka Tolstopyataya.

Meanwhile, from the outlying suburbs reassuring replies were reaching the town. They were all agreed that treason should be uprooted and that they should start by purging themselves. The answer from the Dimwitty district was particularly moving. 'Brethren, look but diligently within yourselves', wrote the inhabitants, 'so that in your hearts the nest of treason be not made, and that you be whole, and before the face of your superiors not evilly-intended, but zealous for good, full of niceness and worthy of praise.' As this reply was being read, sobbing could be heard in the crowd, and a woman called Mangy Aksinya, being fired with great zeal, tipped two twenty-kopek pieces from her purse and opened a fund for the capture of Dunka.

But Dunka would not give in. She fortified herself in the 'greater bug-house' and armed herself with a cannon, which she used like a musket.

'The bitch, see how she handles that cannon!' said the Glupovites, not daring to advance.

'May the bugs get you!' cried others.

But even the bugs appeared to be on her side. She dispatched whole swarms of them against the besiegers, who fled in terror. They decided to try and keep them off with pitch, and this did have some effect. Indeed, the bug sorties ended, but an attack on the house was still impossible owing to the mass array of defending bugs and to the fact that Dunka still operated the cannon with deadly effect. An attempt was made to set the house on fire, but there was little agreement among the besiegers, since no one wished to take the responsibility of command – and the attempt came to nothing.

'Give in, Dunka! We'll not hurt you!' shouted the besiegers, hoping to win her by deceitful words.

But Dunka only answered with some crudity.

Thus it went on until evening. When night fell, the besiegers judiciously retired, leaving a line of pickets at the bug-house in case anything occurred.

It turned out, however, that the stratagem of using pitch against the bugs had some effect after all. The bugs, unable to leave the stronghold in search of food, and attracted by the smell of human flesh, streamed back indoors to satisfy their thirst for blood. In the very dead of night Glupov was rent by a hideous cry of anguish: it was Dunka Tolstopyataya giving up the ghost as the bugs consumed her. They found her body next day lying in the middle of the house. It was nothing but a piece of raw flesh. Nearby lay the cannon and a multitude of squashed bugs. The bugs that remained, as if chastened by their exploit, had taken refuge in cracks between the boards.

It was now the seventh day since the uprising began. The Glupovites were triumphant. But, although the internal enemies had been defeated and the Polish intrigue confounded, the inhabitants were rather uneasy, for there was still neither sight nor sound of a new town-governor. They drifted about like dying flies, not daring to undertake anything, because they did not know how pleased a new governor would be by their recent escapades.

Finally, at two o'clock in the afternoon of the seventh day, he arrived. The newly appointed governor was Semen Konstantinovich Dvoekurov, a State Councillor and knight of an order.

He at once walked on to the square where the rioters were and called for the ring-leaders. Stepka Gorlasty and Filka Beschastny were handed over.

Lukerya Terentevna, the new governor's wife, bowed graciously in all directions.

Thus did this villainous and ludicrous passage of violence come to an end. It ended and such a thing has never happened since.

Notice concerning Dvoekurov

DVOEKUROV held office as town-governor from 1762 to 1770. No detailed account of his governorship has come to light, but, since it coincided with the first and most brilliant years of Catherine's reign, it must be assumed that this was probably the best period in Glupov's history.

The 'Chronicle of Glupov' mentions Dvoekurov three times: first, in the 'Schedule of Town-governors', secondly, at the end of the description of the time of troubles, and thirdly, in the account of the history of Glupov liberalism (see the account of the governorship of Ugryum-Burcheev). It is clear from these references that Dvoekurov was a progressive man and took his duties very seriously. It is inconceivable that the chronicler would have failed to record such valuable information in the history of the town, and it seems most likely that Dvoekurov's biography was deliberately suppressed by his successors on account of its too liberal tone and the temptation it might offer to students of our history to look for constitutionalism where, in fact, there exists only the principle of liberal flogging. This supposition is partly confirmed by the fact that in the Glupov archives there is a single page which is obviously part of a full biography of Dvoekurov. It is so defaced that despite every effort the editor could only make out the following: '. . . being of considerable stature . . . gave great hopes of . . . But being seized with terror . . . unable to fulfil . . . With this memory he passed his life in sadness'. And that is all. What is the meaning of these enigmatic words? It is, of course, impossible to give a definite answer to this question, but if one may hazard a guess on such an important matter then one or two possibilities might be suggested: either, that Dvoekurov, with his considerable stature (some six feet six inches), was supposed to possess some special ability (for example, to be agreeable to women), which he failed to make use of, or, that he was entrusted with some task which he hesitated to carry out – and then passed his life in sadness.

Whichever it was, Dvoekurov's rule in Glupov was undoubtedly fruitful. The fact alone that he introduced the brewing of mead and beer and made obligatory the use of mustard and bay-leaf proves that he was a direct forerunner of those bold innovators, who, three-quarters of a century later, waged war in the name of the potato.[38] But the most important product of Dvoekurov's governorship was undoubtedly his memorandum on the need to found an academy in Glupov.

Fortunately, this memorandum has survived intact* and enables us to pass fair and impartial judgement on Dvoekurov's contribution to the cause of enlightenment. The editor is of the opinion that the ideas contained in this document, apart from showing that even in those distant times there were people with a right view of things, can also still serve as a guide for carrying out similar projects. Of course, our modern academies have a somewhat different character from that proposed by Dvoekurov, but since what matters is not the name, but the final purpose of the project – which is no more than 'the survey of learning' – then, clearly, as long as learning is only to be 'surveyed' Dvoekurov's project will lose none of its force as an educational document. The fact that names may be entirely fortuitous and very rarely change the substance of a thing was very well demonstrated by Borodavkin, one of Dvoekurov's successors. He also asked for the establishment of an academy, but when his request was refused, promptly built a gaol instead. The name was different, but what he had intended was achieved, and Borodavkin wished for nothing more. And, after all, who can say how long Borodavkin's academy might have survived, or what fruits it might have borne? It might have turned out to be built on sand; perhaps, instead of 'surveying' learning, it might have dared to propagate it. One simply cannot tell. But in the case of a gaol, you know exactly where you are. It is built on a firm foundation and will never depart from its expected function.

That is the idea which Dvoekurov develops in his project with that indisputable clarity and consistency, which, alas, none of our modern planners possess. Of course, Dvoekurov was not as resolute a man as Borodavkin, that is, he did not build a gaol instead of an academy, and in fact resoluteness seems to have been generally lacking in his character. Should he be condemned for this deficiency? Or should one rather see in it a secret leaning towards constitutionalism? The answer to this question is left to modern students of our national past, who are referred by the editor to the original document.

* It is printed in full among the Supporting Documents at the end of the present volume. (In fact, Saltykov did not include Dvoekurov's memorandum in this section. I.P.F.).

The Hungry Town

FOR Glupov the year 1776 began with omens of the greatest good fortune. For six whole years the town had suffered neither fire nor famine, epidemic nor cattle-plague, and this unprecedented prosperity was ascribed by the citizens, and not without reason, to the simplicity of their governor, Brigadier Petr Petrovich Ferdyshchenko. And, indeed, such was his simplicity that the chronicler finds himself obliged more than once to emphasize this quality as offering the most natural explanation for the pleasure the Glupovites enjoyed during the Brigadier's administration. He interfered in nothing, was content with modest offerings of tribute, liked to drop in to the taverns for a chat with the tapsters, and in the evenings would come out on to the porch of his residence in a greasy dressing-gown to play cards for nose-taps[39] with his subordinates. He liked greasy food, drank *kvass*, and was fond of embellishing his speech with an affectionate 'my dear good sir'.

'And now, my dear good sir, lie down and be flogged!' he would say to an inhabitant guilty of some misdemeanour.

Or:

'My dear good sir, you know, you'll have to sell that cow of yours, because, my dear good sir, it's a sacred duty to pay your taxes!'

Naturally, after the antics of the Marquis de Sanglot, who had flown in the air in the municipal gardens, the tranquil administration of the aged Brigadier must have seemed both 'prosperous' and 'worthy of wonder'. For the first time the Glupovites breathed freely and realized that to live 'without restraint' was better by far than living with it.

'It's no matter that he doesn't have parades and come on us with armies', they said. 'Under him, our good master, we've seen the light. Now when you go out, you can sit down if you fancy, or go where you will. But before there were so many rules – that the Lord preserve us!'

But in the seventh year of his rule Ferdyshchenko was possessed by a devil. This kindly, rather indolent ruler suddenly became active and resolute in the extreme: he cast off his greasy dressing-gown and took to going about the town in uniform. He demanded that the inhabitants should not be idle, but keep alert, and ended by creating such a state of turmoil that things might have gone badly for him, if at the height of their aggravation the Glupovites had not realized that this would only get them into trouble.

It so happened that at this time in the outlying suburb called Dunghills there lived a certain Alenka Osipova. And she was in the full flower of her beauty. She was evidently that type of luscious Russian beauty at the sight of which a man is not fired with passion, but feels his whole being slowly melt. She was plump and of middle height, with a pink and white complexion; she had large grey protruding eyes, and there was something in the way they looked that was not exactly wanton, nor yet exactly modest; she had full lips like cherries, thick, well-marked eyebrows, and plaited auburn hair which reached to her ankles; as she walked down the street she was as splendid as a grey goose. Her husband, Dmitry Prokofev, was a stage-driver, and a good match for his wife – young, strong, and handsome. He wore a velveteen jacket and a sheep-skin cap decked with peacock's feathers. Dmitry was devoted to Alenka, and Alenka was devoted to him. They often went along to the neighbouring tavern and sang together in their happiness. The Glupovites were delighted to see them living so contentedly together.

How long they lived in this way is no matter, but at the beginning of 1776 the Brigadier called in at the tavern where they happily spent their leisure hours. He drank half a bottle of vodka and enquired of the tapster whether drunkenness was on the increase, but just then he caught sight of Alenka and felt his tongue cling to his throat. However, too abashed to declare himself in public, he went into the street, beckoning Alenka to follow.

'How would you like to come and live with me?' asked the Brigadier.

'And what would I want with you . . . you old coot?' replied Alenka, looking him brazenly in the face. 'I've got a good husband of my own.'

These were the only words to pass between them, but they were not pleasant ones. Next day the Brigadier sent two militiamen to take up quarters in Dmitry Prokofev's house, with instructions to be 'restrictive'. Then he donned his uniform and went to the market. To condition himself to severity he shouted in fury at the stall-holders:

'Who is your governor? Answer me! Or perhaps you think I am not your governor?'

As for Dmitry Prokofev, instead of submitting and bringing his wife to see reason, he gave vent to villainous words, while Alenka armed herself with the oven-fork and chased off the militiamen, shouting for the whole street to hear:

'That Brigadier's a fine one! Crawling like a bug into a married woman's bed!'

It is understandable how upset the Brigadier must have been on hearing that he had been spoken of in these flattering terms. But, since these were liberal times and there was talk abroad of the value of the elective principle, the old man was wary of acting on his own authority. He therefore assembled the most favoured Glupovites, put the matter briefly to them, and demanded the immediate punishment of the recalcitrant parties.

'It's for you to say, my dear good sirs', he added like a true liberal, 'you fix how many lashes apiece – I'll agree to anything you say. For we live in a time when to everyone his own, as long as there is still some flogging!'

After some noisy discussion, the citizens made the following reply:

'Give them as many lashes as there are stars in the sky, your honour. That'll teach these scoundrels a lesson.'

The Brigadier began counting the stars ('great was his simplicity', remarks the chronicler again), but before reaching a hundred he lost count and turned and asked his orderly. The orderly replied that there were hundreds and thousands of stars.

Evidently this answer was good enough for the Brigadier, for when Alenka and Dmitry returned home after their punishment they staggered like drunken men.

But still Alenka refused to give in, or, as the chronicler puts it, 'took to herself no benefit from the Brigadier's lashes'. On the contrary, she seemed to grow only more vehement, as was proved when, a week later, the Brigadier again came into the tavern and beckoned her.

'Well, you stupid hussy, have you made up your mind?' he asked.

'You've got it bad, haven't you, you old dog! Just take your filthy eyes off me!' snapped Alenka.

'Very well!' said the Brigadier.

However, the old man's persistence caused Alenka to have

second thoughts. Coming home after this conversation, she was completely distraught and could not settle to her usual tasks. Then she collapsed against Dmitry and wept bitterly.

'It's no good. I can see there's nothing for it but for me to be the Brigadier's woman', she said in a flood of tears.

'You just do that, and I'll . . . tear you limb from limb!' said Dmitry, breathing heavily, and was just about to go to the bed where he kept his leather rein-straps when he stopped. Shaking all over, he dropped to the bench and let himself go.

He shouted, rapidly, at the top of his voice, there was no telling what he was shouting, but one thing was clear – that here was a man in revolt.

The Brigadier, hearing that Dmitry was in revolt and twice as bitter as before, had the rebel put in irons and carried off to gaol. Alenka rushed, like a woman demented, to the Brigadier's house, but was incapable of speaking clearly. All she did was to rend her dress and cry wildly:

'There, you dog! Now you can get your filthy teeth into me!'

Surprisingly, the Brigadier was not offended, and gave Alenka a ginger-bread and a jar of pomade, just as if nothing had happened. At the sight of these gifts Alenka seemed overcome. She no longer shouted, only sobbed quietly. Then the Brigadier had his new uniform brought, and, putting it on, appeared before Alenka in all his splendour. At the same time his old housekeeper ran out and began remonstrating with her.

'What are you so worried about, you jade? Have some sense', said the smooth-tongued crone. 'The Brigadier will bathe you in honey-water, you know.'

'It's Dmitry I'm sorry for!' Alenka answered, but with a note of uncertainty in her voice that indicated she was beginning to think of giving in.

That night there was a fire in the Brigadier's house. Fortunately, they were able to put it out as soon as it started, and all that was burnt was the archive-room, which was temporarily occupied by pigs being fattened up for feast-days. Naturally there was suspicion of incendiarism, and the person suspected was none other than Dmitry. It was learnt that he had made the gaolers drunk and had gone off in the night, no one knew where. The criminal was apprehended and tortured, but, arrant scoundrel and villain that he was, he would admit nothing.

'I don't know a thing about it', he said. 'All I know is that you've carried off my wife, you old dog, and that I'll forgive you . . . take her!

But they still would not believe him, and the case being urgent, the proceedings were carried out in simplified form. Within a month Dmitry had been knouted on the town square, branded, and dispatched to Siberia, in company with other inveterate scoundrels and brigands. The Brigadier was triumphant. Alenka quietly sobbed.

However, the Glupovites had to pay for all this. As is the rule, the sins of the Brigadier were visited first of all on them.

From that time on things in Glupov were never the same. Each morning the Brigadier would run in full uniform from stall to stall in the market, carrying off all he could lay his hands on. Even Alenka began lifting things as she passed, and then flatly demanded that people should respect her for what she was – not the wife of a stage-driver, but the daughter of a priest.

But this was not all. Nature itself ceased to look favourably on the Glupovites. 'This new Jezebel', says the chronicler of Alenka, 'brought drought upon the town.' From St. Nicholas's Day in the spring when the floods subsided right up to Elias's Day there was not a drop of rain. The old inhabitants could remember nothing like it and, not without some justification, saw the reason for it in the Brigadier's fall from virtue. The sky became burning hot and breathed down a torrent of heat on every living thing; the air appeared to quiver, and there was a smell of burning; the ground cracked and was hard as stone, so that neither plough nor spade could turn it; the grass and young vegetables withered; the rye matured and eared unusually early, but it was so sparse, and the grain so meagre, that nobody expected to harvest enough even for seed; the spring corn simply failed to come up at all, and the fields where it had been sown lay as black as pitch, depressing the sight of the inhabitants with their hopeless bareness; even the goosefoot[40] did not grow; the animals chased about, lowing and neighing, and, finding no food in the fields, they ran into the town and filled the streets. The people grew lean and went about with drooping heads. Only the potters were pleased at the hot, dry weather, but even they thought differently when they saw that there were plenty of pots, but no pottage.

However, the Glupovites did not despair, for they still did not realize the full extent of the evil in store for them. As long as they had last year's stock, many in their folly went on eating and drinking and giving banquets as though there was no end to their supplies. The Brigadier went about the town in his uniform and gave strictest instructions that anyone looking dispirited should be brought to appear before him at the lock-up. To put heart into the people, he told the tax-contractor to organize a picnic with fireworks in the woods outside the town. The picnic was held, the fireworks let off, 'but no bread was provided to the people by these means'. Then the Brigadier called together the most favoured citizens and ordered them to raise the people's spirits. So they set about visiting their neighbours, and there was no person in despair whom they failed to comfort.

Some said 'Oh, we're old hands – we can take it! Why, you could put us all in a heap and light us at the corners – and we wouldn't give a murmur.'

'Think nothing of it', added others, 'We can take it – we know we've got good men over us!'

'What do you think?' a third group asked cheerfully. 'You don't suppose the high-ups are asleep, do you? No, no, my friend, they're having a doze with one eye, but there's nothing they don't see with the other one!'

But when the hay was gathered in it was clear there would be no fodder for the animals; and when the corn harvest was over it was clear there would be nothing to feed the people with either. The Glupovites were alarmed and started going up to the Brigadier's house.

'What of the bread, sir? Will you be seeing about it?' they asked him.

'I'm seeing to it, my dears, I'm seeing to it', answered the Brigadier.

'That's well, then. Do what you can.'

At the end of July the rain came down in useless torrents, and in August people started dying because they had eaten all the food there was. They thought of ways to fill their bellies – they mixed flour and chopped rye-straw, but it was not at all filling; they tried it mixed with ground pine bark to see if it was any better, but this too, they found, had no real substance.

'It's true enough, when you eat it your belly seems to fill, but you've got to admit – there's no goodness in it!' said the Glupovites one to another.

The markets were deserted – there was nothing to sell and no one to sell it to, for the town was now empty. 'Some died', says the chronicler, 'and some took leave of their senses and fled where they would.' But the Brigadier still would not desist from his iniquities, and bought Alenka a fine new kerchief. When the Glupovites heard of this, they again stirred and crowded outside the Brigadier's house.

'You know, Brigadier, what you're doing isn't right – living with a married woman that you've taken from her husband!' they told him. 'And the powers that be didn't send you here to make us poor folk suffer for your follies!'

'Patience, my dears! There'll be plenty of everything!' said the Brigadier, hedging.

'To be sure, we'll be patient – we've seen hard times before. But just you think over what we've been saying, Brigadier, because you never know: we shall be patient all right, but even among us there's foolish chaps in plenty. We wouldn't want anything to happen!'

The crowd dispersed quietly, but the Brigadier set to thinking. He could see for himself that Alenka was the cause of all the trouble, but he could not part with her. He sent for the priest, thinking a talk with him might bring some comfort, but the priest only upset him more by recounting the story of Ahab and Jezebel.

'And when she was eaten by the dogs, the people had all perished to the last man!' the priest ended his story.

'See here, Father, you don't mean Alenka should be given to the dogs?' asked the Brigadier in alarm.

'That's not why I am saying this', explained the priest, 'but still it would not be inexpedient to dwell on the following circumstance: we have an indifferent flock, our means are small and food is dear . . . where, sir, will the shepherd find food?'

'Ah! it's for my sins that God has sent me this trouble in my old age!' moaned the Brigadier, and he began to weep bitterly.

Then he immediately sat down to his writing once again. He wrote at length, addressing a letter to every town.

He wrote as follows: if you can't send bread, at least send a detachment of soldiers.

But to none of these letters was there any response.

And every day the Glupovites grew more and more importunate.

'How about it, Brigadier? Have you had an answer?' they would ask with unprecedented insolence.

'No, I've not, my dears', the Brigadier would reply.

The Glupovites would look him in the eye 'in manner unbefitting' and shake their heads.

'You're an old coot, that's what!' they reproached him. 'They don't answer you, because you aren't worth bothering about!'

In short, the Glupovites began to ask very delicate questions indeed, for the time had come when their bellies started to have their say, and no argument or trickery can stand against that.

The Brigadier thought to himself: 'No, you'll never get anywhere with these people by persuasion. It's not persuasion that's needed here, but one of two things: either bread – or soldiers!'

Like all kindly governors, the Brigadier admitted this latter possibility with the very greatest regret. But he gradually entered into the idea of it so well that he reached the stage where he not only confused soldiers with bread, but even began to wish for the arrival of the former rather than the latter.

He would get up early in the morning and sit by the window listening for the blaring 'Tantara' of a trumpet:–

'Scatter, my hearties!
'To rock or bush!
'In column of twos!'

But no, there was no sound.

'It seems that God himself has forgotten us!' said the Brigadier.

And the Glupovites, meanwhile, went on living.

Every single one of the young people had fled. 'Many ran in flight', says the chronicler, 'but arriving nowhere, received the crown of martyrdom; many were taken captive and put in chains; these reckoned themselves lucky.' The only people to stay at home were the old and the young children whose legs lacked the strength to run away. At first it was easier for those who stayed, since the rations of those who fled increased the portion of those who were left. Thus they lived for another week or so, but then people started dying again. The women wailed, the churches overflowed with coffins, and corpses of the common people lay uncollected in the streets. It was difficult to breathe in the infected atmosphere; there were fears that plague might add to the devastation of famine and, as a precaution, a committee was formed and a plan drawn up for an emergency hospital with ten beds; a quantity of lint was prepared and a report sent to all parts. But, despite such evident solicitude on the part of the authorities, the inhabitants had hardened their hearts. Not an hour went by without one of them giving the Brigadier the fig or calling him a 'coot' or a 'toad' or something similar.

As a crowning misfortune, the Glupovites took to thinking for themselves. Following their old seditious habit, they assembled round the bell-tower and began to weigh and consider. In the end they elected a spokesman, their choice falling on Evseich, the oldest man in the whole town. For a long time the assembly and Evseich bowed low to each other, the assembly begging him to do this service, and he begging to be excused. In the end the assembly said:

'See how many years you've lived in the world, and how many governors you've seen – and still you are alive!'

At this even Evseich could not restrain himself.

'Many years have I lived!' he exclaimed in a sudden burst of ardour. 'Many governors have I seen! And I am alive!'

And, saying this, he wept. 'And his old heart was moved to do this service', adds the chronicler. And so Evseich was made spokesman. He decided that he would examine the Brigadier three times.

'Brigadier,' he said on the first occasion, 'do you know that all we poor folk in the town are dying?'

'Yes, I do', replied the Brigadier.

'And do you know for whose villainous wickedness such a thing has come to pass amongst us?'

'No, that I don't'.

The first examination was over. Evseich returned to the bell-tower and gave a full account of it to the assembly. 'And the Brigadier, seeing the severity of Evseich, was in great fear', says the chronicler.

Three days later Evseich went to the Brigadier for the second time, 'but having now lost his former firmness of countenance'.

'I live content in any place where there is righteousness!' he said. 'If right is on my side you can send me away to the end of the world, and with righteousness I shall be content even there.'

'True enough,' replied the Brigadier, 'you can live content with righteousness, only I would say this – it's better for an old man like you to stay at home with your precious righteousness than go around looking for trouble!'

'No! I cannot stay at home with righteousness, for righteousness will out. You try to steal into another man's bed, but there it is, good righteousness, driving you out . . . that's the way it is!'

'What of it? So be it, as far as I'm concerned! But just look out that this righteousness of yours doesn't run you into deep water!'

The second examination was over. Once more Evseich returned to the bell-tower and gave a full account to the assembly. 'And the Brigadier, seeing Evseich prate vainly about righteousness, feared him now but little', says the chronicler. In other words, Ferdyshchenko realized that if a man talks about righteousness in such a round-about fashion as this, it means that he himself is not altogether sure that he won't get a flogging for it.

Three days later Evseich came to the Brigadier for the third time and said:

'And do you know, you old dog . . .'

But before he had properly opened his mouth, the Brigadier himself had shouted:

'Put this old fool in irons!'

Evseich was dressed in convict's garb and, 'like a bride going to meet her bridgroom', was led off to gaol by two antiquated militiamen. As the procession approached, the assembled Glupovites drew aside.

'Never mind, Evseich, never mind!' people said all round. 'You can live content anywhere with righteousness.'

Evseich meanwhile was bowing in all directions.

'Forgive me, brave hearts', he said, 'if I've given offence or sinned before anyone, or ever told an untruth . . . forgive me all my wrongs!'

'God will forgive you!' came the answer.

'And if I've spoken out of turn to my superiors . . . if I've been a trouble-maker . . . that too, forgive me, for Christ's sake!'

'God will forgive you!'

And from that moment old Evseich vanished as though he had never been. He disappeared without trace, as only the 'zealots' of Russia know how to disappear. However, the Brigadier's severity had still only temporary effect. The town was quieter for a few days, but there was still no bread ('no worse affliction is there than this!' says the chronicler) and the Glupovites had no other recourse but to assemble once more by the bell-tower. The Brigadier observed this 'riotous fury' of the inhabitants from his porch and thought to himself: 'Now would be the time to grab them quick – one, two, three! – and that would be an end to it!' But the Glupovites had no thought of rebellion. They assembled and quietly discussed how they might provide for themselves, but they could think of nothing but to choose another spokesman.

The new spokesman, Pakhomych, took a different view from that of his unfortunate predecessor. As he saw it, the safest thing was to write a petition and send it to all parts of the land.

'There's a man I know', he said to the Glupovites. 'We could go and ask him to help us.'

Hearing this, the majority were delighted. However great their distress, they all seemed relieved at the thought that somewhere there was a person prepared to 'show zeal' for everybody else. They were all agreed that nothing could be done without some show of 'zeal', but they all thought it would be best if the zeal were not theirs, but somebody else's. The crowd was just about to move off in order to follow Pakhomych's advice, when the question arose of which way they had to go – right or left? This moment of indecision was exploited by the conservative faction.

'Brave hearts, wait!' they said. 'We don't want the Brigadier coming down on us. Shouldn't we first ask what kind of man this is?'

'Someone who knows all the tricks of the trade, that's what he is! An expert!' Pakhomych reassured them.

On enquiry it turned out that the man was none other than the retired clerk Bogolepov, who had been expelled from the service because of the 'shaking of his right hand' – the result of strong drink. He lived somewhere in the district called the 'Bog' in the tumble-down cottage of a woman whose frivolous ways had earned her the nicknames of 'Cow' and 'Loving Cup'. Bogolepov had no proper occupation and spent his days from morning till night writing slanderous reports, holding his right hand steady with the left. Nothing else was known about him and nothing else seemed to be necessary, for the majority were already inclined to put complete trust in him.

However, the question put by the conservatives had some effect, and when the crowd eventually moved off in the direction indicated by Pakhomych, a few detached themselves and made their way straight to the Brigadier's house. A split had taken place. There appeared the so-called 'defectors', that is, those far-sighted people who were intent on sparing their backs such shocks as the future promised to bring. These 'defectors' came to the Brigadier's house, but they said nothing – they simply hung about to show that they were well-intentioned.

However, despite the split, the business undertaken by the Glupovites in the 'Bog' was going ahead.

Bogolepov thought for a minute, as though he had first to clear his head of some old hangover. But this lasted only a moment and then he snatched his pen from the ink-well, sucked it, spat, and, grasping his right hand firmly with the left, began to write:

'To All Parts of the Russian Empire

The people and men of all ranks of the unfortunate town of Glupov in deep humility and great distress make petition on the matter contained in the following paragraphs:

1. We hereby notify all persons and places in the Empire of Russia that we poor folk are dying, one and all. About us we see that those in authority over us are without competence, strict in exacting dues, but lax in providing succour. And we further give notice that the stage-driver's wife, Alenka, who is living with Brigadier Ferdyshchenko, has without doubt been the cause of all

our misfortunes, and we see no other cause than this. When Alenka lived with her husband, the stage-driver Dmitry, then was our town peaceful, and we lived in plenty. We can suffer still longer, but we do fear that if we all die, the Brigadier and Alenka will make false report against us and bring doubt on us in the eyes of authority.

2. There are no more paragraphs.

To this petition the people of Glupov subscribe their crosses, two hundred and thirteen.'

When the petition was read through and signed everyone felt that a load had been taken from their minds. The document was put into an envelope, sealed and taken to the post.

'There it goes!' said the old men as they watched the *troika* disappearing with their petition into the unkown. 'Now we'll not have to suffer much more!'

And, indeed, all was quiet in the town again. The Glupovites raised no new rebellions, but sat about outside their cottages, waiting. If people passing through the town asked how things were, they answered:

'We're all right now, friend. We've sent off a paper about it.'

But a month went by, then another – and no reply came. But still the Glupovites went on living and still found something to chew. Their hopes were rising and every day they seemed more likely of fulfilment. Even the 'defectors' began to feel their fears had been misplaced and pressed to have their names included in the list of petitioners. Very likely the matter would have simply died down, if the Brigadier himself had not roused public opinion by his administrative ineptitude. Deceived by the outward tranquillity of the town, he found himself in a very delicate situation. On the one hand, he felt there was nothing he could do; on the other, he felt he ought to do something. He therefore lighted on a middle course, which was rather like a game of spillikins: he dropped his hook among the Glupovites, pulled out a conspirator and put him in gaol. In went the hook once more, up came another conspirator and likewise into gaol. And all the time he never stopped writing. The first to be put in gaol was, of course, Bogolepov, who was so terrified that he implicated a large number of other conspirators, and these in turn implicated still more. The Brigadier was in his glory. But the Glupovites were not only unalarmed, they simply laughed as they asked each other what new game the old dog was up to now.

'Wait!' they thought. 'The letter will be here any day now.'

But no letter came, and the Brigadier continued to weave his net, until little by little he had the whole town entangled in it. The weft and warp of intrigue are dangerous things if you once start pulling at the ends, and with the aid of two old militiamen the Brigadier had soon ensnared and dispatched to gaol the greater part of the town. There was not a household without one or two of its members among the conspirators.

'This way, neighbours, he'll have us all in a fix', said the Glupovites as they saw the way things were going, and this thought alone was enough to pour oil on the dying fire.

Quite spontaneously, the hundred and fifty 'crosses' who had so far escaped the Brigadier's clutches gathered on the square (the 'defectors' had again prudently made themselves scarce) and stopped before the Brigadier's house.

'We've come for Alenka!' roared the crowd.

The Brigadier saw that things were now out of hand and that the best thing he could do was to go and hide in the archives. This he did. Alenka hastened after him, but it so happened that the very moment the Brigadier passed through the door of the archives it slammed shut behind him. The lock clicked and Alenka was left on the outside, her arms thrown wide apart. She was in this position when the crowd came upon her. They found her pale, trembling all over and near-demented.

'Spare my tender skin, good people!' said Alenka, her voice faint with terror. 'You know he forced me from my husband.'

But the crowd were past hearing.

'Witch!' they cried. 'By what spell did you bring drought upon our town?'

Alenka seemed to take leave of her senses. She twisted and turned, as though convinced of the inevitable outcome of her situation. She could say nothing but repeat:

'I'm sick . . . oh! oh! . . . I'm sick!'

Then an unprecedented thing took place. As one man, the Glupovites lifted Alenka as though she were a puff of down, carried her to the topmost gallery of the bell-tower – and from there they threw her to the ground – a hundred feet or more below . . . .

'And of the Brigadier's sweet comforter not a single morsel remained. In the winking of an eye she was carried off by ravenous stray dogs.'

And just at the moment when this spontaneous bloody drama was enacted, far away on the highroad a thick cloud of dust was seen.

'It's the bread coming!' cried the Glupovites, their fury turning suddenly to joy.

'Tantara! Tantara!' The sound came clearly from the middle of the dust-cloud.

'Into column
'Double march!
'We'll let our bayonets
'Give the alarm!
'Double! Double! Double!'

The Town of Straw

THE town had scarcely begun to recover when the Brigadier was inspired by a new folly: he became enamoured of the accursed Domashka, a woman from the Musketeers' suburb.

The Musketeers of that period were no longer the genuine Musketeers of the time before Peter's reign,[41] but they still had memories of the past. Their grim, rather sardonic character did not yield lightly to the civilizing efforts of the authorities, however much the latter tried to impress on them that turmoil and rebellion could under no circumstances be tolerated as 'regular occupations'. The Musketeers lived in a special district outside the town called the Musketeers' suburb. At the opposite end of the town was situated the Cannoneers' suburb, and there lived the Cannoneers,[42] who had incurred Peter's disfavour, together with their descendants. The fact that they were both in disgrace did not, however, unite them, and there were continual conflicts between them. Apparently there were certain old scores which they could not forget, and which for each side boiled down to the fact that but for the other's villainy, they would still be walking freely in dear mother Moscow today. These scores loomed particularly large in their minds at hay-making time. Each suburb had its own fields, but the boundaries between them were defined like this: 'in the place "where Long Peter was flogged" is a plot of land, and likewise in two'. Each year at hay-making time the Musketeers and Cannoneers would go out and at first behave like reasonable people, trying to find such and such a gully, such and such a stream, and the twisted birch-tree that had once been a clear enough boundary-mark, but had been cut down these thirty years. When they failed to find any of these, they would start talking of 'villainy' and end by gradually bringing their scythes into action. The battles which took place were very serious affairs, but the Glupovites were so accustomed to them that they were not in the least scandalized. Eventually, however, the authorities became concerned and ordered the scythes to be confiscated.

65

Then they had nothing to cut the hay with and their animals died from lack of fodder. 'And it profited the Musketeers and the Cannoneers nothing, and only gave the land-surveyors pleasure at their discomfiture', adds the chronicler.

Ferdyshchenko himself turned up at one of these battles with a fire-hose and a tub of water. At first he was quite energetic and played a steady stream of water over the brawlers, but then he caught sight of Domashka. She, armed with a hay-fork and wearing only a shift, was in the forefront of the action, and his 'evil-inflamed' heart burned so fiercely that he forgot all about the oath he had taken and the purpose for which he had come. Instead of stepping up his drenching tactics, he settled himself down with the utmost calm on a small hillock, lit his pipe, and engaged in a titivating conversation with the land-surveyors. And there he sat, devouring Domashka with his eyes, till evening came and the contestants were forced by the gathering dusk to go home.

The Musketeer woman Domashka was quite a different type from Alenka. If Alenka had been soft and feminine in all her movements, Domashka was harsh, resolute, and masculine. Indifferently washed, unkempt and slovenly, she was a good example of that hoydenish type of woman who swears indiscriminately and misses no opportunity to embellish her speech with some indecent gesture. Her voice sounded through the suburb from morning till night, cursing and swearing a variety of oaths, and it only stopped when she was lulled into a stupor by vodka. The younger Musketeers pursued her quite recklessly, but did not fight over her, and she was known to all as the 'Sugar-bowl' and the 'Open road'. The Cannoneers feared her, but also secretly coveted her. She was quite uncommonly bold. She would go straight up to a man, as if to say to him: 'Now then, let's see if you can get the better of me?' – and, needless to say, it was a matter of pride to everyone to prove to this 'Glutton' that they could 'get the better' of her. She did not bother about clothes, for she seemed to know by instinct that her strength lay not in bright coloured frocks, but in that inexhaustible flow of youthful brazenness which burst irrepressibly through in her every movement. Rumour had it that she had a husband, but since she mainly slept around the barns and outhouses and rarely spent a night at home, and since she had no children, this husband was soon forgotten, and it seemed she had come into the world as she was – a woman of no family and a woman free to all.

But, in fact, it was this, the utter impudence with which she came straight to the point that attracted the 'evil-inflamed' heart of the pernickety old man. The luscious, melting wantonness of Alenka was forgotten; a more piquant stimulus was needed, one more capable of arousing an old man's declining sensibilities. 'We tried one who was sweet and gentle', he said to himself, 'Now we'll try a testy one.' And saying this, he sent a constable to the Musketeers' suburb, for the sake of form giving him a dispatch-register to carry. The constable found Domashka half tipsy by a store-shed behind the cottage gardens, surrounded by a crowd of young Musketeers. When she heard she was ordered to appear before the governor, she seemed surprised, but since it was really all one to her ('priest or padre – where's the difference?'), after a moment's hesitation she got up to follow the messenger. But this roused the young Musketeers, who took her away from the constable.

'He's getting very fancy!' they shouted. 'It's not so long since he carried off Alenka from her husband, and now he thinks he will help himself to Domashka, who belongs to us all!'

Of course, the Brigadier should have thought better of it, but there might have been a devil urging him on. He ran about the town like a scalded cat, bawling and shouting. Nothing made any difference to him – neither the lessons of the past, nor his own conscience, which told him clearly that he would not be the one to pay for his sins, but, as usual, the entirely innocent Glupovites. However much the young Musketeers resisted, however much Domashka herself tried to escape by claiming that she 'dare not go against the community', force, as usual, gained the upper hand. Twice the Brigadier had the recalcitrant Domashka thrashed, and twice she stood up to this unmerited punishment, but when they began the third time, she gave in . . . .

Then the Cannoneers came out and taunted the Musketeers with not being able to save one of their own women from the Brigadier's lashes. 'The Cannoneers were fools,' explains the chronicler, 'for they saw not that in laughing at the Musketeers they were laughing at themselves.' But the Musketeers did not care if the Cannoneers acted from foolishness or not. As men who had received a mortal insult and could not revenge themselves on the real culprit, they worked off their feelings on those who reminded them of it. There were fights, brawls, and maimings. They fought in single combat, they fought in pitched battles, but it was the town which suffered most from this hatred, for it lay right between the warring camps. But the Brigadier was past hearing or noticing anything. He took Domashka to the top floor of his house and celebrated the first day of his triumph by drinking himself into a stupor with this new victim of his lechery . . . .

And it was not long before a new and terrible calamity overtook the town . . . .

On the seventh of July, on the eve of the Feast of the Virgin of the Don, fire broke out.

Until July things could not have been better. There had been some rain, but it had been so soft and warm and timely that everything had sprouted and filled and ripened with astonishing rapidity, as if some magic power were forcing it through the ground. Then it became hot and dry, but this was also just right, since the time for field-work was coming. The citizens rejoiced, hoping for a plentiful harvest, and quickly got on with their work.

On the sixth of July the holy fool Arkhipushko went into the square and, standing in the middle of the market, began fanning the air with his rough cloth shirt.

'I'm on fire! I'm on fire!' he shouted.

The old men who had been chatting nearby stopped and gathered round the holy fool.

'Where is it you are on fire, good master?' they asked.

But the prophetic fool was muttering some confused rigmarole:

'The musket fires, it burns with fire, it chokes with smoke. You'll see the sword of fire, hear the voice of the archangel . . . I'm on fire!'

They could get nothing else out of him, because immediately after this rigmarole he disappeared completely and nobody ventured to hold him back. Nevertheless, the old men fell to thinking.

'He said something about a musket!' they said, nodding their heads in the direction of the Musketeers' suburb.

But this was not the end of the matter. Within an hour the holy fool Anisyushka also appeared on the square. She carried a little bundle in her arms, and, sitting in the middle of the market, began poking a hole in the ground with her finger. The old men came and gathered round her too.

'What's that you're doing, Anisyushka? What are you making a hole for?' they asked.

'Burying my things!' she replied, looking at them with the inane smile which seemed to have had since birth.

'Why should you bury them? Why, there's no need for that. Nobody would take anything from a godly old woman like you.'

But she muttered:

'I'm burying my things . . . eight ribbons, eight cloths . . . eight silken kerchieves, eight golden studs . . . eight jewel earrings . . .

eight emerald rings . . . and eight amber beads . . . and eight cotton threads . . . and a ribbon of red – that's nine . . . he-he-he!' she quietly laughed in her childish way.

'Lord! Something terrible is going to happen!' whispered the terrified old men.

They turned round, and there was the Brigadier, drunk as a lord, watching them from his window, while Domashka drew pictures on his face with a piece of charcoal.

It was on the tip of their tongues to say 'There's a ravenous dog the Devil's sent us!' but, as though he had taken their meaning, the Brigadier roared in a terrible voice:

'Rebelling again! Still not come to your senses?'

The Glupovites took themselves home with heavy hearts, and that day there was no laughing, singing or talking in the streets.

The next morning the weather was rather unsettled, but as there was urgent work to be done (reaping was starting), everyone set off for the fields. But the work went sluggishly. It may have been because tomorrow was a feast-day, or because they all felt some vague sense of unease, but everyone moved as though half-asleep. And so it continued until five o'clock, when they set off home to put on their best clothes and go to vespers. Towards seven the church bells began to ring and the streets filled with people. In the sky there was a single small white cloud, but the wind was rising, and this only increased the general feeling that something was going to happen. Before the chimes rang for the third time, the sky was completely overcast and there was such a deafening peal of thunder that a shudder passed through all who were at prayer. The first peal was followed by two more and then, in the distance, there was the sound of an alarm-bell. People poured from the churches, thronging the exits, and crushing one another, especially the women-folk, who bewailed in advance the loss of their stock and possessions. The Cannoneers' suburb was on fire, and a dense mass of sand and dust drifted from it towards the crowd.

Though it was barely after eight, the sky was so full of storm-clouds that the streets were quite dark. Above the town was black, unlimited space, split and sundered by lightning; the air was choked with swirling dust – indescribable chaos reigned, and in the background there was the no less terrible fire. Far in the distance people could be seen stirring. They were not rushing about in anguish and despair, but seemed to be clustering instinctively together. Wisps of burning straw from the roofs spiralled in the air, and it was as though one were witnessing some fantastic entertainment and not that worst of all those evils which the unconscious forces of nature provide in such abundance. One by one the wooden buildings caught fire and seemed to melt away. At one place the fire was already at its height; a whole building was enveloped in flames and every moment grew smaller and smaller, its outline taking a succession of different patterns and shapes which were then hollowed and eaten out by the terrible element. At the side a point of light shone forth, then disappeared in dense smoke. A moment later a tongue of flame leapt from the smoke, was gone, then leapt again – and took control. A new point of light, and another . . . where it had been black was now bright orange; there formed a whole chain of glowing lights, then a veritable sea, in which all details were submerged, a sea of fire that swirled within its banks, with that sound of cracking, hissing, and roaring which it alone possesses. You could not distinguish the burning, the weeping, the suffering – everything burned, everything wept, everything suffered . . . . Even the groans were not heard as separate sounds.

People groaned, however, only in the first minute, as they ran distracted to the place of the fire. At that moment they recalled all that was ever dear to them, all that was sacred and cherished and loved, all that had helped them to accept life and to bear its burdens. A man becomes so accustomed to these ancient idols in his heart, he puts his best hopes in them for so long, that the possibility of losing them never really occurs to him. Then the moment comes when he sees their loss not as an abstraction, not as a figment of his fearful imagination, but as a plain fact, which there is no going against. Confronted with this reality, a man cannot at first bear the pain it brings. He groans, stretches out his hands, complains and curses, still hoping that the evil might pass him by. But when he sees that the evil is already done, he suddenly calms down and wants only one thing – silence. A man comes home and sees his house engulfed with fire, the flames darting from every joint, and it gradually dawns on him that this is that *end of everything* of which he has sometimes vaguely dreamed and which, did he but know it, he has been expecting all his life. What can he do at such a moment? What is there for him to undertake? He can only tell himself that the past is over, that he now has to start on something fresh, a thing he would gladly put off, but which he cannot escape, because this something will anyway come – 'tomorrow'.

'Are you all here?' came a woman's voice from the crowd. 'One, two . . . Nikolka, where are you?'

'Here, Mummy', came the frightened lisp of a child who was hiding behind his mother's skirts.

'Where's Matrenka?' cried a voice somewhere else in the crowd.

'Matrenka – she's still in the house!'

At this, a young man came out of the crowd and rushed headlong into the flames. One agonized minute passed, then another. One after another, beams crashed down, the ceiling creaked. At last the young man reappeared in clouds of smoke – his cap and jacket were smouldering. His arms were empty. There was a wail of 'Matrenka! Matrenka! Where are you?', then words of comfort and suggestions that Matrenka had very likely been frightened and run off into the vegetable patch . . . .

Suddenly, from the depths of an empty shed nearby came a loud inhuman wailing, on hearing which even that distracted crowd crossed themselves and cried 'Lord save us!' All, or practically all, rushed in the direction of the cry. The shed had only just caught fire, but already it was impossible to get near it. The fire had gained hold of the wattle walls and encircled every stick; in a minute the dark smouldering mass was a glowing, incandescent bonfire. They could see someone inside. He was dashing and running about, rending his shirt and tearing at his breast with his nails, then he suddenly stopped and straightened up, as if to take breath. They saw sparks showering over him like water; his hair caught light, he tried to put it out, but then suddenly began spinning round and round . . . .

'Heavens above, it's Arkhipushko!' cried the people, recognizing him.

It was, indeed, he. In the midst of the glowing timbers his dark, half-wild figure seemed illumined. What they saw was not the filthy Arkhipushko with the dull wandering eyes they were used to, nor yet Arkhipushko writhing in torment of death, vainly struggling, like any other mortal, against the inevitable end. The Arkhipushko they saw was rather like some devotee fainting in the fullness of rapture.

'Open up the door, Arkhipushko! Open it!' they shouted in pity from where they stood.

But Arkhipushko did not hear and went on twisting and shouting. It was clear that he was now fighting for breath. Then, at last, the posts supporting the thatched roof burnt through. A great cloud of flame and smoke crashed to the ground, covering Arkhipushko, then spiralled away upwards. For a moment the glow was turned to darkness. All instinctively crossed themselves . . . .

Before the Cannoneers had recovered from this spectacle, there was a new horror: the bells of the main church began to din, then all of a sudden the very biggest of them came thundering to the ground. They rushed to the spot, but as they arrived they saw that the whole district was now in flames and began thinking how they might save themselves. Those who were without shelter, food or clothing, swarmed into the town, only to find there too a state of general confusion. Although the flames had evidently now taken hold of all that they could take hold of, to the townsfolk watching the fire from the other side of the river it seemed to be still increasing and the glow in the sky looked even more intense. The air was filled with brightly burning objects, among which firebrands and wisps of burning straw twisted and spiralled. 'Where will they land? Who will they drop on?' wondered the awe-struck townsfolk.

This created a general panic. Everybody rushed to save his property, and the streets were soon jammed with carts and people on foot, packed and loaded with household goods. This column moved hurriedly, though with little noise, in the direction of the town common. When they were a safe distance from the town, they began to settle themselves down. At this moment the long-awaited rain poured down and turned the soft black earth into a sea of mud.

In the meantime the Cannoneers stopped in the town square and decided to wait there till daylight. Many crouched on the ground and gave free rein to their tears. One of them who was versed in the scriptures struck up 'By the waters of Babylon', but he wept and was unable to finish. Someone mentioned Domashka, the Musketeer woman, but there was no response. They seemed to have forgotten all about the Brigadier, though some claimed they had seen him wandering about with the one and only fire-hose trying to save the house of the priest. The priest was there with the others and muttered complaints.

'Verily have we sinned!' he said.

'You, Father, should have done a bit more praying and had a bit less fun with your wife!' came the bold-faced reply, after which the subject was dropped.

Towards daybreak the fire did in fact begin to abate, partly because there was nothing more to burn, and partly because of the pouring rain. The Cannoneers trudged back to the scene of the fire and were met by the sight of charred beams and ashes lying in heaps, under which the fire still smouldered. They fetched grapnels, brought the hose from the town, and then, unhurriedly, set about dragging aside anything still intact and putting out what was left of the fire. Everyone rummaged in his own house, seeing what they could find; many actually found the things they were looking for and crossed themselves. The number of people who had died in the fire was a dozen or so, among them two grown-ups; the little Matrenka who had been lost the day before was found asleep among the vegetable beds. Gradually the day took on the course of a normal working day. There was little reckoning of losses – everyone tried first to establish what he still had, not what he had lost. One person's cellar had escaped, and there was gladness that some *kvass* and yesterday's loaf of bread remained. By some miracle, the fire had missed another person's outhouse, where his brown mare had been shut up, and the people around praised the mare for her smartness in surviving.

The townspeople also gradually came back to their dwellings from the emergency camp. But they did not stay long. About midday the alarm was rung once more from the church of Elias the Prophet in the part of the town known as the 'Bog'. Fire had broken out in the barn of that same woman called 'the Cow', in whose house the chronicler introduced us to the clerk Bogolepov in the last chapter. It is thought that Bogolepov was smoking his pipe when drunk and dropped a spark in the chaff, but since he himself was burnt to death on this occasion, there was never any definite confirmation of this. In fact, the fire was not a very serious one and could quite easily have been stopped from spreading, but the Glupovites were so worn and shaken by the events of the preceding day that the very word 'Fire!' was enough to throw them into a fresh panic. Once more they rushed to their houses, dragged what they could from them and fled to the common. And the fire meanwhile continued to spread.

We shall not describe the course of this disaster, since it was similar in every way to the one already described. Suffice it to say that the town burnt for two days and that during this time two suburbs were completely destroyed: Boglands and the one called Drabhouses, which had a bad name as the district where soldiers' wives lived and plied their shameful trade. Only on the third day, when the fire shifted towards the central church and the market quarter, did the Glupovites come a little to their senses. Spurred on by the rebellious Musketeers, they left their camp and went in a crowd to the governor's house. They called on Ferdyshchenko to come out.

'How much longer are we to go on burning?' they asked, when after some hesitation he appeared on the steps.

But the wily Brigadier only temporized. He said it was not for him to go against the will of God. 'We don't want you to go against the will of God', said the Glupovites. 'What would an old coot like you be doing raising himself up against God! But you just tell us this – for whose sins is it that we poor folk must now be dying?' The Brigadier was suddenly contrite. His heart was filled with a mighty shame, and he stood before the Glupovites and poured forth tears. ('And all his tears were the tears of a crocodile', says the chronicler, anticipating later events.)

'Didn't you torment us enough last year? Didn't you kill enough of us with your folly and your floggings?' continued the Glupovites, seeing that the Brigadier acknowledged his guilt. 'Think better of it, an old man like you! Put aside your foolishness!'

Then the Brigadier knelt down before the whole community and repented. ('And his repentance was the repentance of a serpent', says the chronicler, once more anticipating the events that were to follow.)

'Forgive me, brave hearts, for Christ's sake!' he said, bowing at the feet of the community. 'I'll put aside my foolishness and hand over to you the one who's caused it all. Only don't treat her badly! For the love of Christ, take her in good faith back to the Musketeers!'

Saying this, he led Domashka out to the crowd. When they saw the jaunty Musketeer woman, the Glupovites heaved a huge sigh. She stood there before them, as unwashed and unkempt as ever, and as she stood there, a tipsy smile spread over her face. And one cannot describe the affection which the Glupovites suddenly felt for this Domashka.

'How are you doing, Domashka?' roared the citizens with a single voice.

'Hallo there! have you come to turn me loose?' cried Domashka in reply.

'Will you go back to the Musketeers of your own accord?'

'With the greatest of pleasure!'

Then they took Domashka and led her arm in arm back to the very barn from which, a little while before, she had been carried off by force.

The Musketeers were jubilant and ran through the streets, beating basins and frying-pans and shouting their familiar battle-cry of 'Shame to the foe!'

And a feeling of great joy and cheerfulness came over the Glupovites. They felt as if a weight had been lifted from them and that henceforward they had only to live in happiness. Led by the Brigadier, they went to tackle the fire, and in a few hours they had demolished a whole street of houses and dug a deep ditch round the area of the fire. By the next day the fire had burnt itself out.

But the chronicler's hints about events to come had not been given for nothing: the Brigadier's tears turned out in fact to be crocodile tears, and his repentance was indeed that of a serpent. As soon as the danger was passed, he sat down in his office and began a report for dispatch to all places. A full ten hours he dipped his pen in the ink-well, and the more he dipped it, the more venomous it became.

'On the tenth day of July', he wrote, 'a mighty rebellion was raised against me by all the citizens of Glupov. On the occasion of a great fire which took place in the suburb of Drabhouses the citizens of all classes assembled before my house and attempted to constrain and force me to kneel down and beg forgiveness of their villainous selves. Which, though, I fearlessly refused to do. I now reckon thus: that if this villainy of theirs is to be tolerated now and indulged in the future, then what will prevent it from recurring again and in a form far less capable of being suppressed?'

When he had finished, the Brigadier sat by the window and began to listen for any sound of a trumpet. At the same time he was affable and courteous in his dealings with the citizens who were enchanted by the kindness of his manner.

'My dears, my dears!' he would say to them. 'Now why did you want to get angry with me, you silly dears! There now, God has taken away, but God will give again! Our Lord in Heaven has many mercies! He has indeed, my dear good fellows!'

Now and then, however, a dubious kind of smile lit on his face, which boded no good . . . .

And, lo, one fine morning a cloud of dust appeared on the highroad. It came gradually closer, until finally it reached Glupov.

From this mysterious cloud clearly came the sound: 'Tantara! Tantara!'

'The trumpet sounds,
'The time has come
'To crush the foe!'

The Glupovites stood transfixed.

The Fantastic Traveller

HARDLY had the Glupovites had time to recover, when the Brigadier's folly nearly brought a new disaster upon them. Ferdyshchenko took it into his head to go travelling.

It was a strange idea, since the only territory in his jurisdiction was the town common, which possessed no treasures of any kind, either above the ground or below. Of course, there were dung-heaps lying about in various places, but there was nothing of interest in them, not even for an archaeologist. 'Where is there to travel here? What is there to travel for?' – were the questions all reasonable people asked themselves, and they found no satisfactory answer. Even the Brigadier's housekeeper was much put out when Ferdyshchenko told her of his plan.

'What do you want to go wandering off for?' she said. 'You'll walk into the first dung-heap and get stuck in it. For the Lord's sake, give up this childishness!'

But the Brigadier was not to be moved. He imagined that as soon as he rode on to the common, the grass would grow greener and the flowers bloom brighter. 'The fields will wax fat, mighty rivers will pour forth, ships will sail out, animal husbandry will flourish, and there will be means of communication', he mumbled to himself, and he cherished his plan like the apple of his eye. 'He was a simple man', explains the chronicler, 'so simple, that after these many disasters he still did not leave his simple ways.'

Evidently, in this particular matter he was following the example of his patron and benefactor, who had also been fond of making journeys and being fêted wherever he went (in the 'Schedule of Town-Governors' Ferdyshchenko is mentioned as 'former orderly to Prince Potemkin').[43]

The plan he drew up was far-reaching. He proposed going first to one corner of the common, then right across it to the far end, then back again to the middle, and then in a straight line; after that they would just follow their noses. Everywhere along the route he would receive greetings and gifts.

'As soon as I come in sight you bang on your basins', he told the inhabitants. 'Then you can greet me, as though you don't know where I've come from.'

'Yes, sir', answered the well-schooled Glupovites. But to themselves they were thinking: 'Lord, see that he doesn't go burning down the town again!'

He set off on the Feast of St. Nicholas, straight after early mass, leaving word at home that he would not be back for some time. He had with him his orderly, Vasily Chernostup, and two old militiamen. The cavalcade set off at a walking pace and headed for the right-hand corner of the common. However, as this was only a short distance away, no matter how much they loitered, in half an hour they were already there. The waiting Glupovites, four in number, banged their basins, and one rattled a tambourine. After this they presented their gifts: a belly-piece of salted sturgeon, a piece of dried *sevryuga*, [44] and some ham. The Brigadier stepped down from his carriage and complained that this was not enough ('And anyway you can't call these gifts, they're not fresh'), and that such offerings were an insult to his honour. At this, each of the Glupovites produced a fifty-kopek piece and Ferdyshchenko calmed down.

'Now then, old fellows,' he said kindly. 'Show me what places of interest there are here.'

They walked up and down the common, but could find nothing of interest, except for a single dung-heap.

'This is from last year. We camped here in the fire and there were all kinds of animals here then', explained one of the old men.

'It would be a fine thing to build a town here', said the Brigadier. 'We could call it Domnoslav in honour of Domashka, that Musketeer woman you upset so needlessly on that occasion.'

Then he asked:

'Well, and what about under the ground?'

'We can't say about that', answered the Glupovites. 'We reckon there must be all manner of things in plenty down there, but we're too scared to find out, lest anybody should see us and report us!'

'You're scared?' scoffed the Brigadier.

In short, within half an hour the inspection was completed, and that easily. Ferdyshchenko saw that a lot of time remained to be filled (he was not due to leave this particular spot until the following day), and he started complaining and upbraiding the Glupovites for not being sea-faring folk and having no ships, no mining, no mint, no means of communication, nor even any statistics – nothing at all, in fact, that might gladden a governor's heart. And worst of all – they were so unenterprising.

'You ought to be building yourselves ships, exporting coffee and sugar', he said. 'But what do you do!'

The old men exchanged glances. They saw there was a measure of sense – and a good dose of nonsense – in what the Brigadier said, so after a moment's hesitation they took out another fifty kopeks each.

'Thanks', said the Brigadier. 'And for what I was saying about sea-faring, forgive me!'

At this point one of the citizens, anxious to ingratiate himself, stepped up and said that he had in his coat a little wooden cannon on wheels and a small stock of dried peas. The Brigadier was quite delighted with this toy and sat down on a patch of grass to fire it. They fired it for a long time, until they were even quite exhausted, but it was still an age to dinner-time.

'Oh, damnation! Even the sun seems to go backwards here!' said the Brigadier, looking indignantly at that luminary, which was moving slowly towards its zenith.

At last, however, they sat down to dinner. But the Brigadier had been drinking heavily since the episode with Domashka and now too became rolling drunk. He started ranting and pointing to the wooden cannon, with which he threatened to shoot down every one of his present Amphytrions. Then his orderly, Vasily Chernostup (who was also drunk, though not to excess), intervened on behalf of their hosts.

'You're talking through your hat!' he said, cutting the Brigadier short. 'If it wasn't for me, you'd never give a peep, you old coot. A fat lot of good you'd be with that gun!'

Meanwhile, time continued to drag hopelessly. They ate long and they drank long, but still the sun was high in the sky. They went to sleep and they slept long. After sleeping off their drunkenness, they at length got up.

'The sun's got up very high!' said the Brigadier, waking up and mistaking west for east.

However, this was such an obvious mistake that even he realized it. They sent one of the old men into Glupov to fetch some *kvass*, which might help the time to pass more quickly, but in the twinkling of an eye he was back again with a whole jar of *kvass* on his head and never a drop spilt. First they drank the *kvass*, then they went on to tea and vodka. Finally, when it was still scarcely dark, they lit an oil-lamp to light up the dung-heap. The lamp smoked and flickered and gave off a foul smell.

'God be praised! We didn't see the end of day!' said the Brigadier, wrapping himself in his greatcoat and lying down to sleep for the second time.

The next day they travelled diagonally across the common. By good fortune they met a shepherd on the way. They demanded of him who he was and what he was up to, loitering in these lonely parts, and did he not have some design in doing so. At first the shepherd was too timid to speak, but then he admitted everything. So they searched him and found a small piece of bread and a scrap of cloth from a legging.

'Tell us what villainy you were up to?' demanded the Brigadier fiercely.

But to all his questions the shepherd responded only by moaning, and the travellers were compelled to take him with them for further questioning. And thus they came to the far corner of the common.

Here too there was banging of basins and presentation of gifts, and now the time passed more quickly, since they were able to occupy themselves interrogating the shepherd and discharging the little cannon. In the evening they again lit the lamp, which made such a pother that it gave them all a headache.

The third day they released the shepherd and set off for the middle of the common, where a regular triumph awaited the Brigadier. The fame of his journeys was increasing hourly, and, it being a feast-day, the Glupovites had decided to make an occasion of his arrival. They put on their best clothes and formed a square to await the arrival of the governor. They banged basins and rattled tambourines, and even had a fiddle to play as well. A little way off there were steaming pots in which were being boiled and baked such a quantity of sucking-pigs, geese, and other fowl, that even the priests were envious. For the first time the Brigadier realized that the people's affection is a force with comestible connections. He stepped from his carriage and wept.

And all who were there wept, and they wept for grief, and they wept for joy. One ancient woman in particular wept copiously (it was said she was a granddaughter of an illegitimate daughter of Marfa Posadnitsa).[45]

'And what are you crying for, old dear?' asked the Brigadier, patting her kindly on the shoulder.

'Ah, good master! How should we not cry, our good protector? All our lives we cry . . . all our lives!' the old crone sobbed in reply.

At midday tables were set up and they sat down to dinner. But the Brigadier was rash enough to dispatch three glasses of prime vodka before the meal had even begun. His eyes suddenly fixed and stared into space. Then, after the first course (cabbage soup and salt beef), he had two more glasses and said that he would have to be going.

'Now, where would you be rushing off to?' asked the honoured Glupovites on either side of him, intending to dissuade him.

'To follow my nose!' he muttered, evidently recalling these words from his itinerary.

After the second course (sucking-pig and sour cream) he felt unwell, but mastered himself and went on to the goose and cabbage. After this, however, his mouth did a violent contraction.

One could see on his face the twitching of some administrative nerve; it twitched for a time, and then stopped . . . . In confusion and alarm the Glupovites sprang from their places.

The end had come . . . the end of this signal governorship, which had twice in recent years been darkened by punitive measures against the Glupovites. 'Was there any need for these chastisements?' the chronicler asks – unfortunately, though, leaving the question unanswered.

For a time the Glupovites simply waited. They feared they might be accused of deliberately overfeeding the Brigadier, and that once more there would come out of the blue 'Tantara!'

'So close your ranks! –
'The better
'To defeat the foe!'

On this occasion, however, their fears fortunately proved groundless. A week later a new governor arrived and, by the excellence of his administrative measures, caused them to forget all the past governors, including Ferdyshchenko. The new governor was Basilisk Semenovich Borodavkin, and it is with him that the golden age of Glupov properly begins. Fears were dispelled, good harvests followed one after the other, there was no sign of any comets, and money was so plentiful that everyone rolled in it – for it was paper money.

The Wars of Enlightenment

BASILISK Semenovich Borodavkin, who succeeded Brigadier Ferdyshchenko, was the complete opposite of his predecessor. As Ferdyshchenko was dissolute and slack, so Borodavkin impressed by his efficiency and by the astonishing administrative thoroughness which he displayed with particular energy in all matters of trivial importance. With his buttons always done up to the top, his cap and gloves always in hand, he represented that type of town-governor whose legs are ready at any moment to go running off to some unknown destination. In the day-time he flitted through the town like a fly, making sure the inhabitants were looking jolly and cheerful, and at night he would be putting out fires, raising false alarms, and generally catching people unawares.

He shouted on all occasions, and he was an uncommon shouter. 'So great was the shout in him', says the chronicler, 'that many Glupovites were thrown by it into an everlasting state of fear for themselves and for their children.' This remarkable testimony is confirmed by the fact that the authorities later had to grant various privileges to the Glupovites, precisely 'on account of their great terror'. His appetite was good, but he always ate in haste and grumbled as he did so. Even to go to sleep he only shut one eye – a habit which caused some consternation to his wife, for, though they had lived together for twenty-five years, she never failed to shudder at the sight of his other, unsleeping eye, which was perfectly round and always fixed enquiringly on her. When there was nothing to do, that is, when there was no need to flit through the town or catch people unawares (such painful moments occur in the lives of even the most energetic administrators), he either promulgated laws, or marched up and down in his office, observing the rise and fall of the toes of his boots, or else went over in his mind the various army bugle calls.

Borodavkin had one other peculiarity: he was a writer. Ten years before his arrival in Glupov he had started on a draft

'Concerning the expansion of our Armies and Navies in all places, by which the return (*sic*) of ancient Byzantium to the protection of the Russian State may be brought closer to attainment', and each day he added another line to it. In this way he had compiled a quite thick copy-book, containing three thousand six hundred and fifty-two lines (there had been two leap-years). He would show this book to his visitors with some pride, saying as he did so: 'Here, sir, you can see the full extent of my plans.'

Political day-dreaming was generally much in vogue at that time, and Borodavkin was also caught up in the general current of the day. The Glupovites would often see him sitting on the balcony of his residence, gazing into the distance with tear-filled eyes at the bastions of Byzantium. The common pastures of Glupov and Byzantium bordered so close to each other that the Byzantine sheep were continually getting mixed up with those of Glupov, which created constant wrangles. All that was needed was a call to arms . . . . And Borodavkin waited for this call, he waited with passion, with an impatience verging on indignation.[46]

'First, we'll deal with Byzantium', he day-dreamed. 'And then, sir, . . .

'To the Drava, and Morava, and the distant Sava too,
'And to the quiet blue Danube . . .'[47]

Yes, indeed, sir!'

If the whole truth were told, he had even secretly drawn up a rather strange memorandum, addressed to K. I. Arsenev, the noted Russian geographer. 'It is proposed to your honour', he wrote, 'that in future all geography books should contain the following entry on the place known to you as Byzantium: "*Constantinople,* formerly Byzantium, now the provincial capital Ekaterinograd, stands at the emergence of the Black Sea into the ancient Propontis. It was taken under the protection of Russia in 17—, with the introduction of a monetary union (which means that Byzantine money has currency in St. Petersburg). Because of its extensive area, the town is administered by four town-governors, who continually dispute with each other. There is trade in walnuts, it has a soap factory and two tanneries".' But, alas, the days went by, Borodavkin's dreams grew even larger, but still the call did not come. Soldiers – infantrymen and cavalry-men – passed on their way through Glupov.

'Where to, my boys?' Borodavkin would ask with emotion.

But the soldiers trumped their trumpets and sang their songs, the shining toes of their boots rose and fell, raising a column of dust in the streets, and still they passed on without end.

'There's millions of them!' said the Glupovites, who presumed that soldiers were a special kind of men, created by nature to march without end in all directions, descending from one plateau in order to climb to another, crossing one bridge in order to pass over another farther on. And another bridge, and another plateau, and another, and another . . . .

In this situation Borodavkin realized that it was still not yet time for larger political enterprises and that he must limit his activities to the so-called 'urgent needs' of his own district. The first of these was, of course, the need of civilization, or, as he defined it, 'the realization of the need for every brave son of the Russian Empire to be firm in misfortune'.

Full of these vague dreams, he came to Glupov, and his first act was to make a thorough study of the aims and achievements of his predecessors. But on looking at the records, he was simply horrified. There they were in succession – Klementy, Velikanov, Lamvrokakis, Baklan, the Marquis de Sanglot, Ferdyshchenko, but what they had done, what they had thought, what objects they had pursued, there was absolutely no way of telling. It seemed that this whole succession of governors was nothing but a dream, in which faceless figures flit by and muffled cries ring out, like the distant tumult of a drunken throng . . . . Out of the darkness appears a shadow, it deals someone a blow – one, two! – and disappears into the unknown. You look and there is another shadow. It too strikes out at all and sundry, and disappears . . . . 'I'll break you!', 'I'll not have it!' is heard all round, but there is no way of knowing why 'I'll break you!' or what 'I'll not have'. You would like to get out of the way, to flatten yourself into a corner, but you cannot escape or hide in a corner, for from every corner comes the same cry 'I'll break you!', and you are driven to another corner, where it overtakes you yet again. The rule of these governors was a wild force devoid of meaning, so that even Borodavkin, for all his efficiency, had some doubts about its virtue. Only State Councillor Dvoekurov showed to advantage among this motley group of administrators, only he displayed a subtle and perceptive intellect, and, in general, revealed himself as a continuer of the cause of reform which had marked the beginning of the eighteenth century. And naturally it was he that Borodavkin took as his model.

Dvoekurov had achieved a great deal. He had paved the two main streets, had collected the tax arrears, had been a patron of learning, and had petitioned for the establishment of an academy in Glupov. But his greatest achievement was the introduction of mustard and bay-leaf. This latter deed so impressed Borodavkin that he promptly conceived the bold idea of doing the same for olive oil. He made enquiries about the measures Dvoekurov had taken to achieve success, but since, as usual, relevant archives turned out to have been burnt (perhaps even deliberately destroyed), he had to be satisfied with the legends and stories which people told about him.

'There was a great to-do!' the old inhabitants told him. 'They flogged them in the gauntlet, and they flogged them ordinary fashion . . . . A lot even went to Siberia over that business!'

'So there were rebellions?' enquired Borodavkin.

'There were rebellions all right! We've a sure way of telling that, sir: whenever there's flogging, you can bet your life there's a rebellion!'

On further enquiry it became clear that Dvoekurov had been a persistent man, who, once he took a thing into his head, saw it through to the end. He always acted in a thorough-going way – when he suppressed the inhabitants or scattered them abroad, there were never any survivors. At the same time, however, he understood that mass measures were not enough in themselves, and for several years he also launched separate attacks on the houses of the Glupovites and suppressed each inhabitant individually.

In general, throughout the history of Glupov it is a striking fact that one day the Glupovites will be all scattered and utterly destroyed, and then the very next day you see them appearing again, and usually there will even be so-called 'old fellows' making speeches at assemblies (very forward for their age they must be). How they manage to grow up in the time is a mystery, but a mystery which was perfectly understood by Dvoekurov, and so he had never spared the birch. As a true administrator, he had distinguished two different kinds of flogging: 'discriminate' flogging and 'indiscriminate' flogging, and he prided himself on being the first of the town-governors to introduce discriminate flogging, – while all his predecessors had flogged at random, often even flogging quite the wrong people. And, indeed, by reasonable and constant application he had achieved the most brilliant results. In the whole course of his governorship the Glupovites never once sat down to table without mustard, and, moreover, they even established extensive mustard plantations to meet the demands of the outside market. 'And that village flourished like the lily of the field, sending forth this bitter produce to the uttermost parts of Russia and receiving in exchange precious metals and furs.'

But in 1770 Dvoekurov had died, and the two governors who followed him not only failed to maintain his reforms, they can be said to have made a thorough mess of them. And, most remarkable of all, the Glupovites now showed a lack of gratitude. They manifested no regret at the abandonment of the civilization implanted by the authorities and they even seemed to rejoice at it. They stopped eating mustard altogether and ploughed up the plantations to grow cabbages and peas. In short, there took place what always happens when enlightenment comes too early to a nation which in civic matters is young and immature. Even the chronicler makes a somewhat ironical reference to this: 'Many years did he (Dvoekurov) spend in raising this cunningly contrived edifice, but never did he guess that he built on sand.' But the chronicler is evidently forgetting that the underlying purpose of human activity lies precisely in building houses 'on sand' one day, so that when they fall down on the following day a new building can be raised on the same 'sand' again.

It appears, therefore, that Borodavkin came in the nick of time to save this dying civilization. The passion for building 'on sand' rose in him to a state of frenzy. Days and nights on end he pondered what he could build that would fall down at the moment of completion and fill the whole world with dust and debris. He thought this way and that, but could think of nothing suitable. Finally, having no ideas of his own, he followed literally in the footsteps of his distinguished predecessor.

'My hand are tied', he complained bitterly to the Glupovites. 'Otherwise I'd give you something to remember me by!'

Then, very opportunely, he heard that the Glupovites had through sheer neglect completely given up the use of mustard. To begin with, he did no more than declare its use obligatory, and punish them for their backsliding by making compulsory the use of olive oil too. At the same time he mentally resolved never to abandon the struggle as long as a single waverer remained in the town.

But the Glupovites were not found wanting. With great presence of mind they countered the force of action by the force of inaction.

'Do what you will with us!' said some, 'Make mincemeat of us if you like, and eat us in your porridge – but we still won't use it!'

'You can't take anything from us!' said others. 'We're not like other people who are fat in the body! We've got nothing for you to pinch on!'

Saying this, they remained obstinately on their knees.

A curious phenomenon results when these two opposing forces meet. There is no rebellion as such, nor is there any real obedience. It is something between the two. We used to see examples of it in the old days of serfdom. A beetle might get into the mistress's soup, and she would call the cook and command him to eat the beetle. The cook would put the beetle in his mouth and visibly chew it, but swallow it he would not. So it was now with the Glupovites: they chewed all right, but they refused to swallow.

'I'll break them down!' said Borodavkin, and, slowly and unhastingly, considered his plan.

And the Glupovites knelt and waited. They knew they were in revolt, but they could not help kneeling. Heavens! what thoughts passed through their heads at this time! They knew that if they started eating mustard now, at some time in the future they might be forced to eat some other such filth; if they did not, they would feel the lash. In the present instance it seemed that kneeling was a middle course which might lessen the severity of both possibilities.

Suddenly they heard the blare of a trumpet and the beating of a drum. Full of mettle, Borodavkin, with his buttons all done up, rode out on a white horse, followed by cannon and muskets. The Glupovites supposed he was on his way to subjugate Byzantium, but, as it turned out, he had decided on subjugating them . . . .

Thus began that remarkable series of events which the chronicler describes under the general heading of the 'Wars of Enlightenment'.

As has been said, the first war of 'enlightenment' was brought about by mustard and it began in 1780, almost immediately, that is, after Borodavkin's arrival in Glupov.

Nonetheless, Borodavkin did not begin shooting straightaway – he was too much of a pedant to commit such an obvious administrative error. He began with gradual measures, and first of all assembled the Glupovites and tried to win them by persuasion. In the speech he made to the inhabitants he spoke in some detail concerning the bases of society in general, and of mustard as a basis of society in particular, but – either because what he said contained more personal faith in the cause he was defending than real power of conviction, or because, as was his habit, he did not speak, but shouted, his exhortations resulted only in the Glupovites being seized with terror and again falling on their knees.

'And the Glupovites had good cause for their terror', says the chronicler. 'Before them stood a man not great in stature, nor stoutly built, a man who spoke not in words, but only shouted and roared.'

'Have you understood, old men?' he asked, addressing the terrified inhabitants.

The crowd bowed low and remained mute, which, of course, only enraged him the more.

'Have you understood that I'll . . . see you dead . . . , you scoundrels!'

But this fresh rumbling had hardly escaped his lips when the Glupovites leapt hastily from their knees and fled in all directions.

'I'll break you!' he cried after them.

Borodavkin moped the whole of that day. He walked in silence through the apartments of the town-governor's house, and only occasionally muttered 'Villains!'

More than anything else, he was concerned about the Musketeers' suburb, which even under his predecessors had been noted for its unshakeable recalcitrance. The Musketeers had developed the force of inaction to a state of refinement. Not only did they fail to attend the assemblies called by Borodavkin, but also whenever they saw him coming they simply disappeared completely. So he had nobody to exhort, and nobody to question. Somewhere someone was audibly trembling, but where it was and who it was that trembled remained a mystery.

Meanwhile there could be no doubt that the root of all the evil lay in the Musketeers' suburb. The most depressing rumours reached Borodavkin about this nest of sedition. A preacher appeared there who had transposed the name 'Borodavkin' into numbers and proved that if you missed out the letter 'r', you would have 666, that is, the number of the Prince of Darkness. Polemical works passed from hand to hand, which explained that mustard was a plant that had grown from the body of a dissolute girl of notorious profligacy, from whose name the word 'mustard' was derived. Verses were even composed which went so far as to mention the town-governor's mother and refer to her in very unfavourable terms. The Musketeers listened to these songs and interpretations in a state of near rapture. Arm in arm, they roamed the streets, roaring at the tops of their voices as though bent on driving the spirit of humility from their midst once and for all.

Drop by drop, Borodavkin felt his heart brim with bitterness. He neither ate nor drank, but only cursed and swore, as if in order to keep up his spirits. The question of the mustard had seemed so simple and straightforward that refusal to accept it must result from some evil intent. And the more Borodavkin had to restrain the impulses of his passionate nature, the more tormenting was this knowledge to him.

'My hands are tied!' he repeated, as he pensively chewed his dark moustache, 'Otherwise I'd show you a thing or two!'

He reckoned – not without reason – that the natural outcome of any such collision is, after all, flogging, and he was fortified by this knowledge. While awaiting this outcome, he attended to his work, and secretly wrote a statute 'On the Non-constraint of Town-governors by Laws'. The first and only paragraph in this statute ran as follows: 'If you feel that a law puts an obstacle in your path, remove it from the table and place it underneath you. It is now invisible, and your course will be greatly eased.'

However, as yet his statute lacked official confirmation and so there was no way of avoiding these constraints. A month later, Borodavkin again summoned the inhabitants. He again started shouting, but he had scarcely uttered the first two syllables of his greeting ('of which, for very modesty, I will say nothing', says the chronicler), when the Glupovites again fled, this time without even waiting to fall on their knees. Only then did Borodavkin decide on the introduction of true civilization.

First thing in the morning he set out on his campaign, letting it look as though he were merely going out on some simple military exercise. The morning was bright and fresh, with a slight frost (these events took place in mid-September). The sun reflected on the soldiers' helmets and muskets; a light covering of hoar-frost lay on the streets and roof-tops; the stoves were being lit, and a merry flame could be seen through the windows of every house.

Although the main target of the campaign was the Musketeers' suburb, Borodavkin had recourse to subterfuge. He did not move straight forward, nor did he go left, or right. He manoeuvred. One by one, the Glupovites emerged from their houses and gave approving shouts to encourage the skilful commander in his evolutions.

'The Lord be praised! He seems to have forgotten about the mustard!' they said, taking off their caps and piously crossing themselves in the direction of the bell-tower.

Borodavkin, though, went on manoeuvring and manoeuvring, and around midday had reached the Drabhouses suburb, where he made a halt. All those participating in the campaign were given a cup of vodka and told to sing songs, and that evening they took prisoner a young townswoman who had strayed too far from the gate of her house.

The next day, waking early, they went in search of a prisoner who could give them information. All this was done in complete seriousness, with never as much a wink. They brought in a Jew and at first proposed hanging him, but then remembered their purpose in capturing him and spared him. The Jew, with his hand under his thigh, told them they must first go to Dunghills, and then go about in the open country until they came to the landmark called Dunka's Hollow. From there they should pass three turnings, and then follow their noses.

This Borodavkin did. But before his men had covered a quarter of a mile, they felt they were going the wrong way. They could see nothing at all, neither earth, nor sky, nor water. Borodavkin called for the treacherous Jew so that he could hang him, but the Jew had by now vanished (it later transpired that he had fled to St. Petersburg, where, just at this time, he managed to obtain a railway concession).[48] They blundered about like this in broad daylight for a considerable time, and it might have been an eclipse as far as they were concerned, for there stood Dunghills in full view of everybody, but not one of them saw it. In the end real darkness fell. Someone raised a shout of 'thieves!' – it was a soldier in his cups, but it threw everyone into confusion, and, thinking that the Musketeers were coming, they began fighting. They fought hard all through the night, hitting at random, and many were wounded and killed. Only when it was quite light did they see that they had been fighting their own men, and that the scene of this confusion was right under the stockade of the Dunghills suburb. They decided that after the dead were buried they would raise a monument on the site of the battle, and call the day it took place the 'Day of the Born-blind', to be commemorated by an annual ceremony with a whistle-pipe lament.

The third day they made a halt at Dunghills, but here, having learnt by experience, they took hostages. After that they caught all the inhabitants' chickens and held a wake for the dead. The people of Dunghills thought it all very strange – for here was a man playing a game of soldiers, but none the less catching real chickens. However, since Borodavkin did not reveal his secret, they supposed it was 'all in the game' and did not worry.

But when after the wake Borodavkin commanded his soldiers to trample down a field of winter wheat next to the suburb, the inhabitants thought differently.

'Can there really be a game such as this, friends?' they asked each other quietly so that no one could hear, not even Borodavkin, who was keeping a sharp watch on the way their thoughts were tending.

The fourth day they left for Dunka's Hollow, setting off at first light, for they had a long and tiring march before them and were anxious not to be late. They marched for a long time, and as they went, kept asking the hostages if they were nearly there. Great was their astonishment when suddenly, in the middle of open country, the hostages cried: 'This is it!' They had good cause to be astonished, for all around there was not a sign of habitation; on every side bare fields stretched into the distance, and only in the distance did the ground sink away into the deep ravine, into which, according to legend, Dunka from the Cannoneers' suburb had once fallen, as she hurried in a drunken state to meet her sweetheart.

'Where's the suburb?' Borodavkin asked the hostages.

'There is no suburb here!' answered the hostages. 'There used to be, there used to be suburbs everywhere, but the soldiers destroyed them all!'

But they would not believe it and decided to flog the hostages until they showed them where the suburb was. But strangely enough – the more they flogged them, the less sure they became themselves of finding the suburb they wanted. At this unexpected turn Borodavkin rent his uniform, and, raising his right hand to heaven, shook a threatening finger and said:

'I'll give it you!'

They were in an awkward situation. Darkness had fallen, it was cold and damp, and wolves had appeared in the fields. Borodavkin, in a fit of rationality, ordered that no one should sleep or shiver the whole night.

The fifth day they set out to return to Dunghills, trampling down another field of winter wheat on the way. They marched all day, and only reached the suburb towards evening, when they were tired and hungry. But there was no one there when they arrived. On seeing the approaching soldiers, the inhabitants had fled, driving away all their livestock, and entrenching themselves in an impregnable position. This position had to be taken by storm, but since Borodavkin's gunpowder was not real gunpowder, all the shooting of his soldiers did no harm, except to create a most awful smell.

The sixth day Borodavkin intended continuing the bombardment, but already he saw signs of treachery. The hostages had been released in the night and many of the real soldiers had been sent home and replaced by lead soldiers. When he asked why the hostages had been released, he was referred to some regulation which apparently said that 'hostages shall be flogged, but any hostage who has been flogged shall not be detained more than twenty-four hours without being sent home for treatment'. Whether he liked it or not, Borodavkin had to agree that correct action had been taken, but at the same time he called to mind his draft 'On the Non-constraint of Town-governors by Laws' and wept bitterly.

'And what are these?' he asked, pointing at the lead soldiers.

'For convenience, your honour!' they replied. 'They ask no victuals, and can march with the best of them!'

This too he had to accept. Borodavkin shut himself up in a peasant's cottage and held a solitary council of war. He wanted to punish the people of Dunghills for their insolence, but he could not help thinking about the siege of Troy which had lasted ten whole years – even though Achilles and Agamemnon had been on the side of the besiegers. It was not the privations that he feared, not the anguish of parting from his beloved wife, but the fact that in ten years his absence from Glupov might be noticed and give rise to unfavourable comment. In this connection he recalled a history lesson he had heard as a child, which had deeply impressed him. 'For all the benevolence of Menelaus', the history teacher had said, 'the Spartans were never so happy as during the siege of Troy; for although there were many documents that went unsigned, there were, on the other hand, many backs that went unlashed, and the latter omission made more than ample amends for the former . . .'

'No, sir! That's not right, sir!' said Borodavkin, walking about the hut in agitation, and protesting to his invisible companion. 'Nothing should go unsigned, sir! No back should go unlashed, sir! That is the way of order!'

As a crowning blow, the autumn rains began steadily falling and threatened to disrupt communications and stop the supply of provisions.

'Why the Devil didn't I go straight for the Musketeers!' exclaimed Borodavkin with bitterness, looking out of the window at the puddles, which grew larger every minute. 'I could have been there in half an hour!'

For the first time he realized that in some cases excess of cleverness can have the same effect as lack of it, and on seeing this, he decided to beat the retreat, and keep the lead soldiers as a dependable reserve.

The seventh day they set off at dawn, but as the road had been washed away during the night, the going was difficult and the guns kept getting stuck in the rutted black earth. On the way they had to attack the Hill of Svistukha – the order was given 'Charge!' and the front ranks rushed gallantly forward, but the lead soldiers made no move to follow. And since their faces had been hastily drawn with only a bare outline of features (and very haphazardly at that), from a distance it looked as though they were smiling ironically. And from irony to sedition is but a single step!

'Cowards!' Borodavkin grated through his teeth, but he could hardly say this aloud, and was forced to withdraw from the hill with losses.

They set off to make a detour, but on their way encountered a bog, which no one had any idea was there. Borodavkin looked at the map of the common – everywhere there was cultivated land, meadows in the watered parts, a patch of scrubland and some stony ground, but no bog was marked, and that was that.

'There is no bog here! You're lying, you villains! Quick march!' ordered Borodavkin, and climbed on to a hillock to have a better view of the crossing.

The men advanced into the marsh and immediately all the cannon sank to the bottom. The soldiers themselves somehow managed to scramble out in a very muddy state. Borodavkin got muddy too, but he was too preoccupied to pay any attention to that. He surveyed his lost artillery, and at the sight of the cannon half submerged, their barrels pointing to the sky as if threatening to shoot it down, he gave way to sorrow and affliction.

'How many years did I scrape and save and lavish care!' he complained. 'What shall I do now? How shall I rule without my cannon?'

The troops were by now completely demoralized. They crawled out of the morass and were confronted once more by a vast plain, again with no sign of habitation. In some places human bones lay about, and piles of bricks rose from the ground. All this indicated that at some time there had existed here a quite vigorous civilization (it later transpired that this civilization had been destroyed by an earlier town-governor, Urus-Kugush-Kildibaev, who while drunk had mistaken it for some kind of rebellion), but since then many years had elapsed, and no town-governor had ever bothered about its restoration. Strange shadows flitted across the countryside; mysterious sounds came to the ear. Something magic was taking place, rather like the third act of *Ruslan and Lyudmila*, when Farlaf comes running on to the stage in terror. Although Borodavkin was braver than Farlaf, even he could still not help shuddering at the thought that at any moment the wicked Naina might come out to meet him . . . .[49]

Only on the eighth day, at about midday, did his exhausted force come into view of the Musketeers' suburb and joyfully sound their bugles. Borodavkin remembered that before conquering his enemies, the Grand Prince Svyatoslav Igorevich[50] always sent a messenger to say: 'I am coming against you!' and, following his example, he dispatched his orderly to the Musketeers with the same greeting.

The following day, scarcely had the sun gilded the tops of the thatched roofs, when the troops, led by Borodavkin, were already entering the suburb. But there was no one there, except for a supernumerary priest, who at that particular moment was wondering whether it might not be more profitable for him to join the Schismatics. The priest was an ancient man, and better fitted to inspire despair than courage into a man's heart.

'Where are the inhabitants?' asked Borodavkin, flashing his eyes at him.

'They were here a minute ago', mumbled the priest toothlessly.

'What do you mean – a minute ago? Where have they run off to?'

'Where should they run? Why should they run away from their own homes? They must be somewhere about hiding from you, I suppose.'

Borodavkin stood quite still, grinding his feet into the ground. There was a moment when he began to think that the force of inaction must triumph.

'I should have begun my campaign in the winter!' he regretted in his heart. 'Then they wouldn't have hidden from me!'

'Hey! Who's there? Come out!' he shouted, in such a voice that even the lead soldiers shuddered.

But the suburb was silent as the dead. From somewhere came a sound of sighing, but the mysterious way in which these sighs escaped from unseen beings increased still more the annoyance of the exasperated town-governor.

'Where are these swine who are sighing?' he raged, looking hopelessly round in all directions, and evidently completely baffled. 'Find the first swine who sighs and bring him to me!'

They rushed to search, but look as they might they found nobody. Borodavkin himself walked along the street, peering into every cranny, but there was no one there. He was so perplexed that his head suddenly swarmed with the most incongruous ideas.

'If I destroy them now by fire . . . no, it would be better to starve them', he thought, letting his mind wander from one absurdity to another.

Then he suddenly stopped dumbfounded before the lead soldiers.

Something quite extraordinary was happening to them. Their eyes gradually suffused with blood, and, previously fixed, suddenly they began to roll and display anger. The soldiers' moustaches, which had been carelessly painted so that some pointed one way and some another, fell into proper place and began to bristle; their lips, a thin pink line which had been almost washed off in the late rain, pursed and made ready to speak. Nostrils, which had previously not been there at all, now took shape and flared with impatience.

'What do you say, men?' Borodavkin asked.

'Houses . . . houses . . . break down!' said the lead soldiers incoherently, but in a manner somehow sinister.

The means had been found.

They started with the house at the end. With shouts of glee, the lead soldiers rushed on to the roof, and at once set frenziedly to work. Down came bundles of thatch, wooden poles, and sticks. Clouds of dust went swirling upwards.

'Quiet! Quiet!' shouted Borodavkin, suddenly catching the sound of moaning close by.

The whole suburb moaned. It was an indistinct, but all-pervasive humming, in which no individual sound was to be distinguished, but which as a whole expressed the near intolerable anguish of a human heart.

'Who's there? Come out!' shouted Borodavkin again with all his might.

The suburb hushed, but no one came out. 'The Musketeers hoped', says the chronicler, 'that this new device (that is, suppression by means of demolishing houses) was but an illusion, like everything else, but they could not long console themselves with that sweet hope.'

'Carry on', said Borodavkin firmly.

There was a sound of crashing and splintering. One after the other, the timbers were removed from the walls and, as they fell to the ground, the moaning was renewed and grew louder. A few minutes later the end house had completely disappeared, and the lead soldiers were already ferociously attacking the next one. When, after a brief interval, the hiding Musketeers heard again the blows of the axe continuing its work of destruction, their hearts quaked. They all came out together, old and young, men and women. Lifting their hands to heaven, they fell on their knees in the middle of the square. At first Borodavkin drew back to launch a charge at them, but then remembered the words of the instruction: 'in carrying out pacifications, efforts should be made to persuade, rather than to destroy', and this calmed him. He saw that the hour of triumph had come, and that the triumph would be the greater if it involved no pulped noses or crushed cheek-bones.

'Do you accept the mustard?' he asked clearly, doing his best to suppress any threatening note in his voice.

The crowd bowed silently to the ground.

'I am asking you: do you accept it?' he repeated, all ready to boil over.

'Yes, yes, we accept it!' answered the crowd in a low drone, like a whispered murmur of malice.

'All right. Now tell me which of you insulted the memory of my dear mother in those verses?'

The Musketeers hesitated. It seemed wrong that they should betray a man who had given them comfort in the more bitter moments of life; but after a minute's hesitation they decided again to do as they were told.

'Go on, Fedka! Don't be afraid! Go on!' said voices in the crowd.

A fair-haired young man came forward and stood before the town-governor. His lips quivered, as if about to smile, but his face was as pale as death, and his teeth chattered.

'So it's you?' said Borodavkin with a loud laugh and stepped back a little, as though wanting to take a proper look at the offender, then he repeated: 'So it's you?'

It was obvious that a struggle was going on inside him. He was wondering whether to smash Fedka's face in or punish him in some other way. Finally, he decided on what might be called a 'mixed' punishment.

'Listen!' he said, administering a slight modification to the set of Fedka's jaw. 'Since you abused the memory of my dear mother, from now on you will write verses every day in her honour and bring them to me!'

Saying this, he ordered the retreat to be sounded.

The rebellion was over, ignorance was suppressed, and en-lightenment established in its place. Half an hour later, Borodavkin, laden with spoils and dragging behind him a multitude of prisoners and hostages, rode in triumph into the town. Since among his prisoners there were certain captains and other persons of high rank, he gave orders that they should be treated gently (though to be on the safe side, he had their eyes put out); the others were sent to penal servitude.

95

The same evening, Borodavkin closeted himself in his office and made the following entry in his journal:

'Today, the 17th September, after a hard, but glorious campaign of nine days' duration, the joyful and long-cherished event took place. The use of mustard has now been confirmed in all places and for all time, without the loss of a single drop of blood.'

To which the chronicler adds ironically: 'But for that which was shed by the stockade of Dunghills, in commemoration of which the ceremony of the whistle-piping is still celebrated.'

It may well be that much of the above narrative will seem too fantastic to the reader. Why should Borodavkin carry out a nine-day campaign, when the Musketeers' suburb was on his very doorstep and could be reached in half an hour? How could he get lost on the town common, with which, as town-governor, he must have been fully familiar? Is it possible to believe the story of the lead soldiers, who appear not only to have marched, but even, later, to have become suffused with blood?

Fully appreciating the importance of these questions, the editor considers they can be answered in the following way. The history of the town of Glupov is concerned, first and foremost, with a world of miracles, which can only be rejected if the existence of miracles is rejected altogether. But there is more to it than that. There are some miracles in which, on careful examination, one can detect a quite clear basis in fact. We all know the legend of Baba Yaga with the Bony Leg,[51] who rode in a mixing bowl and drove herself along with a mop, and we see these journeys of hers as one of the miracles which have been created by popular fancy. But nobody asks himself why popular fancy should have created this particular tale rather than another. If only students of our country were to look into this question, they might well be expected to discover much that has been previously shrouded in mystery. Thus, for instance, it would very likely be found that the legend of Baba Yaga originated in a purely administrative context, and that Baba Yaga was no more than the ruler of a town or, perhaps, an elected governess, who chose this particular method of travelling about her territory simply in order to inspire a salutary sense of fear in the inhabitants. During journeys she would snatch up any peasant Ivanushkas who came her way and declare on arriving home: 'I'll have a ride, and I'll have a roll, when I've eaten the flesh of Ivanushka'.

This, it seems, should be enough to convince the reader that the chronicler is concerned with matters which are far from fantastic, and that everything that has been said about

96

Borovadkin's campaigns can be taken as a perfectly reliable record of fact. Of course, at first it may seem strange that Borodavkin should spend nine whole days roaming the common, but it should be remembered, first, that he had no reason to hurry, since one could tell in advance that his enterprise was bound to succeed, and, secondly, that every administrator will readily have recourse to evolutions in order to impress inhabitants. If one could imagine the ceremony known as 'physical correction' taking place without the preliminaries – such as the removal of the clothing, the injunctions on the part of the corrector, the pleas for mercy on the part of the correctee – what would one be left with? Nothing but an empty formality, the point of which would be lost on all but the person suffering it. The same must be true of any campaign, whether for the conquest of a kingdom or simply for the collection of tax arrears. If you take away the 'evolutions', what are you left with?

Borodavkin might certainly have avoided many very serious mistakes. For instance, the episode the chronicler calls the 'Day of the Born-blind' was a very bad lapse indeed. But let us not forget that success is bound to involve losses, and that if we remove from the skeleton of history that tissue of falsehood with which time and prejudice overlay it, then we invariably find a greater or smaller number of 'slain'. Who are these 'slain'? Were they in the right, or in the wrong, and to what extent? How did they come to be among the 'slain'? All this will be answered later. But the 'slain' are indispensable, for without them – there would be no excuse for a wake!

So the only question that remains is that of the lead soldiers. But this is another question which is clarified to some extent by the chronicler. 'Very often do we remark', he says, 'that objects apparently quite inanimate (as if of stone), feel desires when presented with scenes accessible to their inanimate condition.' And he cites the example of a neighbouring landowner, who was paralysed and lay for ten years in his chair unable to move, but who still made happy moaning noises when the quit-rent was delivered.

There were altogether four wars of 'enlightenment'. One of them has been described above; of the remaining three, the first was aimed at demonstrating to the Glupovites the value of building houses on stone foundations; the second arose from the inhabitants' refusal to grow feverfew for making flea-powder; and the third was caused by a rumour about founding an academy in Glupov. It is generally obvious that Borodavkin was a Utopian, and that if he had lived longer, he would most likely have ended either by being exiled to Siberia for liberalism or else by setting up a phalanstery[52] in Glupov.

There is no need to give a detailed description of these brilliant achievements here, but it would not be superfluous to give some idea of their general character.

In Borodavkin's later campaigns one notices a considerable step forward. He prepared the ground for the uprisings with more elaborate care, and he suppressed them with greater speed. The most difficult campaign, that caused by rumours of an academy, lasted only two days, the others no more than a few hours. As a rule, Borodavkin would give the call to arms after his morning tea; the lead soldiers would assemble at the double, be promptly infused with blood and hasten to the appointed place. Borodavkin would be home in time for dinner and sing a *Te Deum*. By this means he brought it about that in a few years there was not a single Glupovite who could point to any part of his body which had not been flogged.

The inhabitants continued in a state of utter bewilderment. From the chronicler's account it is clear that they would have been just as happy not rebelling, but this was something quite beyond them, for they never understood what a rebellion actually was. And, indeed, Borodavkin was extremely clever in confusing them. Usually he gave no explanations and simply made his wishes known by proclamations, which were secretly posted at night on the end houses of every street. These proclamations were written in the manner of the advertisements one sees today for Kach's store, in which large letters are used for words of no importance at all and the essential matter is written in the smallest possible print. In addition to this, he also used Latin names – for example, feverfew was not called feverfew but *Pyrethrum roseum*, otherwise pellitory or Alexander's foot, belonging to the *Compositae* family, etc. The result of this was that the literate Glupovites who were usually charged with reading out these proclamations shouted loudly only those words which were in capital letters and glossed over the rest. So, for instance, the proclamation about feverfew read thus:

IT IS WELL KNOWN
what damage is caused by bugs, fleas, etc.

NOW FINALLY DISCOVERED !!!
Men of enterprise have imported from the Far East, etc.

Of all this the common people caught only 'It is well known' and 'now finally discovered'. And when these words were proclaimed, they took off their caps and sighed and crossed themselves. In this there was obviously nothing rebellious – it was more like the fulfilment of the authorities' aims. The people brought to a state of sighing – what more could be asked!

Consequently, it was all a matter of the Glupovites not understanding, and this conclusion is reinforced by the fact that even today the Glupovites do not know the meaning of the word 'academy', even though this particular word was written by Borodavkin in large letters (see No. 1089 in the 'Complete Collection of Proclamations'). The chronicler shows, however, that the Glupovites did make serious efforts themselves to persuade Borodavkin to lighten the darkness of their minds, but without success. This was entirely the fault of the town-governor. Quite often the whole community would go to the governor's house and say to Borodavkin:

'Open our eyes. Tell us what it's all about!'

'Get away, you ruffians!' was Borodavkin's usual reply.

'Us ruffians! You don't know what real ruffians are then! Come on, tell us!'

But Borodavkin said nothing. Why was he silent? Was it because he thought that the Glupovites' failure to understand was just a blind to conceal their stubborn resistance? Or was it because he wanted to give them a surprise? One cannot say for sure, but it must be supposed that some element of both was involved. No administrator who himself clearly understands the value of a measure he is undertaking ever imagines that it can be obscure or dubious to anyone else. On the other hand, every administrator is bound to be a fatalist and believe that, however he continues his administrative course, in the end he is certain to come up against the human body. Consequently, if you try to avert this inevitable end by elaborate explanations at the outset, do you not simply end by making the inevitable conclusion even more painful and violent? Finally, all administrators want to capture the people's trust, and what better way is there for people to show trust than by unprotestingly fulfilling something they do not understand?

Be this as it may, the fact remains that the Glupovites learnt the object of Borodavkin's campaigns only after their conclusion.

But however brilliant the results of these campaigns, they were in fact far from beneficial. Admittedly, contumacy had been destroyed, but then so also had prosperity. The inhabitants hung their heads and seemed to be ailing. They half-heartedly worked in the fields, half-heartedly returned home, half-heartedly sat down to their meagre repast, and wandered aimlessly about as though weary of everything.

On top of all this, the Glupovites sowed so much mustard and feverfew that their market price fell to an unbelievably low level. There followed an economic crisis, and there was no Molinari or Bezobrazov[53] to explain that the ruinous state they were in was in reality a state of true prosperity. The inhabitants not only received no precious metals and furs for their produce, but they even lacked the means to buy themselves corn.

However, until the year 1790 things kept going somehow. The inhabitants went from full rations to half-rations, but they did not fall into arrears with their taxes, and even showed some inclination towards enlightenment. In 1790 the Glupovites took mustard and feverfew to the main markets, but no one would buy – they had all taken pity on the fleas. Then the inhabitants went on to quarter-rations – and stopped paying their taxes. Just at this time, as though on purpose, the Revolution broke out in France, and everyone realized that 'enlightenment' is beneficial only when it is 'unenlightened' in character. Borodavkin received a document instructing him 'on the occasion of the event which is known to you to actively ensure that this incorrigible evil is outrooted in all its parts'.

Only then did Borodavkin pause and realize that he had been advancing too fast, and in quite the wrong direction. When he began collecting the taxes, he was surprised and indignant to find that the cottage-yards were empty, and that such chickens as he did come across were likewise lean from lack of food. But, as was his wont, he failed to appreciate the true cause of this and interpreted it in his own particular way – that is, he saw in it a rebellion, brought about now not by ignorance, but by excessive enlightenment.

'You've taken up with free-thinking! You've got too fat!' he cried, losing control of himself. 'Following after the French you are!'

And there now began a new series of campaigns – this time against enlightenment. In the first of these Borodavkin burnt down the suburb of Dunghills, in the second he destroyed Drab-houses, and in the third liquidated the district called the 'Bog'. But still the taxes were not paid. The moment was approaching when Borodavkin would be left with no one but his secretary on the ruins of the town, and for this moment he was actively preparing. But Providence stepped in to prevent it. In 1798 the combustible materials with which the whole town was to be burnt down were all ready to hand, when Borodavkin suddenly died. 'He had scattered everyone abroad', says the chronicler, 'So that there were not even priests to attend his parting. They had to summon the chief constable from the next district, who duly witnessed the passing of his restless spirit.'

The Period of Release from Wars

IN 1802 Negodyaev fell. He fell, according to the chronicler, because of his disagreement with Novosiltsev and Stroganov[54] on the question of a constitution. But this would seem to be only a plausible pretext, for it can scarcely be supposed that Negodyaev would have refused to introduce a constitution if his superiors had seriously demanded it of him. Negodyaev was one of the so-called 'fledgling' school of administrators, who did not care a button what they introduced. In view of this, the real reason for his dismissal most likely lay in the fact that he had at one time been a stoker in Gatchina, and so to some extent represented the democratic principles of that place.[55] Besides this, the authorities evidently realized that the wars of enlightenment, which had then become wars against enlightenment, had left Glupov so exhausted that there was a palpable need for the town to have some respite from wars altogether for a time. That the suggestion relating Negodyaev's fall to the constitutional question was no more than a baseless rumour is proved, first, by the most recent researches on the subject, and secondly, by the fact that Negodyaev was replaced as town-governor by the Circassian Mikaladze, who scarcely had any clearer notion of constitutions than Negodyaev.

Of course, it must be admitted that efforts to embody the constitutional principle were made, but this apparently meant nothing more than that the police inspectors improved their manners to the extent that some people at least were allowed to pass without being grabbed by the collar. This was the only constitutional measure considered possible in the then immature state of society. The prime object was to accustom people to courteous treatment, and only then, when their characters had been softened, would they be given what are supposed to be 'real' rights. In theory, of course, this view is perfectly correct. On the other hand, there is the no less acceptable view which says that, however attractive the theory of courteous treatment might be, by itself it gives absolutely no guarantee against the sudden intrusion of the theory of discourteous treatment (as was later shown by the appearance of such a person as Ugryum-Burcheev on the historical scene), and that, therefore, if we really wish to establish courteous treatment on a lasting basis, we must still first provide people with what are supposed to be 'real' rights. And this, in turn, proves how unreliable theories are in general, and how sensible are those military commanders who put no trust in them.

The new town-governor saw this, and consequently set out to win the Glupovites' hearts by the single means of elegant manners. Though he was an officer, he paid no attention to matters of uniform, and even spoke with bitterness on the subject of discipline. He always went about with his coat unbuttoned, presenting an alluring view of his snowy-white *piqué* waistcoat and turned-back collars. He liked to offer his left hand to his subordinates, he liked to smile, and not only did he avoid extremes of sharpness in his assertions, but, when receiving reports, was fond of using such expressions as 'And so, you were pleased to say' or 'I have already had the honour of informing you', etc. Only once, when his patience was exhausted by the persistent contrariness of his assistant, did he allow himself to say: 'I have already had the honour of telling you, you swine' . . ., but he immediately remembered himself and promoted the official in question to the next grade. Being passionate by nature, he gave himself up with zest to the society of women, and in pursuit of this passion he came to his untimely end. In the work which he left entitled 'Concerning the Agreeable Outward Aspect of Town-governors' (see below, among the Supporting Documents) he expounded his views on this subject in some detail, but he seems to have been somewhat disingenuous in linking his success among the ladies of Glupov with certain political and diplomatic ends. Most likely, like Antony in Egypt, he was ashamed of the very pampered existence he led, and wished to prove that even a pampered existence can have some administrative and juridical point. Confirmation of this is provided by the fact that in the chronicler's account there is no clear indication that there were frequent arrests or merciless floggings during his governorship, – which would, of course, have been indispensable if his amorous activities had really been aimed at maintaining public security. Hence one can say with fair certainty that he was fond of love-affairs for their own sake and admired the attractions of women simply as such, without any political ends in mind. The 'political ends' he invented simply in order to protect himself in the eyes of the authorities, who, despite their undoubted liberalism, still did not neglect to enquire occasionally whether the time was not ripe for another war. The chronicler says of this: 'And he, out of pity for the tears of orphans, answered always: "It is not time, for the material which I am gathering is not yet ready". And he died, without ever having gathered it.'

However this may be, the appointment of Mikaladze was still a most happy event for the Glupovites. Though his predecessor, Captain Negodyaev, had not been an essentially evil-tempered man, he had nonetheless considered himself to be a man of principle and, as such, was continually attempting to discover whether the Glupovites were sufficiently resolute in misfortune. The result of his intensive administration was that by the end of his governorship Glupov consisted of nothing but a disorderly huddle of blackened, dilapidated huts, in the midst of which only the watch-tower of the gaol rose proudly towards the sky. There was no proper food, and no decent clothing. The Glupovites had lost all sense of shame, fur had grown all over their bodies, and they sucked their fists.

'But how can you live in such a way?' Mikaladze asked the inhabitants in astonishment.

'We live like this because we've got no proper way to live', answered the Glupovites, half-laughing and half-crying.

In the face of such moral dissolution, the first concern of the new governor was, understandably, to free the Glupovites from fear. And, undoubtedly, he showed some skill in the way he went about this. A number of measures were taken aimed specifically at achieving this purpose, which can be summed up as follows: (1) enlightenment and its attendant chastisements were to be temporarily suspended, and (2) no laws were to be promulgated. From the very first the results were astonishing. Before the end of a month, the fur covering the Glupovites had vanished completely, and the Glupovites were ashamed of their nakedness. At the end of another month they stopped sucking their fists, and six months later, for the first time in many years, an evening of song and dance was held in Glupov, attended by the governor in person, who presented ginger-breads to all the ladies.

By such peaceful accomplishments did Mikaladze distinguish himself. Like any other truly fruitful period of activity, Mikaladze's tenure as governor was neither glorious nor brilliant;

it was marked neither by conquests abroad nor by upheavals at home; but it answered the needs of the moment and entirely succeeded in attaining those modest ends which it had set itself. There were few visible events, but innumerable consequences. 'Wise men of the world!' exclaims the chronicler in this connection, 'give earnest thought to this matter, and let not your hearts be troubled at the sight of the scourges and other instruments wherein you, in your high-mindedness, suppose the power and light of enlightenment to reside!'

In view of all this the editor finds it quite natural that the chronicler's account of Mikaladze's governorship should not be very rich in detail. Mikaladze is important not for doing anything in the ordinary sense, but for being the first pioneer along that peaceful path which the civilization of Glupov came so near to taking. The benefits of his activity were elusive, for such measures as shaking hands, smiling kindly, and generally treating people gently are felt only in their immediate effect, and leave no specially strong or evident traces in history. They produce no revolutions in the economic or intellectual situation of a country, yet if you compare these administrative measures with measures as, for instance, calling your subordinates 'swine', or giving them continual floggings, then you will have to admit that there is an immense difference between them. Many people, looking back over the actions of Mikaladze, find some cause for reproach. They say, for example, that he had no right to suspend enlightenment – and this is true. If, on the other hand, enlightenment is necessarily accompanied by various forms of chastisement, then surely reason demands that even in a cause so obviously beneficial some short periods of respite ought to be allowed. And then they say that Mikaladze had no right not to promulgate laws, and, of course, this also is correct. And yet, do we not see that even the most educated nations reckon themselves happiest on Sundays and holidays, at times, that is, when those in authority consider themselves relieved of the obligation to write laws?

One can hardly ignore these lessons of experience. The chronicler's account may suffer from a lack of hard and palpable facts, but we see none the less that Mikaladze was the first governor of Glupov to establish that most valuable of all administrative precedents – the precedent of singing praises gently and without swearing. Let us grant that this precedent represents nothing very positive and was in its later development subjected to many more or less cruel circumstances, but the fact remains that, once introduced, it never died out completely, and even occasionally gave a reminder of its existence. Is this really a small achievement? This worthy governor possessed one weakness: an uncontrollable, almost feverish passion for the female sex. The chronicler dwells in some detail on this peculiarity of his hero, but it is notable that there is no hint of bitterness or anger in his account. Only on one occasion does he say: 'and great was the ruin he caused to the women and maids of Glupov', which seems to imply that, in his opinion, it would have been better if they had not been ruined. But there is nowhere any sign of outright indignation. However, we shall not follow the chronicler's description of this weakness, since those who wish to learn more of it can obtain all the information they need from the work personally written by Mikaladze, 'Concerning the Agreeable Outward Aspect of Town-governors', which is found at the end of this volume. It is only fair to say, however, that this work fails to mention one rather important event recorded in the 'Chronicle'. This is the following: that one night Mikaladze had made his way to the wife of the town treasurer and had hardly had time to cast aside his fetters (it is thus that the chronicler refers to his uniform), when he was surprised by the jealous husband. A battle ensued, in which Mikaladze not so much did battle as had battle done to him, but since he afterwards washed himself, of course, no traces of his dishonour remained. Apparently, this was the only such failure he ever suffered, and so it is understandable why he did not mention it in his composition. It was such an insignificant detail in the vast series of his herculean achievements in this field that it did not cause him ever to reconsider his strategy to ensure better success in future operations . . . .

Mikaladze died in 1806 from exhaustion.

When the ground had been sufficiently broken by courteous treatment, and when the people had had some respite from enlightenment, naturally, the next concern was for legislation. The answer to this need was Feofilakt Irinarkhovich Benevolensky, a State Councillor and friend of Speransky, with whom he had attended the same seminary.

From his earliest youth Benevolensky had been irresistibly inclined towards legislation. While still a pupil in the seminary, he had drafted a number of laws, among which the most notable were: 'Every man shall have a contrite heart', 'Every spirit shall tremble', and 'Every cobbler shall stick to his duly appointed last'. But as the gifted youth grew older, so this innate passion grew more irresistible. No one had the least doubt that he would become a legislator. It was only a question of the kind of legislator he would become – whether he would recall the profundity and administrative perspicacity of Lycurgus, or simply be firm, like Dracon. He was himself fully aware of the importance of this question, and in a letter 'to a certain friend' (is this not Speransky?) he describes his uncertainty on the subject in the following manner:

'I am sitting', he writes, 'in my gloomy solitude and thinking constantly of what laws are the most valuable and expedient. There are wise laws which, though they contrive towards the happiness of man (such, for example, as the laws of universal human nourishment), are not, in some circumstances, always useful; then there are unwise laws, which, while not contriving to anybody's happiness, are still, in some circumstances, useful (I will mention no examples: you know them well enough!); and there are, thirdly, intermediate laws, which are neither very wise, nor yet very unwise, and neither useful, nor useless, but are still expedient in the sense that they make for the greater fullness of human life. For instance, when in moments of forgetfulness we begin to think ourselves immortal, how refreshingly are we affected by the simple phrase *"memento mori"*! So is it in the present case. When we think our happiness unbounded, because wise laws are no concern of ours and because from unwise laws we are immune, then it is that intermediate laws are helpful, reminding all men alive that there is not one breath of air on earth for which a law of some sort has not in due time been written. And, my friend, will you believe me when I say that the more I think of it, the more I incline towards intermediate laws? They beguile my spirit, for they are not really laws at all, but rather, you might say, the *shadows* of laws. On entering their sphere, you feel that you are in communion with legality, but cannot comprehend the nature of this communion. It happens without conscious thought; you think of nothing, you see nothing, yet at the same time you feel a certain vague unease which has no foundation in fact. It might be compared to an apocalyptic letter, which can only be understood by the person who receives it. Intermediate laws have the advantage that anyone reading them will say: "What nonsense!" – but at the same time everyone will strive wholeheartedly to carry them out. If, for example, you were to promulgate a law which said: "Every man shall eat", then this would be an example of those intermediate laws which everyone strives to fulfil without the least constraint. My friend, you will ask me: then why promulgate laws which are carried out anyway? And my answer will be: the object of promulgating laws is twofold: some are promulgated for the better ordering of nations and countries, and others are promulgated to save legislators from wasting in idleness . . . .'

And so on.

Thus, when Benevolensky arrived in Glupov, his views on legislation were already formed, and they were formed in precisely the manner most fitted to the needs of the moment. Accordingly, the well-being of the Glupovites, which had been inaugurated under Mikaladze, not only continued undisturbed, but received further consolidation. What the Glupovites needed was precisely 'shadows of laws', that is, laws which can usefully occupy the leisure hours of legislators, but cannot impinge upon the lives of other people. Occasionally such laws are even termed 'wise' laws, and, in the view of competent authorities, the term is neither exaggerated nor unwarranted.

But at this point an unforeseen circumstance was encountered. Benevolensky had scarcely set about promulgating his first law when it was discovered that he, as a mere town-governor, had no right to promulgate laws of his own. When he was first told this by his secretary, he refused to believe him. They hunted through the Senate Orders, but although they searched the whole archives, no order empowering the Borodavkins, Dvoekurovs, Velikanovs, Benevolenskys, etc. to promulgate laws of their own creation came to light.

'You can do what you like without a law!' said the secretary. 'But you cannot make your own laws.'

'Strange!' said Benevolensky, and straightway wrote to the authorities, explaining the difficulty he had encountered.

'I have arrived in Glupov', he wrote, 'and though I found the inhabitants brought by my predecessor into a state of fatness, yet I have discovered such a paucity of laws that the inhabitants make no distinction between law and nature. And thus, without any visible beacon to guide them, they wander in the darkness of night. In this extremity I ask myself: if one of these wanderers should miss his footing, or fall into the abyss, what shall keep him from falling? Although there is an abundance of laws in Russia, they have all been filed away in various archives and it is even highly probable that the greater part of them have perished in the various fires that have occurred in the past. On account of this, it is a matter of urgency and expedience that I, as town-governor, should be able to promulgate laws of my own composition, even though they be not laws of the first class (I would not presume even to think of that!), but of the second and third. I am strengthened in this opinion by the fact that Glupov is, by its very nature, what might be termed a "second-class" district in the legal aspect, and has no need of laws which are burdensome or profound in content. In expectation of a favourable reply to my present request, I remain . . .', etc.

To this application an answer soon came.

'In reply to your application', said the letter, 'for the town of Glupov to be regarded as a district requiring laws of the second class, the following is submitted for your consideration:

1. In the event of many such towns appearing in which the town-governors compose second-class laws, will this not result in some harm being done to the governmental structure of the Russian State?

2. In the event of town-governors being allowed to compose second-class laws in their capacity as town-governors, will it not then be necessary to permit village constables in their capacity as village constables to compose similar laws, and to what class would such laws belong?'

Benevolensky realized that these questions were an indirect refusal to his request, and was much saddened. His contemporaries explain his grief by claiming that his heart was infected by the poison of autocracy, but that can hardly be the case. When a man can do anything he likes with no laws at all, it is strange to suspect him of ambition for doing something which would not only not increase, but actually restrict his capacity to do so. For all laws (even such laws, for instance, as 'Every man shall eat' or 'Every spirit shall tremble') have a restricting effect, and this never appeals to ambitious people. It is clear, therefore, that Benevolensky was not really a man of ambition, but a well-meaning doctrinaire, who thought it reprehensible even to wipe his nose if there was no law which clearly stated that 'Every man requiring to wipe his nose shall wipe it'.

Whatever the case, Benevolensky was so upset by this refusal that he retired to the house of the merchant's widow, Raspopova (whom he admired for her skill in baking pies), and, to give some satisfaction to his consuming thirst for intellectual activity, devoted himself to writing sermons. For a whole month the priests read these masterly sermons in all the churches of the town, and for a whole month the Glupovites sighed as they listened to them, – they were written with such sensibility! The governor himself instructed the priests on how to deliver them.

'A preacher', he said, 'must have a contrite heart, and must therefore incline his head slightly to one side. His voice should not be strident, but languid, as though he were sighing. He should not make violent gestures with his hands, but first place his right hand near his heart (that true source of all our sighs), then gradually stretch it forward and return it again to the same point. In passages of especial feeling he should not cry out or add unnecessary words of his own, but only sigh the louder.'

In the meantime the Glupovites grew fatter and fatter, and Benevolensky was not only not upset by this, he was actually glad. Never once did the thought of letting blood from these contented people enter his mind. On the contrary, as he looked from the windows of Raspopova's house and saw the inhabitants going contentedly about the streets, he even wondered whether their happiness was not due to their being undisturbed by laws of any class whatever. But such an idea was too distressing for him to dwell on. Scarcely had he turned his eyes from the jubilant Glupovites, than he was again possessed by his longing for legislation.

'My dear Marfa Terentevna,' he would say to Raspopova, the merchant's widow, 'I just cannot tell you what I might achieve and how much happier these people would be, if only I were allowed to promulgate just one law a day!'

At last, he could stand it no longer. One dark night, when not only the watchmen, but even the dogs were asleep, he crept into the street and scattered a large number of paper bills containing the first law written by him for Glupov. And although he knew this to be a most reprehensible way to publish laws, his long-restrained passion for legislation so clamoured for satisfaction that its voice silenced even the dictates of reason.

The new law had evidently been written in haste, and this would account for its unusual brevity. The following day the Glupovites picked up the paper bills as they went to market and read the following:

'Every man shall walk circumspectly; and the tax-contractor shall bring gifts.'

That was all. But the meaning of the law was clear, and the very next day the tax-contractor called on the governor. An explanation took place between them. The tax-contractor explained that even in the past he had been 'prepared' within the bounds of possibility, while Benevolensky replied that he could not remain in his previous undefined position, that an expression such as 'the bounds of possibility' meant nothing either to the intellect or to the heart, and that only the law was clear. They settled for three thousand roubles a year, and it was ordained that this should be the lawful figure until such times as 'circumstances should require a change in the law'.

After recounting this incident, the chronicler questions whether this law was of any use, and replies in the affirmative. 'The mention of walking circumspectly', he says, 'caused the Glupovites no disquiet, since they had always possessed a great and natural capacity for acting in this manner, and practised it in all places. But the tax-contractor genuinely benefited from this legislation, for when Benevolensky's successor, Pryshch, demanded double the usual three thousand, the tax-contractor replied with great boldness that he could not do it, since by the law he was not bound to give more than three thousand. And Pryshch said: "Then we shall change this law". And he changed it.'

Encouraged by the success of his first law, Benevolensky made active preparations for the issue of his second. The fruits of these preparations came soon after, when by the same mysterious means a new and more extensive law appeared in the streets of Glupov. It read thus:

STATUTE

CONCERNING THE PROPER BAKING OF PIES

1. On feast days every person shall bake a pie, nor shall he desist from the baking of pies likewise on ordinary days.

2. Every person shall employ such filling for his pie as befits his station, thus: a fish caught in the river may so be used; meat, finely chopped, may likewise so be used; cabbage, chopped, may also so be used. Those without means may use tripe.

Note. The making of pies from mud, clay, and building materials is forbidden for all time.

3. After the insertion of the filling and the enrichment of it by a proper quantity of butter and eggs, the pie shall be placed in a moderate oven until brown.

4. On the removal of the pie from the oven, every person shall take to hand a knife and cut out a portion from the centre, the same to be taken as a gift to the governor.

5. On fulfilment of the above, the pie shall be eaten.

The Glupovites grasped the import of this new regulation the more readily, as they had of old been accustomed to presenting a portion of their pies to the governor. Although in more recent times – during the liberal administration of Mikaladze – this custom had fallen into neglect and lapsed, they made no complaint about its renewal, since they hoped it would still further strengthen the amicable relations existing between them and the new governor. They all hastened to be the first to afford pleasure to Benevolensky, bringing him the very best portion and some even giving him the whole pie.

After this there was a bustle of legislative activity in Glupov. Not a day passed by without the appearance of some new anonymous document bringing the Glupovites new cause for rejoicing. Finally, the time came when Benevolensky even began thinking of a constitution.

'I can tell you, my dear Marfa Terentevna,' he said to the merchant's widow, Raspopova, 'a constitution is not nearly so daunting a thing as uninformed people imagine it to be. The import of any constitution is as follows: that every man shall live in peace and contentment in his own home. And what, madam, is there terrible or presumptuous in that?'

And he considered his plan. But the more he thought, the more confused he became in his ideas. The thing that caused him most trouble was that he could reach no clear definition of the word 'rights'. He knew perfectly well what 'duties' were, and on that subject he could have written reams, but 'rights' – what are 'rights'? Was it sufficient to define them by saying: 'Every man shall live in peace and contentment in his own home'? Would that not be too brief? On the other hand, if one launched into explanations, would it not be too long and burdensome for the Glupovites themselves?

These doubts were resolved by Benevolensky's issuing, as a provisional measure, a 'Statute concerning the Benevolence proper to Town-governors', which, in view of its length, has been placed among the Supporting Documents at the end of this volume.

'I know', he said to Raspopova, 'I know that this document falls short of being a true constitution, but, dear madam, I beg you to consider – that no building, not even a chicken-run, is ever built all at once. With time, we shall carry out the remainder of our agreeable task, and find present consolation by putting our trust in God!'

There is no reason to doubt that Benevolensky would sooner or later have brought his plan to fulfilment, but the storm clouds were already gathering over him. It was all on account of Bonaparte. The year 1811 came, and Russian relations with Napoleon grew extremely strained. Still, the fame of this new 'scourge of

God' had not yet waned, and it even reached Glupov. There, among his many female admirers (it is remarkable how particularly devoted females were to the Enemy of Mankind) the most fanatical enthusiasm was displayed by the merchant's widow, Raspopova.

'How I'm taken with that Bonaparte!' she used to say to Benevolensky. 'I think there is nothing I wouldn't give just to peep at him once!'

At first, Benevolensky would grow angry, even saying that this was silly woman's talk. But Marfa Terentevna would not desist and grew even more importunate, insisting that Benevolensky should produce her Bonaparte at once, and in the end he gave way. He realized that it was impossible not to do what the 'silly woman' wanted, and gradually he even came to see nothing reprehensible in it.

'What of it! Let the silly ceature have her way!' he consoled himself. 'Who's the loser by it!'

So he entered into secret relations with Napoleon.

Heaven alone knows by what means these relations were discovered, but it would appear that Napoleon himself let the cat out of the bag to Prince Kurakin[56] at one of his *petits levés*. And so, one fine morning, Glupov learned with astonishment that they were ruled not by a town-governor, but by a traitor, and that a special commission was on its way from the provincial capital to investigate his treason.

Now it all came out: that Benevolensky had secretly invited Napoleon to come to Glupov, and that he had promulgated laws of his own creation. His only defence was to say that the Glupovites had never enjoyed such a state of fatness as during his term as governor, but this justification was rejected, or, more accurately, it elicited the reply that 'he would have been less guilty if he had brought them to a state of utter leanness, as long as he had desisted from promulgating those absurd scribblings which he had the effrontery to call laws'.

It was a warm moonlit night when the carriage drove up to the governor's house. Benevolensky came out on to the porch with a firm step and was on the point of bowing to all sides, when he noticed to his confusion that, except for two gendarmes, the street was empty. Now again the Glupovites, as was their wont, astounded the world by their lack of gratitude, for as soon as they discovered the town-governor was in trouble, they promptly withdrew their support. However bitter this cup was, Benevolensky drained it with a cheerful spirit. In a clear, distinct voice he uttered the one word 'Scoundrels!' and, taking his seat in the carriage, drove safely off to that distant land of no return.

Thus ended the administrative career of a town-governor in whom there was continual conflict between a passion for legislation and a passion for pies. The laws which he promulgated have no validity today.

But, apparently, there was to be no end to the good fortune of the Glupovites. In place of Benevolensky came Lieutenant-Colonel Pryshch, bringing with him an even simpler system of administration.

Pryshch was no longer a young man, but he was unusually well-preserved. He was broad-shouldered and built like an ox, and his whole figure seemed to say: 'Pay no attention to my grey whiskers. I am capable! I am still very capable!' He was ruddy-complexioned, with succulent red lips, which parted to reveal a row of white teeth; he walked with a lively, purposeful step, and gestured rapidly with his hands. The whole was embellished with glittering colonel's epaulettes, which at his every movement literally danced on his shoulders.

Following the usual custom, he went to pay his respects to the various authorities of the town and to the other notables of both sexes, and on these occasions he unfolded to them his programme.

'I am a simple man, sir,' he would say to some, 'and I didn't come here to issue laws. No, sir. My duty is to see that the laws are preserved in good order and are not left lying about the tables. Of course, I also have a plan of campaign, but my plan is as follows: to rest, sir!'

To others he spoke thus:

'I have, thank God, a decent substance. I had, sir, a command, so I did not squander my substance – I increased it. And so the laws concerning such matters I know, and have no wish to issue new ones. Of course, many in my position would storm into the attack, and would perhaps even organize a bombardment, but I am a simple man, sir, and see no pleasure for myself in attacking people.'

To a third group he explained his position thus:

'I am not a liberal, and never have been a liberal, sir. I always act in a straightforward way, and that's why I keep well clear of the laws. If it is a difficult case I have them look one out, but one thing I do insist on is that the law should be an old one. I don't care for new laws, sir. There's a lot left out in them, and some things are not even mentioned at all. When I was leaving to come here, I said: Spare me the new laws and the rest I shall hope to carry out to the letter.'

Finally, to a fourth group he depicted himself in the following colours:

'All I can say about myself is this: I have not been in any battles, no, sir, but I have been seasoned on parade to a most uncommon degree. I don't understand new ideas. I don't even understand why anyone should understand them.'

That was not all. On the first feast day he called a general assembly of the Glupovites and gave them formal confirmation of his administrative views.

'Now, old fellows,' he said to the inhabitants, 'Let's live in peace. You leave me alone, and I'll leave you alone. Plant and sow, eat and drink, start having factories – why not? It would be all for your good, sirs! As far as I'm concerned, you can build monuments – I shan't stand in your way! Only, for the Lord's sake, be careful how you handle fire, because that can easily lead to trouble. You burn your property, you burn yourselves – and what's the good of that?'

However much the Glupovites had been spoiled by their last two governors, such unbounded liberalism as this made them wonder whether it was not some kind of trap. So for some time they were on their guard, trying to find out more, talking in whispers, and generally 'walking circumspectly'. It seemed rather strange that the town-governor should not only not interfere in the affairs of the inhabitants, but even declare that the very essence of his administration lay in this non-interference.

'And won't you even issue laws?' they asked him doubtingly.

'No, I won't even issue laws. Live in peace!'

'All right, then. Do us a kindness and don't issue any. See what it got that swine (thus they referred to Benevolensky). If you start on that again, we might all have to answer for it, you and us as well!'

But Pryshch was quite sincere in what he said and firmly followed his chosen path. He put an end to all official business and spent his time in visiting, accepting invitations to dinners and balls; he even got himself a pack of hounds with which he coursed for hares and foxes on the town common, and on one occasion caught a very pretty little woman from one of the trades-men's districts. He used to speak somewhat ironically of his predecessor, now languishing in captivity.

'Filat Irinarkhovich', he would say, 'liked to make paper promises that under him the inhabitants would rest in peace and contentment in their own homes, but I shall give them this in actual fact . . . yes, sir!'

And it was true. Despite the fact that the Glupovites had greeted Pryshch's first steps with mistrust, before very long they found that they had twice and three times as much of everything as they had before. The bees swarmed so uncommonly well that the amount of honey and beeswax dispatched to Byzantium was almost as great as in the time of Prince Oleg.[57] Although there were no plagues to kill the cattle, there were great quantities of hides, and, as the Glupovites still found it more comfortable to cut a figure wearing bast-shoes rather than leather boots, all the hides were disposed of to Byzantium as well, and everything paid for in good solid paper-money. And since everyone was now at liberty to produce manure, the corn grew in such abundance that, apart from what was sold, some even remained for their own use. 'It was not as in other towns', says the chronicler with bitterness, 'where the railways* can scarcely shift the gifts of the soil destined to be sold, while the inhabitants themselves wax lean from lack of food. In Glupov at this happy time not only the master, but every hired man ate real bread, nor was it uncommon to have cabbage soup with a piece of meat cooked with it.'

Pryshch rejoiced at the sight of this happiness – and indeed he could hardly help rejoicing, since the general plenty was reflected in his own prosperity. His barns were bursting with offerings in kind; his chests could not contain all the silver and gold, and the paper money simply littered the floor.

So another year passed, during which the Glupovites' goods were no longer two or three times, but four times what they had been. But as liberty developed, so its old enemy – analysis – developed accordingly. With the increase in material well-being came leisure, and with leisure came the ability to examine and investigate the nature of things. This always happens, but the Glupovites used this 'their newly manifested ability' not to further their well-being, but to undermine it.

Unused to governing themselves, the Glupovites came to attribute their well-being to the agency of some unknown power. And as in their language 'unknown power' was another name for devilry, they began thinking too there was something unwholesome about the present situation and that the Devil doubtless had a hand in it. They began to watch Pryshch and discovered certain doubtful features in his behaviour. For instance, it was said that

* Railways had not even been thought of then, but this is one of those harmless anachronisms which occur so frequently in the Chronicle.

someone had found him sleeping on a couch with mousetraps arranged all round his body. Some went further and claimed that every night Pryshch took himself off to sleep in the ice-house. All this suggested something mysterious, and although no one asked himself what business it was of his that the town-governor slept in the ice-house rather than an ordinary bedroom, it was none the less disturbing. The general suspicion increased still more when it was noticed that the local Marshal of the Nobility had for some time been in an unnatural state of excitement, and that every time he met the town-governor he would start writhing about and make unseemly motions with his body.

It cannot be claimed that the Marshal possessed any special qualities of intellect or feeling, but he had a stomach of grave-like capacity into which disappeared morsels of every possible kind. This somewhat elemental natural gift had become for him a source of the most lively pleasure. Early each morning he would set out on an expedition round the town, sniffing the smells from the Glupovites' kitchens. In a short time his sense of smell had become so refined that he could guess unerringly the ingredients of the most complicated force-meat mixture.

The very first time that he met the town-governor the Marshal felt that there was something not quite usual about this dignitary – namely, that he smelt of truffles. For a long time he struggled against this idea, taking it to be a figment of his gastronomically-fired imagination, but the more often he met him, the more tantalizing became his doubts. At last, he could hold out no longer, and communicated his suspicions to Polovinkin, the Clerk of the Gentry Court of Wards.

'There's a smell about him!' he said to his astonished confidant. 'A smell! Just like a delicatessen-store!'

'Perhaps his honour uses a truffle-scented brilliantine?' suggested Polovinkin sceptically.

'That, my friend, is stuff and nonsense! If you say that, then every sucking-pig will be telling you to your face that he's not a sucking-pig at all, but only uses sucking-pig scent!'

On the first occasion their conversation had no further consequences, but the Marshal was deeply moved by the idea of sucking-pig scent. He wandered about the town in a state of gastronomic melancholy, like a man in love, and if he happened to catch sight of Pryshch anywhere, he slobbered in a most unseemly fashion. Once during a joint meeting to discuss the organization of some extra-special gastronomic occasion at Shrovetide the Marshal, moved to a state of frenzy by the piquant smell emanating from the town-governor, lost control of himself and leapt from his seat with a cry of: 'Fetch the vinegar and mustard!' Then, falling on the governor's head, he began sniffing it.

The astonishment of those present at this bewildering scene was unbounded. It also seemed odd that the governor should say (admittedly through his teeth, but none the less rather rashly):

'He's found out, the swine!'

Then, checking himself, he added with obviously affected casualness:

'It would seem that our worthy Marshal has taken my head to be a stuffed one . . . Ha, ha!'

Alas! this indirect admission contained the most bitter truth!

The Marshal fainted and was ill with a fever, but he forgot nothing and grew none the wiser. A number of scenes took place which bordered on the indecent. The Marshal fussed and twisted about Pryshch until finally, finding himself alone with him on one occasion, he took the bull by the horns.

'Give me a piece!' he moaned to the governor, closely observing the look in his chosen victim's eyes.

At the first murmur of a request so clearly formulated, the governor shuddered. His position had now suddenly become clear with that finality which makes all idea of compromise useless. He glanced timidly at his tormentor and, seeing his determined gaze, at once lapsed into a state of profound melancholy.

Nevertheless, he still made some feeble effort to resist. A struggle developed, but the Marshal was now in a state of uncontrollable frenzy. His eyes flashed, his stomach ached with sweet pangs of yearning. He gasped and moaned, he called the governor his 'dear' and his 'darling' and other names unbefitting to the governor's dignity. He licked him and sniffed him, and so on. At last, in a state of utter fury, the Marshal threw himself on his victim, cut a piece from his head with a knife and promptly swallowed it . . . .

The first piece was followed by a second, then a third, until not a single scrap was left . . . .

Then the town-governor suddenly leapt up and began wiping with his hands those parts of his body which the Marshal had sprinkled with vinegar. He then spun round and all at once crashed bodily to the floor.

The next day the Glupovites learned that their town-governor had had a stuffed head.

But nobody guessed that this was the very reason why the town had been brought to such a state of prosperity, the like of which was unknown in the chronicles from its very foundation.

The Worship of Mammon — and Repentance

THE life of man, say the spiritualist philosophers, is a dream, and if they were to be entirely logical, they would add that history also is a dream. Of course, viewed absolutely, both statements are equally inept, but one is inevitably conscious that at certain times in history there do seem to be gaps, before which the intellect pauses in bewilderment. The stream of life appears to break off its natural course to form a whirlpool, which twists and spumes until covered with a muddy scum, through which it is impossible to distinguish any clear characteristics or individual phenomena. Confusing, meaningless events succeed each other without connection, and people seem to pursue no other end than to survive the passing day. They tremble and triumph by turns, and the deeper their humiliation, the more vengeful and cruel is their triumph. The source of the disturbance is now clouded with mud; the principles in the name of which the struggle arose can no longer be discerned; there remains only struggle for the sake of struggle, art for the sake of art – that art which invented the rack, the gauntlet, and other such things.

Of course, the main centre of disturbance is on the surface, though it can hardly be claimed that meanwhile all is well at the bottom. What is taking place at those various levels which lie just beneath the surface and lower down, right to the bottom? Are they still tranquil, or does the disturbance on the surface affect them too? We cannot say for sure, since we are not much accustomed to looking deep into things that go far beneath the surface. But it must be fairly certain that the pressure is felt there too. It has its effect partly in the form of material damage and loss, but chiefly in greater or lesser delays in social development. And although it is only afterwards that the real pain of these losses is felt, it can still be assumed that people living at the time regard the pressures that bear down on them with no special pleasure.

It was most likely one of these difficult periods in history that Glupov was passing through at the time described by the chronicler. The real inner life of the town lay hidden in the depths, while on the surface appeared certain malignant exhalations, which completely dominated the historical scene. From top to bottom Glupov was enveloped in spurious, extraneous elements, and though it can be claimed that these spurious elements contributed something to the general economy of the town's existence, it can be said with equal truth that those who lived under their yoke were not particularly fortunate people. To suffer a Borodavkin for the sake of discovering the benefits of using certain kinds of herbs; to suffer an Urus-Kugush-Kildibaev for the sake of learning the nature of true valour – say what you will, such a fate cannot be called truly normal or particularly gratifying: although this is not to say that some herbs are not indeed beneficial, or that there is anything wrong with valour, when displayed at a proper time and place.

In such conditions one cannot expect from the inhabitants any outstanding achievements in the field of public welfare or morality, or any particular successes in the arts and sciences. For them such periods in history are years of training, when they put themselves to the test for the single purpose of seeing how much they can endure. This is just how the chronicler presents his fellow-citizens. It is evident from his account that the Glupovites submitted to the caprices of history without murmur, and their actions provide no factual basis for us to form an estimate of their readiness for self-government. On the contrary, it is clear that they rushed hither and thither without plan, as though driven by some unaccountable fear. It is an unflattering picture, no one will deny, but it cannot be otherwise, since its subject is a man who is being buffeted on the head with astonishing regularity, as a result of which, of course, he becomes dazed. The chronicler describes the history of these states of dazedness with that truth and lack of artifice which are typical of the accounts of our life and customs given by the archivists. And, in my opinion, we can ask no more of him. There is no intended ridicule in his account; on the contrary, in many passages one can even detect sympathy for the poor creatures who exist in this state of dazedness. As for the Glupovites, the fact that, despite their life and death struggle, they go on living is sufficient testimony to their power of endurance, and worthy of the serious attention of historians.

Let us not forget that the chronicler writes mainly about the so-called common people, who even today are still regarded as being outside the bounds of history. In his mind's eye the chronicler sees, on the one hand, a force which has crept up from the distance and achieved strength and organization, and, on the other hand, poor defenceless creatures who have scattered and sheltered in corners and are for ever being taken unawares. Can there be any doubt of the relationship which must arise when two such disparate elements are brought together?

That the force of which we are speaking is not an imaginary one is proved by the fact that its description has actually led to the establishment of a whole school of historians, the members of which declare with complete sincerity that the more you liquidiate the inhabitants, the happier they will be, and the more brilliant their history.[58] Of course, this is not a very sensible view, but how will you prove that to people so complacent that they will neither hear nor accept argument? Before you can prove anything, you have to make yourself heard, and how will you do that, when the inhabitants are not altogether sure themselves that they ought not to be exterminated?

'I kept asking him', says the victim, '"What's your reason, sir, for beating me?" But all he did was punch me in the teeth and say: "There's a reason! And there's a reason!"'

In such circumstances there is no other formula for relations between the two. There is no reason to beat him, but there is also no reason for not beating him – as a result of which we are left with the sad tautology which explains a cuff on the ear by a cuff on the ear. Of course, this tautology hangs by a thread, a single thread, but how can it be broken? That is the whole question. The view suggests itself that it is probably best simply to put all one's hopes in the future. This is not a very sensible view either, but what else can you do, if no other views have been thought of? And this, evidently, was the view taken by the Glupovites.

Likening themselves to eternal debtors in the hands of eternal creditors, they reckoned there were all kinds of creditors in the world, reasonable ones, and unreasonable ones. A reasonable creditor helps the debtor out of his straitened circumstances and, for his reasonableness, he has his debt repaid. The unreasonable creditor puts his debtor into prison, or beats him unceasingly, and gets nothing in return. Reckoning thus, the Glupovites waited for the time when all creditors would become reasonable ones. And they are still waiting to this day.

Because of this, I see nothing in the chronicler's narrative detrimental to the dignity of the inhabitants of Glupov. They are people like any other people, except that their natural qualities have become overlaid with a mass of extraneous particles, beneath which practically nothing can be seen. It is a question, therefore, not of actual qualities but merely of extraneous particles. Would it be better or more agreeable if, instead of describing Glupov in its disorderly movements, the chronicler had presented it as an ideal centre of legality and right? For instance, when Borodavkin demanded the universal adoption of mustard, would it have been more agreeable to the reader if the chronicler had made the inhabitants not tremble before him, but succeed in demonstrating to him how untimely and inappropriate his plans were?

With all sincerity I assert that such a distortion of the habits of the Glupovites would not only be useless, but even positively disagreeable. And this for the very simple reason that, presented thus, the chronicler's account *would not have been in accordance with the truth.*

The sudden decapitation of Major Pryshch had practically no effect on the well-being of the Glupovites. Because of a shortage of town-governors, the town was ruled for a time by the police-inspectors. But since liberalism still set the tone of life, even they restrained themselves from attacks on the inhabitants, and only walked discreetly round the market, casting tender glances at the more succulent morsels – but even these modest approaches were not always successful, for the inhabitants were now so bold that all they would give willingly was tripe.

The result of this state of prosperity was that in the course of a whole year there was only one conspiracy in Glupov – and even that was not a conspiracy of the inhabitants against the police-inspectors (as is usual), but the opposite – a conspiracy of the inspectors against the inhabitants (which never occurs). What happened was that the inspectors grew so hungry that they decided to poison all the watch-dogs in the market, so as to enter the market stalls at night unhindered. Fortunately, this attempt was discovered in time, and the only result of the conspiracy was that the conspirators themselves for a time forfeited their appointed offering of tripe.

Following this, State Councillor Ivanov arrived in Glupov, but he turned out to be such a small man that he could take in nothing of any size. As though on purpose, his term coincided with a time when the passion for legislation in our country was approaching dangerous limits; government offices overflowed with statutes in a manner never equalled by the fairy-tale rivers which flow with milk and honey, and each order weighed not less than a pound. It was this very fact that brought about the end of Ivanov. The account of his end exists in two different versions. One says that Ivanov died of fright on receiving a Senate decree which he had no hope of ever taking in. The second claims that Ivanov did not die at all, but was dismissed because, owing to the desiccation of his brain (through lack of use), his head had passed into an embryonic state. After that, he allegedly lived for a long time on his own estate, where he founded a whole race of Shortheads (*Microcephales*), who still exist today.

It is difficult to decide which of these two variants is the more credible. It must be said in fairness that the attenuation of a major organ like the head is hardly possible in such a short space of time. But on the other hand, there is no doubt that the *Microcephales* do exist, and according to legend their founder was indeed a certain State Councillor Ivanov. However, for us this is a matter of only a secondary importance. The main thing is that in Ivanov's time the Glupovites continued to enjoy a state of prosperity, and so the defect he suffered from served rather to the advantage than the disadvantage of the inhabitants.

In 1815 the Vicomte du Chariot, a French émigré, came to replace Ivanov. Paris had been taken, the Enemy of Mankind was installed for life on the island of St. Helena; the *Moscow News*[59] declared that with the humiliation of the enemy its task was now complete and promised to end its existence – but the next day made another promise instead, undertaking to cease publication only when Paris had been captured for a second time. There was general jubilation, and the Glupovites rejoiced with everyone else. They recalled the merchant's widow, Raspopova, and how she and Benevolensky had intrigued together to aid Napoleon, and they dragged her into the street and let the urchins make mock of her. The whole day the little rascals pursued the unfortunate widow, called her 'Mrs. Bonaparte', 'Mistress of Antichrist', etc., until at last she flew into a frenzy and began making prophecies. It was only later that the point of these prophecies became clear, when Ugryum-Burcheev came to Glupov and left not one stone standing on another.

Du Chariot was very gay. Firstly, his émigré heart rejoiced that Paris had been taken; and secondly, it was such a long time since he had had a decent meal that the Glupov pies seemed to him like ambrosia. When he had eaten his fill, he asked immediately to be shown to a place where he might *passer son temps à faire des bêtises*, and was highly delighted to discover that in the Soldiers' suburb of the town there was a house of just the kind he wanted. After that he burst into a flow of ceaseless chatter which never stopped until he was deported from Glupov under escort by order of the authorities. But since, after all, he was a child of the eighteenth century, the spirit of enquiry quite often manifested itself in his chattering and this might have had dire consequences, but for the fact that it was very much tempered by the spirit of frivolity. Thus, for instance, he once began explaining to the Glupovites the rights of man, but fortunately ended by explaining the rights of the Bourbons. Another time he began by trying to persuade the inhabitants to believe in the Goddess of Reason and finished by asking them to acknowledge the infallibility of the Pope. All these sentiments, however, were mere *façons de parler*, and, in reality, the Vicomte was prepared to support any principle or dogma, if he thought there were a few kopeks in it for himself.

He was an indefatigable merry-maker, and almost every day was organizing masquerades, putting on fancy-dress, dancing the can-can, and he was especially fond of making himself interesting to men.* He was expert at singing scurrilous songs, which, he claimed, he had learned from the Comte d'Artois (subsequently King Charles X of France), when he was in Riga. At first he ate everything that offered, but when he had begun to grow fat again, he ate mainly what we would call unclean food, his preference being for strangled animals and frogs. But in the way of official business he did nothing and never interfered in matters of administration.

This last circumstance gave promise of continuing the prosperity of the Glupovites indefinitely – but under the burden of their happiness they themselves gave way. They forgot themselves. They had been spoilt by five successive administrations and been brought to a state of obduracy by the crude flattery of the police-inspectors, as a result of which they began to imagine that happiness was theirs by right, and that no one could take it away from them. The victory over Napoleon strengthened them still further in this opinion, and it was likely at this time that the well-known saying 'We'll beat them hollow!' originated, which was subsequently the motto for the Glupovites' achievements on the field of battle.

And there now followed a succession of painful incidents which the chronicler refers to as 'the Glupovites' shameless frenzy', but which would be much better called 'the Glupovites' short-lived folly'.

They began by throwing bread under the table and crossing

* There is nothing surprising in this, for the chronicler tells us that this same du Chariot was later examined and found to be a woman.

themselves in some abandoned fashion. Denunciatory articles of that time are full of the most distressing evidence of this sad fact. 'There was a time', stormed the accusers, 'when the Glupovites by their piety put the Platos and Socrates of old to shame; but now they themselves have become Platos and worse, for even Plato hardly threw bread on the floor instead of putting it in his mouth, which is what the present fashionable conceit commands us to do.' But the Glupovites paid no heed to the accusers and arrogantly said: 'The pigs can eat the bread, and we will eat the pigs – it will be just the same!' And du Chariot did not forbid them to reply thus, but actually saw in such answers the beginnings of a spirit of enquiry.

Feeling themselves free to do as they liked, the Glupovites headed furiously down the slippery path that had opened up before them. They immediately had the idea of building a tower, the top of which was to reach up to the very sky. But having no architects and with carpenters who were uninstructed and not always sober, they stopped half-way, and it was perhaps only because of this that they avoided a new confusion of tongues.

But even this seemed not enough. The Glupovites forgot the true God and took to idol-worship. They remembered that long ago, in the time of Vladimir the Bright Sun,[60] some disused idols had been put away in the archives, so they rushed to the archives and dragged out two of them, Perun and Volos.[61] The idols, which had been left unrepaired for some centuries, were in a terrible state of neglect, and someone had even drawn a moustache on Perun with a piece of charcoal. However, the Glupovites found them so much to their liking that they immediately called an assembly and decided as follows: that the nobility of both sexes should worship Perun and the serfs should make sacrifices to Volos. The clergy too were summoned and required to become soothsayers, – they made no reply and only trembled in confusion to the very hems of their cassocks. Then they remembered that in the Musketeers' suburb there was a man called Kuzma 'the Unfrocked' (the same man, if the reader recalls, who considered becoming a Schismatic in the time of Borodavkin), and they sent for him. By this time Kuzma was completely blind and deaf, but the sniff of a rouble coin was enough to make him agree to anything and he began declaiming some incomprehensible lines from *Rogneda*, the opera by Averkiev.[62]

Du Chariot watched the whole of this ceremony from his window and cried, holding his sides: *'Sont-ils bêtes! Dieu des dieux! sont-ils bêtes, ces moujiks de Glupoff!'*

The corruption of morals went on apace. Dandies and doxies appeared, men took to wearing waistcoats with unprecedented cutaways which completely exposed their chests; women fixed behind them protuberances of suggestive import which roused unconstrained thoughts in passers-by. A new language was created, half-human, half-monkey, but in any case quite useless for the expression of any abstract ideas. The gentry walked through the streets singing '*À moi l'pompon*' or '*La Vénus aux carottes*',[63] while the serfs drifted from tavern to tavern, roaring out the *Komarinskaya*.[64] They imagined that while this gaiety was going on, the corn would grow of its own accord, and they gave up tilling the fields. Respect for their elders disappeared; they debated the idea of eliminating people on reaching a certain age, but their cupidity got the better of them and they decided on selling the old men and women into slavery instead. As a final culmination, they cleaned out the building of a riding-school and staged *La Belle Hélène*, with Blanche Gandon[65] playing the lead.

And despite all this, they continued to reckon themselves the wisest people in the world.

It was in this state that State Councillor Erast Andreevich Grustilov found the affairs of Glupov. He was a sensitive man and blushed when he spoke of relations between the sexes. Just before his arrival he had written a story, entitled 'Saturn halting his Course in the Embraces of Venus', in which, according to contemporary critics, the tenderness of Apuleius and the frivolity of Parny were happily wedded. In the figure of Saturn he had depicted himself, and in that of Venus – Natalya Kirillovna de Pompadour,[66] the famous beauty of the time. 'Saturn', he wrote, 'was bent in form and toiled beneath the burden of his years, but he was still capable of something. It must have been this that caused Venus to notice him and stay on him her look of favour . . .'

But Grustilov's melancholy appearance (the harbinger of his later mysticism) concealed many tendencies within which were undoubtedly depraved. Thus, for instance, when he was serving as Quarter-master with the army in the field, he was somewhat liberal in his use of government property, and only through shedding copious tears as he watched the soldiers eat their mouldy bread was he able to find relief from the reproaches of his conscience. It was known, too, that he had gained favour with Madame de Pompadour not for any special 'quality' he had, but simply by gifts of money, and thanks to her influence he had escaped court-martial and actually been promoted. When the

Pompadour was exiled 'for the lax keeping of some secret matter' and forced to become a nun (with the religious name of Nymphodora), Grustilov was the first to cast a stone at her by writing 'The Tale of a certain Amorous Wife', in which he made some blatant allusions to his former protectress. Besides this, though he was shy and blushed in the presence of women, beneath this shyness was concealed that worst kind of sensuality, which likes some initial titillation and then drives relentlessly to its intended goal. There were many stories told about this masked, but burning sensuality of his. On one occasion he dressed up as a swan and swam up to a girl who was bathing (the daughter of gentlefolk, whose only dowry was her beauty), and while she stroked his head, he ruined her for life. In short, he was thoroughly versed in mythology and, though he liked to make a show of piety, he was in fact a most vicious idol-worshipper.

The moral dissolution of the Glupovites suited him well. Even as he entered the town he met a procession that at once aroused his interest. Six maidens dressed in diaphanous tunics were carrying the idol of Perun on poles; in front was the Marshal's wife wearing nothing but some ostrich feathers and prancing about in a state of exaltation; behind, there followed a crowd of gentlemen and ladies, including some of the more respected members of the Glupov merchantry (peasants, artisans, and tradesmen were at that time worshipping Volos). Reaching the square, the crowd halted. They set Perun on a raised platform and the Marshal's wife knelt and began declaiming in a loud voice Boborykin's *Evening Victim*.[67]

'What's this?' asked Grustilov, leaning from his carriage and stealing a glance at the costume of the Marshal's wife.

'They are celebrating Perun's birthday, your honour!' replied the police-inspectors as one man.

'And girls . . . are there . . . are there any girls?' enquired Grustilov languidly.

'A host of them, sir!' answered the inspectors, exchanging knowing glances with each other.

Grustilov sighed and gave the order to proceed.

Stopping at the governor's residence and discovering on enquiry from the chief clerk that there were no tax arrears, that trade was flourishing, and agriculture improving every year, he thought for a moment, hesitating, as though trying to find words to express some cherished thought. Then, at last, in an unsure voice he asked:

'Are there black grouse here?'

'Yes, certainly, your honour!'

'You know, my dear fellow, I like sometimes to . . . it's nice occasionally to watch them . . . this great joy of nature . . .'

And he blushed. The clerk too was momentarily embarrassed, but he saw at once what was required.

'What better, sir!' he replied, 'Only I will make so bold as to inform your honour that there are even finer things of that sort to be seen here!'

'Hm . . . are there?'

'We have the fancy women here, your honour, who came along in your predecessor's time, and in the theatre, why, it's like a regular mating-ground, sir. They are there every evening, sir, whistling and shaking their legs. . . .'

'That would be interesting to see!' said Grustilov. And he fell into a state of sweet meditation.

In those times the view was that the town-governor was master of the town, and the inhabitants were, so to speak, his guests. The only difference between 'master' in the accepted sense of the word and 'master' of the town was that the latter had the right to flog his guests – which convention did not allow to the master of an ordinary household. When Grustilov recalled this right, his meditation grew sweeter still.

'Is there much flogging here?' he asked the clerk, his eyes still lowered.

'We've given up that fashion, your honour. There's not even been a single case of it since the time of governor Negodyaev. It's all kindness and persuasion now, sir.'

'Well, I'll do some flogging. I'll flog . . . girls!' said Grustilov, suddenly blushing.

Thus the nature of his internal policy was clearly defined. He proposed continuing the activity of the five preceding governors, placing special emphasis, however, on the scurrilous element introduced by du Chariot, with a dash of sentimentality for the sake of appearances. The influence of the army's brief stay in Paris was everywhere felt. The victors, who in their haste had mistaken the hydra of despotism for the hydra of revolution and had defeated it, were now in their turn vanquished by the defeated. The majestic barbarity of former days disappeared entirely, and in place of giants who could bend horse-shoes and break rouble coins in half, there appeared a race of effeminate people who thought of nothing but pleasant improprieties. For these improprieties a special language existed – an assignation between a man and a woman was called a 'voyage to the island of love'; and the coarse terminology of anatomy was replaced by something more refined, which gave currency to expressions such as 'the playful misanthrope', 'the dear recluse', etc.

Nevertheless, life was still relatively easier, and this was particularly welcome to the serfs. The Glupov intelligentsia, now that they had plumped for polytheism tinged with scurrility, were indifferent to anything outside the narrow horizons of 'voyages to the island of love'. They felt happy and contented and, being so, had no wish to stand in the way of the happiness and contentment of others. In the times of the Borodavkins, the Negodyaevs, etc., it was, for instance, thought an unpardonable piece of impudence for a serf to put butter on his porridge. It was impudent, not because it did any harm, but because people like Negodyaev are always die-hard theorists who think the serfs can have only one ability – to be firm in misfortune. So they took the serf's porridge and threw it to the dogs. This view of things was now considerably modified, – a change which was of course due in no small measure to the then fashionable malady of softening of the brain – and the serfs took advantage of the situation to stuff their bellies with buttered porridge. They were then still unaware that man lives not by porridge alone, and so imagined that if their bellies were full, then they themselves must be completely happy. It was for the same reason that they took so readily to polytheism: it seemed more convenient than monotheism. For preference they worshipped Volos or Yarilo,[68] but they bore it in mind that if there were ever a drought or too much rain, then they could always give these favourite gods a thrashing, or daub them with filth, and generally take it out on them. And although it is obvious that such crude materialism can sustain no society for long, as a novelty it was appealing and even intoxicating.

Everyone hastened to live and enjoy himself, and Grustilov did the same. He completely gave up governing the town and limited his administrative activity to doubling the taxes imposed by his predecessors and demanded payment without default at the times appointed. The rest of his time he devoted to the worship of Cypris in the unprecedented variety of forms evolved by the civilization of that time. However, for Grustilov this carefree attitude of his official duties was a grave mistake.

Although in his time as Quarter-master Grustilov had been quite adroit in the diversion of government funds, his actual administrative experience was neither broad nor deep. Many people imagine that if someone can lift the next man's handkerchief from his pocket without being detected, then that alone is enough to make his reputation as a politician or as a sounder of hearts.[69] But this is not the case. Thieves who combine thieving with sounding of hearts are very rarely met with; most often even the most grandiose swindler is remarkable only in this one sphere and shows no ability at all outside it. To be a successful thief one needs only to be skilful and avaricious. Avarice is particularly necessary, since for a mere petty theft you might actually be prosecuted. But whatever names robbery uses to conceal itself, the sphere of the robber is still quite distinct from the sphere of the sounder of hearts, for the latter snatches people, while the former snatches only their note-cases and handkerchiefs. Consequently, a man who embezzles some millions of roubles, even though he later becomes a Maecenas and builds a marble palazzo where all the wonders of art and science are brought together, still should not be called an accomplished public man, but only an accomplished scoundrel.

But these truths were still unknown at that time, and so Grustilov was not debarred from gaining a reputation as a sounder of hearts. Though this was not the case in fact. If Grustilov had really been in command of the situation, he would have realized that his immediate predecessors, in raising parasitism to the level of an administrative principle, had made a very serious error, and he would have known that parasitism as a creative force can really only achieve useful ends when it is concentrated within certain limits. If parasitism exists, then it is a natural corollary that industry exists side by side with it – on this the whole science of political economy is founded. Industry feeds parasitism, and parasitism makes industry fruitful – from the scientific point of view, this is the only formula which can be applied to the whole of life. Grustilov knew nothing of this. He imagined that *everyone* could lead a parasitic life and that the productive forces of the country would not only not decline, but would actually increase as a result. This was his first serious mistake.

His second mistake was that he allowed himself to be too carried away by the more brilliant side of his predecessors' internal policy. Hearing accounts of the benevolent inactivity of Major Pryshch, he was attracted by the picture of general rejoicing that resulted from this inactivity. But he failed to see, first, that even the most mature nations cannot live long in a state of prosperity without the risk of lapsing into crude materialism, and, secondly, that in Glupov, because of the liberalism imported from Paris, there was also the complication of a spirit of unruliness.

It cannot be denied that peoples can and should be given the opportunity to taste the fruit of the tree of knowledge, but this fruit must be held by a firm hand, and held in such a way that it can be at any time removed from lips that prove too eager.

The consequences of these mistakes were very soon felt. Already in 1815 the harvest in Glupov had been distinctly poor, and the following year there was no produce at all, since the inhabitants, corrupted by endless revelry, trusted their luck so much that they scattered the seed at random, without first ploughing the ground.

'It'll come up just the same', they said in the intoxication of pride.

But their hopes were not fulfilled, and when in the spring the fields emerged from their covering of snow, it was not without astonishment that the Glupovites observed that they were quite bare. As usual, they put this down to the action of hostile powers and blamed the gods for not protecting them properly. They flogged Volos, who bore his punishment stoically, and then dealt with Yarilo, and it is said that tears came to his eyes – at which the terrified Glupovites ran off to the taverns and waited to see what would follow. But nothing particular happened. There was rain, then some fine weather, but no corn appeared on the unsown fields.

Grustilov was attending a masked ball (every day then was carnival day for the Glupovites) when the news of the disaster threatening the town reached him. Evidently he had no inkling of it. He was gaily bantering with the Marshal's wife and telling her that there was soon to be a fashion in ladies' dresses which would allow one to look straight down and see the floor beneath the wearer. Then he began talking of the charms of a solitary life and mentioned in passing that he himself hoped one day to find repose within the walls of a religious house.

'A nunnery, of course?' enquired the Marshal's wife, with an arch smile.

'If you will consent to be abbess, I am ready to take my vows this very minute', replied Grustilov gallantly.

But this evening was fated to be a turning-point in Grustilov's internal policy.

The ball was in full swing. The dancers spun frenziedly round and round; bare, white, scented shoulders flashed amidst the whirl of billowing dresses and flying curls. Grustilov's imagination had gradually worked itself up and taken off into a dream-world whither, in his mind's eye, he transported in turn each one of these half-naked goddesses, whose bosoms so deeply stirred his heart. Soon, however, even in his dream-world, it got rather stuffy and he withdrew to a solitary room, where, settling himself comfortably in the greenery of wild-oranges and myrtle bushes, he fell into a state of oblivion.

At this moment a masked figure appeared and placed a hand on his shoulder. He realized at once that this was *she*. She had come up to him so silently that it might have been a sylph, rather than a woman beneath the satin domino, through which, however, the billowing lines of her figure still clearly showed. Fair, almost ash-blonde curls lay strewn on her shoulders; blue eyes looked from behind the mask; and the uncovered chin bore a dimple in which, it seemed, Cupid had made his nest. Everything about her possessed a modest, though not uncalculated elegance, from the *violettes de Parme* sprinkled on her handkerchief to the dainty glove fitting snugly on her tiny aristocratic hand. However, she was obviously in a state of agitation, for her bosom heaved tremblingly, and in her voice, which recalled the music of Paradise, there was a faint tremor.

'Awake, fallen brother!' she said to Grustilov.

Grustilov did not understand. He assumed that she supposed him to be asleep, and to prove this was not the case he put out his arms.

'I speak not of the body, but of the spirit!' continued the masked lady sadly. 'Not your body, but your soul is asleep . . . fast asleep.'

Only now did Grustilov understand what she was speaking about, but his soul being hardened in idolatry, the word of truth could naturally not enter it at once. At first, he even suspected that hiding behind the mask was Aksinyushka, the holy fool who had foretold the great fire of Glupov in the time of Ferdyshchenko, and who had alone remained faithful to the true God when the Glupovites turned to idolatry.

'No, I am not who you think I am', continued the mysterious stranger, as though guessing his thoughts. 'I am not Aksinyushka, for I am unworthy to kiss the dust of her feet. I am just another sinner like yourself.'

With these words she took the mask from her face.

Grustilov was astounded. Before him was the most charming woman's face he had ever seen. Actually, he had once seen a face something like it in the free city of Hamburg, but it was so long ago that the memory of it was blurred. Yes, these were the same ashen curls, the same dead whiteness of the face, the same blue eyes, the same full, trembling bosom; but how different it all looked in these new surroundings, how clearly the better, more interesting aspects of this face stood out! But Grustilov was most astonished by the fact that the stranger had guessed so clearly his suspicions about Aksinyushka.

'I am your inner word! I am sent to reveal to you the light of Tabor, which unknowingly you seek!' continued the stranger. 'But ask me not who sent me, for even I myself cannot tell!'

'But who are you?' cried the alarmed Grustilov.

'I am that same foolish virgin whom you saw with her lamp extinguished in the free city of Hamburg! For a long time I was in torment, for a long time I strove in vain towards the light, but the Prince of Darkness is too clever to let his victim escape at once! But my course was already marked out *there*. Pfeiffer, the Glupov chemist, came and took me in marriage and brought me here. Here I met Aksinyushka – and saw the task of spreading the light so clearly before me that I was filled with rapture. But if only you knew how hard the struggle was!'

She stopped, overcome by her painful memories, while Grustilov hungrily stretched out his hands, as though wishing to feel the touch of this inscrutable being.

'Take your hands back', she said gently. 'To hear what I have to tell you, you must contact me in thought, but not by touch.'

'But would it not be better if we retired to some more private room?' Grustilov asked shyly, as if doubtful himself of the propriety of his suggestion.

However, she agreed, and they withdrew into one of those charming retreats which since Mikaladze's time had been installed in every remotely respectable house in Glupov for the use of the town-governor. What took place between them remained a mystery to everyone, but Grustilov emerged distraught and with tear-stained eyes. The *inner word* had affected him so strongly that he went straight home, with not as much as a glance at the dancers.

This event made a deep impression on the Glupovites. They began enquiring into the origins of Pfeiffer's wife. Some said she was nothing but an intriguer, who with her husband's connivance had planned to gain a hold over Grustilov in order to oust from the town Salzfisch, the other chemist, who was providing Pfeiffer with stiff competition. Others claimed that she had already fallen in love with Grustilov in Hamburg on account of his melancholy appearance, and had only married Pfeiffer at all in order to be united with Grustilov, and become the sole object of that sensitivity which he was wasting on such vain spectacles as the billing-and-cooing of the black grouse and the doxies.[70]

Whichever was the case, there was no denying that she was a very unusual woman. From the correspondence she left, it is evident that she was in touch with all the most noted mystics and pietists of the time, and that Labzin,[71] for example, dedicated to her those choicest parts of his works which were not intended for publication. She also wrote several novels, in one of which, *Dorothea the Pilgrim*, she portrayed herself in the best possible light. 'She was attractive to look at', she wrote of the heroine, 'but although many men desired her caresses, she remained cold and enigmatic. But her soul was constantly athirst, and when in her search she met with a famous scientist (this was how she referred to Pfeiffer), she formed a permanent attachment to him. But with her first sensation of earthly things she realized that her thirst was still unslaked . . .', and so on.

On returning home, Grustilov spent the whole night weeping. In his imagination he saw the pit of sinfulness, at the bottom of which were devils scurrying about. There were doxies there too, and dandies, and even black grouse – and all of them afire. One of the devils crawled from the pit and brought him his favourite food, but his lips had scarcely touched it when the whole room filled with a repulsive stench. And what horrified him more than anything else was the bitter certainty that he had not sunk alone, but that the whole of Glupov had been dragged down with him.

'Answer for all, or save them all!' he cried out, numb with fear. And, of course, he decided to save them.

Early in the morning of the following day the Glupovites were astonished to hear the bell chiming for mattins. It was so long since this sound had been heard that the Glupovites had forgotten all about it. Many supposed there was a fire somewhere, but it was a more moving sight than a fire that met their eyes. They saw Grustilov, hatless, his uniform torn and head bent low, beating his breast, at the head of a procession consisting actually of no one but members of the gendarmerie and fire-brigade. Bringing up the rear came Pfeiffer's wife, without her crinoline, and escorted on one side by Aksinyushka and on the other by Paramosha, the celebrated holy fool who had supplanted in the affections of the Glupovites the equally celebrated Arkhipushko, so tragically burnt to death in the great fire (see 'The Town of Straw').

After mattins, Grustilov emerged from church in better spirits, and, drawing the attention of Pfeiffer's wife to the firemen and constables standing to attention ('who even in the time of the Glupovites' dissoluteness remained covertly faithful to the true God', adds the chronicler), he said:

'When I see the sudden zeal of these men, I know exactly how prompt is the effect of what, madam, you rightly call the "inner word".'

Then, turning to the police-inspectors, he added:

'Ten kopeks all round as reward for their zeal.'

'At your service, sir!' shouted the constables as one man, and marched off in quick time to the tavern.

This was Grustilov's first act after his sudden regeneration. He then went off to see Aksinyushka, for without her moral support no success in the further development of their cause was to be expected. Aksinyushka lived on the very outskirts of the town in a hovel built into the ground, more like a mole's nest than a human habitation. With her lived in chaste union the holy fool Paramosha. Accompanied by Pfeiffer's wife, Grustilov groped his way down the dark stairway and only with difficulty succeeded in finding the door. An astonishing spectacle met his eyes. On the dirty floor were sprawled two half-naked human skeletons (these were the holy ones, already returned from the service), mumbling and shouting inarticulately, at the same time shaking, twisting and writhing, as if in a state of fever. Into this warren a dim light shone through a single tiny window, which was covered with dust and cobwebs; the walls were layered with damp and mould. The stench was so revolting that Grustilov was at first overcome and held his nose. The second-sighted crone noticed this.

'Scent of kings! Scent of Heaven!' she sang in her shrill voice. 'Does nobody want any scent?'

She accompanied this with such a gesture that Grustilov would certainly have wavered, had he not been supported by Pfeiffer's wife.

'Your soul is asleep . . . fast asleep!' she said sternly. 'And you were so recently boasting of your courage!'

'Your soul is asleep on its pillow . . . your soul is asleep on its bed . . . and the dear God goes "knock, knock!" on your head, "knock, knock!" on your crown, "knock, knock!"' shrieked Aksinyushka, throwing bits of wood and earth and rubbish at Grustilov.

Paramosha meanwhile was barking like a dog and crowing like a cock.

'Satan, scat! The cock has crowed!' he mumbled in between.

'Man of little faith, remember the inner word!' urged Pfeiffer's wife.

Grustilov took heart.

'Mistress Aksinya Yegorovna, kindly give me absolution', he said in a firm voice.

136

'Yegorovna I am, I am! Yarilo the bane – Volos the stain – Perun the pain – and Paramon the brain!' screeched the holy Aksinyushka. She then writhed and fell silent.

Grustilov looked round in bewilderment.

'That means you should bow to Paramon Melentich', prompted Pfeiffer's wife.

'Master Paramon Melentich, kindly give me absolution', said Grustilov, bowing to him.

But for some time Paramosha did nothing but writhe and hiccup.

'Bow lower! Lower!' ordered Aksinyushka. 'Don't spare your back! It's God's back, not yours!'

'Sir, kindly give me absolution', repeated Grustilov, bowing still lower.

'No work, no supper!' mumbled Paramosha wildly, and suddenly leapt up.

Aksinyushka immediately followed suit, and they both began twisting round and round. At first they went slowly, sobbing quietly, but their gyrations then grew faster and faster until, at length, they were twisting like a regular whirlwind. There was laughing, screaming, squealing and sobbing, the like of which might only be heard in spring in some pond infested by myriads of frogs.

For some time Grustilov and Pfeiffer's wife stood looking on in horror, but at last they could resist no more. First they trembled and crouched, then gradually began twisting round and round, till suddenly they too were whirling and laughing aloud. This signified that the moment of inspiration had come, and that the absolution which had been asked for was granted.

Grustilov arrived home in a state of exhaustion, though he found enough strength to sign an order for the immediate expulsion of Salzfisch the chemist from the town. The faithful rejoiced and the clergy, who for several years had lived on nothing but worthless herbs, killed a sheep, and not only ate it, hooves and all, but also long afterwards scraped their knives on the table where the meat had stood and hungrily ate the shavings as though afraid of losing a single atom of nourishment. The same day Grustilov put chains on himself (it later transpired that they were simply braces, which were previously unknown in Glupov), and subjected his body to flagellation.

'Today I realized for the first time', he wrote to Pfeiffer's wife, 'the meaning of the words "wound me in sweet torment", which you spoke to me at our first meeting, dear sister in the spirit! At first I beat myself with some restraint, but my ardour gradually increased, and finally I called my orderly and told him to thrash me. And what happened? Even this was not enough, and I found it necessary to wound myself in an inconspicuous place; from this too, though, I suffered nothing, and only experienced a state of rapture. No pain at all! So much did this surprise me that even now I ask myself if this is really suffering, and if there is not concealed therein some special form of self-gratification and indulgence of the flesh. I await your visit, dear sister in the spirit, in order to answer these questions by considering them with you.'

It may seem strange that Grustilov, who had been one of the most frivolous of Mammon-worshippers, should turn so quickly into an ascetic. To this I can only say that people who do not believe in miraculous transformations should not read the chronicle of Glupov. There are plenty enough such miracles to be found there. For example, one superior spat in the eyes of a subordinate, and he saw. Another superior set about flogging a man who had not paid his taxes, supposing that he was merely teaching him a lesson, when quite unexpectedly he discovered that the man being flogged had his fortune hidden in his back.* If such astonishing facts as these do not arouse our disbelief, then should we be surprised at the commonplace transformation that took place in Grustilov?

On the other hand, there is another, more natural explanation of this phenomenon. There is evidence to suggest that Grustilov's asceticism was not nearly so strict as might at first be supposed. We have already seen that his 'chains' were nothing more than braces, and from further statements of the chronicler we see that Grustilov greatly exaggerated his other achievements too, and that these were anyway considerably sweetened by his love in the spirit. The whip with which he scourged himself was made of velvet (it is still preserved in the town archives); his fasting consisted in adding to his normal fare turbot, which he ordered from Paris at the inhabitants' expense. Is it surprising that the scourging caused him rapture, and that even the wounds seemed a delight?

Meanwhile the bell continued sounding the call to prayer at the appointed times, and the number of the faithful increased daily. At first it was only the constables who went, but when they were seen to be going, other people began to go as well. For his part, Grustilov set an example of true piety by spitting on Perun's

* The truth of this is confirmed by the fact that since then flogging has been recognized as the best means of exacting unpaid taxes.

temple every time he passed it. Perhaps the matter would gradually have resolved itself in this way, had not its peaceful conclusion been prevented by the machinations of a few restless and ambitious people, who even in those times were known as the 'extremists'.

This party was led by the same Aksinyushka and Paramosha, who had the support of a whole crowd of beggars and cripples. The beggars' only means of sustenance was begging for alms at the church porch, but as the old piety of Glupov had been for a time abandoned, this source had naturally been much reduced. Grustilov's reforms were greeted by them with loud approval. A dense throng of these poor folk filled the courtyard of the governor's house, some hobbling on wooden legs, others crawling on all fours, all singing hymns of praise, but also demanding that the reform must have immediate effect and that they should have the task of supervising it. In this instance, as always, hunger proved a bad counsellor, and the gradual, but firm and far-sighted measures proposed by Grustilov were subjected to false interpretations. In vain did Grustilov pander to the cripples' appetites by sending them out the remains of his sumptuous repast; in vain did he explain to a deputation of the poor that taking gradual measures was not indulgence but only served a give a firmer foundation to the enterprise in hand. The cripples would hear none of it. They angrily shook their wooden legs and loudly threatened to raise the banner of revolt.

The danger that threatened was serious, for to pacify a crowd of beggars requires far greater courage than it takes to shoot at people who are unhandicapped. Grustilov knew this. Moreover, he felt himself defenceless against the demagogues because they saw in him, as it were, their own creation, and in this respect they had acted extremely cleverly. First, they had surrounded themselves with a network of informers, through whom Grustilov was apprised of every rumour purporting to his discredit, and secondly, they gained the support of Pfeiffer's wife, promising her a cut of the so-called 'scrip-levy' (this was a levy imposed on every beggar's scrip – it was later to become the basis of the entire financial system of Glupov).

Pfeiffer's wife pestered Grustilov day and night, in particular tormenting him with a correspondence which, despite the shortness of time, was already enough to fill quite a large volume. The basic material for her letters was provided by her visions, the content of which varied according to whether she was pleased or displeased with her 'spiritual brother'. In one letter she sees him 'walking on a cloud', and claims that not only she, but Pfeiffer too had seen it; but in another she sees him in Hell-fire, in the company of devils of all possible designations. In one letter she develops the theme that town-governors have the right to absolute bliss in the after life simply by virtue of having been town-governors; but in another she claims that town-governors should pay particular heed to their behaviour, since in the after life they are subjected to twice and three times the torments suffered by other people. The same, in fact, as popes and princes.

In the present instance her letters were threatening. 'I hasten to tell you what I dreamed last night', she wrote in one of them. 'You were standing in a dark and noisome place, tied to a stake. Your bonds were serpents, and on your breast you wore a tablet with the words "Infamous protector of the impious and the sons of Hagar (*sic*)". And demons gathered round and rejoiced, and the righteous stood apart and shed tears as they beheld you. See yourself, whether there is here not some omen not entirely to your advantage.'

Reading these letters, Grustilov became unusually agitated. On the one hand, there was his natural tendency to apathy, on the other – his fear of devils, and all this together threw him into a state of utter confusion and he became lost in a muddle of contradictory propositions and measures. One thing seemed clear – that he would only be happy when every single Glupovite went to vespers, and when Paramosha was appointed inspector in charge of all the schools in the town.[72]

This last condition was particularly important, and the poor were very insistent on it. The corruption of morals was such that the Glupovites even attempted to fathom the mystery of the Creation and openly applauded a teacher of calligraphy, who, straying outside his own subject, had declared in class that the world could not have been created in six days. The poor reckoned, and with very good reason, that if this opinion became established, the whole Glupov philosophy of life would be shattered at a blow. The individual parts of this Glupov philosophy were all so closely linked that to disturb one meant destroying all the others. The important thing was not what was created when, but the fact that to ask this question might lead to the introduction of some completely new principle into their life, which would very likely upset everything else. Travellers of the time all declared how astonished they were at the integrated character of life in Glupov, and they justly attributed this to the fortunate absence there of any spirit of enquiry. If the Glupovites could suffer the most appalling disasters with fortitude and go on living afterwards, this was solely due to the fact that they saw every disaster as something quite outside their control, and so inevitable. In the face of an approaching catastrophe the most you were allowed was to press yourself to one side, to hold your breath, and disappear for the time being while the disaster raged. But even this was regarded as being refractory, and as for struggling or openly going out to meet the catastrophe – the Lord preserve us! If the Glupovites were once allowed to think about things, they might perhaps come to consider such questions as whether there was actually any reason why they should endure even minor disasters such as the brief, though completely senseless governorship of Brudasty (see 'The Music-Box'). But this question being so deep and their wits so shallow, the posing of the question would obviously only shake their fortitude in times of trouble and do nothing to improve their situation.

But while Grustilov hesitated, the poor decided to act on their own. They broke into the apartment of Linkin, the calligraphy teacher, and searched his rooms, in the course of which they found a book entitled *How to destroy Bugs, Fleas, and other Insects.* They triumphantly hustled Linkin out into the street, and, rending the air with their shouts of joy, brought him to the governor's house. At first Grustilov was at a loss what to do. Having inspected the book, he was going to explain that there was nothing in it contrary to religion or morality or even public order, but the beggars were now past listening.

'You can't have read it properly!' they shouted insolently at the governor, and raised such a tumult that Grustilov was alarmed and reckoned it only common sense to accede to the popular demand.

'Did you write this mischievous book yourself? And if you didn't, then who is the infamous rogue and arrant knave responsible for such a crime? And how did you become acquainted with him? And was it from him that you got the book? And if you did, why did you not inform the proper authorities, rather than lose all sense of conscience, and support and follow him in his depravity?' Thus Grustilov began his interrogation of Linkin.

'I neither wrote the book, nor have I ever seen its author', answered Linkin firmly. 'It was printed in Moscow at the University Press for Manukhins, the booksellers!'

This reply was not much to the liking of the crowd, who had anyway expected something quite different. They had supposed that as soon as they brought Linkin to Grustilov, the governor would tear him in two, and that would be the end of it. But instead of that, here was the governor wasting time talking! As a result, scarcely had Grustilov opened his mouth to ask his next question, when the crowd roared:

'What are you nattering with him for? He doesn't believe in God!'

At this Grustilov rent his uniform in horror.

'Is that true? You don't believe in God?' he asked, springing up to Linkin, and in view of the seriousness of the accusation, without waiting for an answer, gave him a tap on the cheek to be going on with.

'I've never said so to anybody', answered Linkin, evading a direct reply.

'There are witnesses! Witnesses!' roared the crowd.

Two witnesses came forward: Karapuzov, a retired soldier, and Maremyanushka, a blind beggar-woman. 'And those witnesses each received five silver kopeks for their false testimony', says the chronicler, who on this occasion clearly takes the part of the persecuted Linkin.

'Not long ago, I can't just remember when it was', said Karapuzov in evidence, 'I was sitting in the tavern having a drink, and not far away from me was sitting this teacher, having a drink as well. And when he'd done with drinking, he said: "Whether we're men or beasts, it comes to the same thing: we shall all die and go to the Devil!"'

'But when . . .', stammered Linkin.

'Just a minute! Don't you be so quick to open your lip! Let the witness finish what he was saying first!' the crowd shouted at him.

'And being as I was tempted by what he said', Karapuzov continued, ' I said to him nicely: "How can that be, your honour?" I said to him. "Can it be", I said, "that men and beasts are the same? And what do you run us down for and say we shall only go to the Devil? The priests", I said, "our spiritual fathers, have told us different, so there!" Well, then he sort of looked at me askance and said: "You limping scoundrel", he said, (it's true, your excellency, I lost a leg at Ochakov[73]). "anybody can tell you work for the police!" And he took his cap and went off out of the tavern.'

Linkin opened his mouth to speak, but this only made the crowd more angry.

'Make him shut up!' they cried to Grustilov. 'He's got too much to say for himself!'

Karapuzov was replaced by Maremyanushka.

'Not long ago I was sitting in the beer-shop', she testified, 'and I came over all bad, poor blind soul that I am. I was sitting there and thinking how much prouder people have got to what they used to be, I thought. They've forgotten God, and never keep the fasts or provide for the needy. You just see, I thought to myself, they'll soon start looking to the sun! It's true. Then up comes this young fellow. "Are you blind, my dear?" he says. "Yes, I'm blind, your good worship", says I. "And what made you blind?" he says. "It came from God, your good worship", says I. "What's it to do with God?" he says, "I suppose it was the small-pox?" "And who", I say, "sent the small-pox?" "All right", he says, "it was God – I don't think! You spend your whole life wallowing in damp and filth", he says, "and it's all God's fault!"'

Maremyanushka stopped and burst into tears.

'And I was that upset', she went on sobbing. 'I can't tell you how upset I was! And I said to him: "What do you mean by insulting God?" I said. But he didn't as much as answer, and just spit straight in my eyes. "Wipe that off", he says, "and perhaps you'll be able to see!" – and then he was gone.'

The facts of the case were now quite clear, but since Linkin demanded that they should at all costs hear the speech of his defending counsel, Grustilov reluctantly allowed his demand. And so it happened. Out of the crowd came a retired scrivener and began to speak. At first he was rather incoherent, but then he warmed to his subject and, to the general astonishment, instead of defending his client, began accusing him. Such was the effect of this on Linkin, that he not only immediately confessed, but even admitted a number of things which had never even happened.

'Once I was by a pond watching some frogs', he said, 'and I was tempted by the Devil, and began villainously wondering if it was true that only man has a soul, and thought that reptiles might have one too. So I took a frog and examined it. And I found that it was true – that frogs also have a soul, but only a small one, and not immortal.'

Then Grustilov, turning to the poor, said:

'You can see for yourselves!' and he ordered Linkin to be led away to the police-station.

Unfortunately, the chronicler does not relate any further details in this story. Only the following lines relating to this affair are preserved in the correspondence of Pfeiffer's wife: 'You men are very fortunate: you can be firm. But I was so affected by yesterday's scene, that Pfeiffer was seriously alarmed and quickly gave me some drops to soothe me.' And that is all.

But this event was important in the following respect – namely, that if Grustilov has previously had doubts about how he should act, from now on these doubts completely vanished. That very evening he appointed Paramosha as inspector of schools in Glupov, while to another holy fool, Yashenka, he offered a chair of philosophy created specially for him in the district institute. As for himself, he energetically set about writing a treatise 'On the Raptures of a Pious Soul'.

In a very short time the face of the town was so changed that it was scarcely recognizable. In place of the former riotousness and dancing a deathly silence reigned, broken only by the sound of the church-bells. The temples were empty, the idols thrown into the river, and the riding-school where Blanche Gandon had performed was burnt down. After this, the streets were all censed with myrrh and frankincense, and only then did the inhabitants take heart and feel that the power of evil was vanquished at last.

But there was still no more corn in the fields, for the Glupovites had simply passed from one kind of inactivity to another – from the inactivity of gay abandon to the inactivity of gloom. They raised their hands to heaven, they imposed on themselves prostrations, they made vows and fasted and organized processions, but all in vain: God did not heed their prayers. One man suggested tentatively that when all was said and done they would still have to take the plough to the fields, but this bold spirit barely escaped being stoned by the others, whose response to this proposal was only to treble their fervour.

Meanwhile, Paramosha and Yashenka carried out their work in the schools. There was no recognizing Parmosha. He combed his hair, took to wearing a velvet jacket, scented himself, and washed his hands quite clean with soap, and thus he went from school to school, rebuking those who put their hope in the Prince of this World. He bitterly mocked the vainglorious, proud, and high-minded, who concerned themselves with the food of the flesh, and took no thought for the food of the spirit, and suggested they should all go into the wilderness. Meanwhile, Yashenka in his lectures declared that the world which we think we see is nothing but a dream sent to us by the Enemy of Mankind, and that we are mere wayfarers, proceeding from the bosom of the Father to return to it again. According to him, the souls of men are as spiritual corn stored in a garner, whence, according to need, they are dispatched for a glimpse of this earthly dream, and, after a little, wing their way once more to the precious garner on high. The essential consequences of this doctrine were:

(i) there was no need to work, (ii) still less was there any need to be provident, heedful or careful, and (iii) one should trust in God and meditate. And that was all. Paramosha even gave instructions on how to meditate. 'For this purpose', he said, 'withdraw into the farthest corner of the room, sit, link your hands beneath your breast, and fix your eyes upon your navel.'

Aksinyushka too was not found wanting, and ravenously ate the bread of idleness. She went from house to house, telling how she had once been led by the Devil through the torments of Hell, and at first took him to be a pilgrim, but then guessed who he was and fought him. The basic principles of her teaching were the same as those of Paramosha and Yashenka – that is, that you should not work, but meditate. 'And above all give to the poor, for beggars care nothing for Mammon and think only of saving their souls', she would add, holding out her hand. Her preaching was so successful that the Glupov kopeks simply showered into her pockets, and before long she had amassed a considerable fortune. And, indeed, one had to give her something, since she would unceremoniously spit in the eye of anyone who refused her alms and, instead of asking pardon, merely said: 'No offence!'

But even this severe regime was not enough to satisfy the local intelligentsia. It gave them only outward satisfaction, and there was nothing in it which caused real pain. Of course, they never said this in public and very scrupulously went through with the ritual, though this was merely an outward show to pander to the common people. As they went along the street with downcast eyes and reverently approached the church-porch, they seemed to be saying to the serfs: 'See! Even your company we do not abhor!' – but in reality their thoughts were far away. Corrupted as they were by the recent orgies of polytheism and sated with the sweets of civilization, faith alone was not enough for them, and they looked for 'raptures' of some description. Unfortunately, it was Grustilov who first embarked on this road to ruin, and he led the others after him. He had noticed on the outskirts of the town a half-derelict building, and in this building Grustilov organized nightly routs, attended by all the so-called *beau monde* of Glupov. They began with readings from the critical essays of N. Strakhov,[74] but as these were so inane, they soon passed on to other activities. The chairman would rise and begin contorting himself, others would follow suit, and gradually they would all begin leaping, twisting, singing and shouting, and continue in this frenzied fashion until they fell prostrate on the floor from exhaustion. And this was what they called the 'moment of rapture'.

Could such a way of life continue? And for how long? It is not very easy to give a positive answer to these questions. The main obstacle to its continuing indefinitely was, of course, the shortage of food, which was a direct result of the prevailing asceticism of the time, although there are certainly instances in the history of Glupov which prove quite clearly that food is not nearly so essential to the happiness of nations as it at first seems. If a man has beef to hand, then, naturally, he will rather live on that than on other, less nutritious foods; but if there is no meat, he will just as readily eat bread, and if bread is short, then he will eat herbs. The food question is still, therefore, a matter of dispute. But be that as it may, the unseemly course followed by the Glupovites was cut short in a much more unexpected fashion and for quite different reasons than those that seemed most likely.

The fact of the matter was that there was a certain staff-officer living in the town, a man of no clear occupation, who once quite by chance had been the victim of a slight. What had happened was this: as long ago as in the days of polytheism, at a birthday banquet at Grustilov's, all the most important guests were given sterlet soup, while the staff-officer was served – of course, unbeknown to his host – with perch soup. The guest swallowed the insult ('only the spoon trembled in his hand', says the chronicler), but in his heart he swore revenge. There began to be differences. At first the struggle went on beneath the surface, but the longer it continued, the more passionate it grew. The matter of the soup was forgotten, but other questions arose, questions of a political and theological nature, and in the end, when, out of politeness, the staff-officer was invited to attend one of the 'raptures', he refused point-blank.

And this staff-officer was an informer . . . .

Although he attended none of the assemblies in person, he kept a close eye on all that went on there. The leaping and twisting, the reading of Strakhov's articles – nothing escaped his penetrating eye. But neither by word nor deed did he express his approval or disapproval of all these activities; he merely waited calmly for the abcess to ripen. And finally the moment he wished for arrived: a copy of Grustilov's book 'On the Raptures of a Pious Soul' came into his possession. . . .

One night the Glupov ladies and their cavaliers had assembled as usual in the disused building of the irregulars' detachment. The reading of Strakhov's essays was already over, and those present were just beginning to shake slightly, but scarcely had Grustilov, as chairman of the meeting, begun to bend his knees and generally perform the preliminary motions required for the enrapturement of the spirit, when a noise was heard outside. The members of the sect rushed in terror to the exits, forgetting even to put out the lights or remove the material evidence . . . . But it was too late.

At the main entrance stood Ugryum-Burcheev, piercing the assembly with a withering look . . .

And what a look it was! . . . Lord, what a look!

Repentance Confirmed. Conclusion

H E was terrible.

But he was little conscious of it, and with a kind of austere modesty explained: 'There cometh one after me who will be more terrible than I'.

He was terrible; he was also laconic, and combined with an astonishing narrowness of outlook a firmness of resolve bordering on idiocy. Nobody could accuse him of having a passion for martial enterprises, of which people had accused Borodavkin, nor of being given to outbursts of insane fury, to which Brudasty, Negodyaev and many others had been subject. Passion was excluded from the elements which made up his nature, and instead he possessed a firmness of resolve which functioned with machine-like precision and regularity. He never gesticulated, raised his voice or gnashed his teeth; he never guffawed, stamped his feet or laughed with that particular caustic laugh which is characteristic of all those in higher office; he seemed quite unaware of the need for such manifestations of administrative zeal. He stated his demands in a totally expressionless voice and confirmed the inevitability of their fulfilment by his staring gaze, which contained a quality of utter shamelessness. The man on whom this gaze was fixed could not withstand it. He experienced a unique sensation, the main part of which was not so much the instinct of self-preservation as a feeling of apprehension for human nature in general. This vague feeling of apprehension mingled with all kinds of presentiments about mysterious and insuperable dangers which were to come. You felt that the heavens would fall in, that the earth would open up beneath your feet, that a whirlwind would come and swallow everything up in a moment . . . . It was a gaze as bright as steel, a gaze entirely devoid of thought and incapable, therefore, of hesitation or of making distinctions. Resolution, plain and simple, nothing more.

As a man of limited vision, his sole object in life was regular formations. The straight line, absence of variety, simplicity carried to the extreme of bareness – these were the ideals he recognized and strove to attain. His conception of 'duty' did not go beyond the principle of universal equality in running the gauntlet; his idea of 'simplicity' was the simplicity of an animal, fulfilling its needs in perfect openness. He rejected reason absolutely and regarded it as his worst enemy, seeing it as something which entangles a man in a web of temptations and dangerous fancies. Faced with anything resembling gaiety or even simple leisure, he stopped in perplexity. Not that these natural expressions of human life roused him to indignation – no, he simply did not understand them. He never raged or fumed, he never took revenge or persecuted anybody; like every other unconscious force of nature, he went forward, sweeping from the face of the earth all that failed to get out of his path. 'Why?' – this was the only word by which he ever expressed any impulse inside him.

All you had to do was to get out of the way in time. The field of vision of this idiot was very narrow: outside it, you could swing your arms, talk aloud, breathe, even walk with your belt unbuckled, and he noticed nothing; but within it, there was no alternative but – to march. If the Glupovites had realized this sooner, they need have done nothing but stand to one side and wait. But they understood it only later, and at first followed the example of all peoples who love their superiors, thrusting themselves in his path, as if bent on destruction. From this came a countless multitude of self-inflicted torments, which spread like a net round the lives of the inhabitants, and it also explains how Ugryum-Burcheev came to be given the quite unmerited nickname of 'Satan'. When the Glupovites were asked what gave rise to this unusual name, they could offer no clear explanation, and merely trembled. They would point in silence to their houses drawn up in straight rows, to the broken fences in front of them, to the uniform overcoats in which every inhabitant was dressed, and with trembling lips whisper: 'Satan!'

Even the chronicler, who as a rule is fairly well-disposed towards the town-governors, cannot conceal a vague feeling of terror, when he comes to describe Ugryum-Burcheev. 'At that time', he says at the beginning of his narrative, 'in one of the churches of the town there was a picture showing the torments of the sinful before the Enemy of Mankind. Satan is depicted standing on the upper step of the throne of Hell, his hand stretched out imperiously before him, and gazing dully into space. Neither in his figure, nor even in his features is any special passion for torture to be seen; one sees only a deliberate abnegation of nature. This abnegation has manifested itself in but a single action – the imperious gesture; centred within itself, it has become fixed. But it is noteworthy that, however fearsome are the tortures and torments that fill the picture, and however much the heart is wrung by the writhings and convulsions of the malefactors for whom these torments are prepared, yet every beholder will surely feel that even their sufferings are less painful than the sufferings of this veritable monster, who has so overcome all natural feeling that he can regard such torments with a cold, uncomprehending eye.' This occurs at the beginning of the chronicle account, and, although it is followed by a gap and the chronicler makes no further reference to the picture, one cannot help supposing that he mentioned it there for a purpose.

A portrait of Ugryum-Burcheev is still preserved in the town archives. It shows a man of medium height, with a wooden face that has clearly never been lit by a smile. He has thick, jet black hair cut short over his cone-shaped skull and framing his narrow, sloping forehead like a skull-cap. His eyes are grey and sunken, shaded by their somewhat puffy lids; his look is clear and unhesitating; his nose is thin, descending in an almost straight line from his forehead; his lips thin and pale, with a bristling trimmed moustache; his jaws are strongly developed, they show no special signs of avidity, but some indefinable suggestion of a readiness to grind to pieces and bite in two. His whole figure is lean, with narrow, raised shoulders, chest thrown unnaturally forward, and long, muscular arms. He is dressed in a top-coat of military cut, buttoned to the neck, and holds in his right hand the 'Order on Resolute Flogging' composed by Borodavkin, but he is clearly not reading it and seems rather to be expressing surprise that there are people in the world who consider that resoluteness in such a matter needs to be secured by regulations. The background of the picture is a desert, in the middle of which is a prison; at the top, instead of sky, there is the lowering grey of a soldier's great-coat . . . .

This portrait makes a very sombre impression. Before the eyes of the viewer there arises the figure of an idiot of the purest water, an idiot who has taken some dark decision and inwardly vowed to put it into effect. Idiots in general are very dangerous people, not because they are necessarily evil (evil and goodness in an idiot are quite indistinguishable), but because they are alien to any kind of reasoning and invariably press on regardless, as though the path which they are on is their own exclusive property. From the distance, they might appear to be men of hard, but well-established principles striving consciouslessly towards some firmly fixed goal. But this is an optical illusion, and one should never be deceived by it. They are nothing but blind, circumscribed beings, trampling their way forward, incapable of recognizing that any connection exists between them and any kind of order of things . . . .

Certain measures are usually taken against idiots to prevent them overturning everything that they meet in their mad rush forwards. But these measures almost always relate to *ordinary* idiots – when to idiocy is attached the power of authority, then the problem of protecting society becomes much more complex. In such cases the danger is proportionately increased by the defencelessness to which life at certain moments in history seems doomed . . . . Where the ordinary idiot breaks his head or rushes against the stake and impales himself, the idiot with authority snaps every stake in two, and performs his, as it were, unconscious misdeeds without let or hindrance. For him there is no lesson to be learned from the futility or patent harmfulness of these misdeeds. He is not concerned with the results of his actions, since they affect not him (he is too lost to feeling to be affected by anything), but some other object, with which he has no organic connection. If through the concentrated efforts of his idiocy the whole world were turned into a desert, even that would not daunt the idiot. Who knows, perhaps a desert is what he regards as the ideal setting for the communal life of man?

It is precisely this hardened, utterly complacent quality of the idiot which strikes the observer in the portrait of Ugryum-Burcheev. On his face there are no questions; on the contrary, in every single feature there is an imperturbably soldier-like assurance that all questions have long since been resolved. What these questions are and how they have been resolved are riddles so perplexing that you might well go through every possible question and every possible answer, yet still not light on those he has in mind. Perhaps it is the already settled question of universal destruction, or perhaps merely the question of everyone standing straight, chest-forward, shoulders-back. Nothing is known. The only certainty is that cost what it may, this unknown question will be given practical effect. This unnatural combination of the certainty of effect and the uncertainty of the question leads only to still greater confusion, and the only possible result of such a situation is – general panic fear.

Ugryum-Burcheev's very way of life was such as to deepen still further the terror inspired by his appearance. He slept on the bare earth, and only in severe frosts allowed himself to shelter in the hay-loft of the fire-station; he put a stone beneath his head as a pillow; he rose at dawn, dressed in his uniform and straightway beat a drum; he smoked such foul-smelling cheap tobacco that even the police-constables blushed when the odour reached their nostrils; he ate horse-meat and readily chewed through beef gristle. To finish with, he spent three hours each day marching up and down in the courtyard of the governor's house, entirely alone, shouting to himself the words of command, and disciplining himself when necessary, even if it meant a flogging ('Doing which, he beat himself not feigning, as his predecessor Grustilov had done, but according to the true spirit of the law', adds the chronicler).

He also had a family, but in all his time as governor none of the inhabitants ever saw his wife or children. There was a rumour that they languished somewhere in the cellar of the governor's residence, and that he personally gave them bread and water once a day through an iron grille. And, indeed, when Ugryum-Burcheev vanished from the administrative scene, some naked and completely wild creatures were found in the cellar, who bit, screamed, and clawed each other and snarled at the people standing round. They were taken out into the fresh air and given hot soup. On seeing the steam, they first snorted and were superstitiously afraid, but then they calmed down and fell with such animal greed on the food that they promptly over-ate themselves and expired.

It was said that Ugryum-Burcheev owed his promotion to a very special circumstance. Apparently, a certain commander was once suddenly afflicted by the thought that none of his subordinates loved him.

'We do, sir!' his subordinates assured him.

'You are only saying that', persisted the commander. 'If it came to the point none of you would sacrifice as much as a finger for me!'

And gradually, despite their protests, this idea became so rooted in the mind of the jealous commander, that he decided to put his subordinates to the test. He called them on parade and announced:

'Whoever will prove his love for me, let him cut off the first finger of his right hand!'

But nobody hastened to respond. Some did not step forward, because they were too soft and knew that cutting off a finger involved a certain amount of pain; others held back through a misapprehension: not having understood what the question was, they supposed they were being asked if they had any complaints, and not wanting to be thought mutinous, simply roared their accustomed reply: 'At your service, your excellency!'

'Who'll prove his love for me? Step forward! Don't be afraid!' the jealous commander repeated his call.

But once more the only response was silence, or shouts which were not an answer to the question. The commander's face at first grew purple, then fell sadly.

'Swi . . .'

But before he could finish, there stepped from the ranks a simple punishment-orderly,[75] his body worn by floggings, and cried in a loud voice:

'I'll do it!'

Saying this, he put his finger across a beam and hacked it off with his blunt short-sword.

Having done this, he smiled. In the whole of his tortured life it was the only occasion when any sign of humanity had ever lighted on his face.

Many thought he had done this deed simply to spare his back from the rod, but no, in the mind of this punishment-orderly a kind of idea had taken shape.

At the sight of the severed finger, which dropped at his feet, the commander was at first overcome with astonishment, and then was filled with tender joy.

'You have loved me', he declared, 'and I shall love you an hundredfold!'

At that time there was nothing definitely known about communists or socialists or about any of those who go by the name of 'levellers'. Levelling, however, did exist, and on a very widespread scale. There were 'Toe the Line' levellers, levellers of the 'Jackboot' and 'Iron Fist' varieties, and so on. But nobody saw in this anything constituting a threat to society or undermining its foundations. It was felt that, if you take a man's life in order to bring him into line with his contemporaries, then though this may not involve any specially happy consequences for him individually, it is still beneficial, and even necessary, for preserving the harmony of society as a whole. The levellers themselves never for a moment suspected that they were levellers at all, and declared themselves benevolent and solicitous organizers, zealously exerting themselves for the happiness of their subordinates and of those they controlled . . . .

Such were the simple ways of those times, that we, who are witnesses of a later age, have difficulty in transferring ourselves even mentally back to those days, not long past, when every cavalry major, though never calling himself a communist, still considered it his honour and duty to be one from head to toe.

Ugryum-Burcheev was one of the most fanatical levellers of this school. He drew a straight line and resolved to make the whole of the visible and invisible world conform to it, with absolutely no allowance for turning backwards or forwards, right or left. It is difficult to say whether he supposed that in doing this he would benefit mankind. It is in fact more likely that he had no suppositions about anything at all. It is only in the most recent times (almost before our eyes) that the idea of combining the principle of the straight line with the principle of bestowing universal happiness has been developed into an administrative theory of some complexity, and not devoid of certain ideological niceties. But the levellers of the old school, such as Ugryum-Burcheev, acted in the simplicity of their hearts, solely in response to their instinctive abhorrence for crooked lines and any kind of zigzag or curve. Ugryum-Burcheev was a punishment-orderly, and all that that implied, not only because he had held that position in his regiment, but also because he was a punishment-orderly in his whole being and in his every thought. The attraction of the straight line for him was not that it was the shortest distance between two points – that did not interest him; its attraction was that one could spend a lifetime marching along it and never reach an end. The brilliance of the straight-line principle rooted itself like a willow stake in his afflicted head and shot out a mass of tendrils and branches. It was like some mysterious forest, full of magical visions. Mysterious shadows moved through it in single file, one by one, buttons done up, hair cropped, in uniform dress, at uniform pace, on they went, and on and on . . . . All with the same face, keeping the same silence and passing out of sight . . . . Where did they disappear to? It seemed that beyond this fantastic dream-world there was some even more fantastic abyss, where all difficulties were resolved, for into it everything fell and disappeared without trace. When this fantastic abyss had engulfed a sufficient quantity of these fantastic shadows, Ugryum-Burcheev would, as it were, turn on his other side and start afresh with another, similar dream. Once more the shadows moved in file, one by one, going on and on . . . .

Long before his arrival in Glupov, Ugryum-Burcheev had prepared a complete mad fantasy, in which the future organization

154

of this ill-fated township was established down to the smallest detail. According to this scheme, the town which he planned to make the model of its kind was envisaged roughly as follows:

In the centre would be a square, with streets running off along the radials, or rather not streets, but, as he termed them, 'company lines'. As they went further from the centre, these company lines would be intersected by boulevards, running in a double belt around the town and serving as a defence against external enemies. Beyond that there would be the outer town, an earthen rampart, and a dark curtain, which would be the end of the world. No river, no stream, no gully, no hillock, – nothing, in short, did he envisage, which might serve as an obstacle to free movement on foot. Each of the company lines would be forty feet wide, no more and no less; each house would have three windows looking out on to a small fenced garden, in which would grow bugle-lilies, crown vetch, beet and soapwort. All the houses would be painted light grey, and, although in the nature of things one side of a street will always face north or east, and the other south or west, no account was taken of this and it was assumed that the sun and moon would shine equally on all sides at once, day and night.

In each house there would be two elderly people, two adults, two adolescents, and two infants; persons of different sexes would feel no shame before each other. People equal in age would also be equal in size. Some company lines would be occupied exclusively by tall people, others exclusively by short people or by sharp-shooters. Children who at birth gave no promise of being firm in misfortune would be put to death; people of advanced age or incapable of working might also be put to death, but only in cases where, in the opinion of the local police authority, the forces of the town as a whole were over strength. In each household there would be one male and one female of every useful animal, whose duty it would be (i) to carry out the work appropriate to their kind and (ii) to breed. On the square would be situated the stone-built public institutions, for example, the government offices, and the various exercise-halls – for gymnastic training, sword-drill, foot-drill, others for the intake of food, for communal genuflections, etc. The government offices would be known as 'headquarters', and the officials working there as 'clerical orderlies'. There would be no schools and no provision for literacy; mathematics would be taught on the fingers. There would be no past and no future, and the calendar would be abolished. There would be two public holidays a year: one in spring after the melting of the snow, called the 'Day of Steadfastness', which would be a preparation for misfortunes to come; the other, to be called the 'Day of the Powers that Be', would be in autumn and dedicated to the memory of misfortunes already endured. The only difference between these holidays and other days would be the increased amount of marching.

Such was the outer framework of this mad fantasy. After this, it was a matter of settling the internal conditions of the living beings caught up in it. In this, Ugryum-Burcheev's fantasy achieved a truly astonishing minuteness of detail.

Each house would be merely a 'habitation unit', with its own commanding officer and spy (Ugryum-Burcheev was particularly insistent on the spy), and would be one of a group of ten such units, to be called a 'platoon'. The platoon, in turn, would have its commander and its spy. Five platoons would make a company, and five companies a regiment. In all, there would be four regiments, forming two brigades, and one division. After that there would be the town itself, which in the case of Glupov would be renamed 'Resolution', and dedicated to 'Grand Prince Svyatoslav Igorevich, of eternal memory'.[76] Over the town, in the midst of a cloud, would hover the town-governor, otherwise designated 'Commander-in-Chief of the Land and Sea Forces of the Town of Resolution', who would be at odds with everyone and see that everyone felt his authority. At his side . . . a spy!

In each habitation unit time would be strictly apportioned. At sunrise all the people in the house would rise. The adults and adolescents would put on uniform (made to a special design approved by the town-governor), tidy themselves and tighten their straps. The infants would take a hasty suck at their mother's breast; the old people would deliver a short homily, invariably ending with some vile oath; the spies would hasten to make their reports. Half an hour later only the old people and infants would be left, the others having already set off to carry out their allotted duties. First they would go to the 'hall of genuflections' and say a quick prayer; then they would take themselves to the 'physical exercise hall', where they would fortify their bodies with sword-drill and gymnastics; lastly, they would go to the 'food intake hall', where they would each receive a piece of black bread sprinkled with salt. After consuming this food, they would form up in the square and from there march off in platoons under their commanders to carry out public work projects. Work would be done to words of command. The inhabitants would bend and straighten in time together; scythe-blades would flash, hay-forks toss, picks tap and ploughs turn the earth – all by orders. When they ploughed, they would try to turn the furrows in such a way as to form the initials of those figures in history most renowned for their steadfastness. By the side of every work platoon a soldier would pace up and down with a musket and every five minutes fire a shot at the sun. Through the midst of those throwing, bending, and straightening would go Ugryum-Burcheev, walking ever in a straight line, bathed in sweat and redolent of the barracks, intoning as he went:

'One – two! One – two!'

– and all the people working would take up after him:

'Heave – one!

'Heave again!'

But as the sun reached its zenith, Ugryum-Burcheev would shout 'Break!'. Once more the inhabitants would form up in platoons and return to the town, where they would march in ceremonial order through the 'food intake hall' and receive a piece of black bread and salt. After a short period of rest (to consist of marching), they would again form up and be led to work as before until sunset. After sunset they would receive a further piece of bread and hurry home to bed. At night the spirit of Ugryum-Burcheev would hover over the town of Resolution and keep vigilant watch on the sleep of the inhabitants . . . .

There would be no God, no idols, nothing . . . .

In this world of fantasy there would be no passions, enthusiasms or attachments. People would spend every minute of their lives in company with others, yet every one of them would feel himself alone. Never for a moment would their lives be diverted from the performance of a multitude of idiotic duties, each calculated in advance and hanging over every man like destiny. Women would have the right to bear children only in winter, since any infringement of this rule might prevent the completion of the summer work. Marriage between young people would be arranged solely according to their height and build, as thus would be satisfied the need to have fine, regular ranks on parade. Levelling, reduced to the issue of a dole of black bread – such was the essence of this cantonist's[77] fantasy . . . .

Nonetheless, when Ugryum-Burcheev expounded this crazy scheme to his superiors, they were not alarmed by it – on the contrary, they regarded this ignorant punishment-orderly, who had conceived a plan to seize the universe, with an astonishment bordering on veneration. The idea of a terrifying mass of energy acting as a single man staggered the imagination. The whole world appeared covered with black dots, in each of which people moved in straight lines to the beat of a drum, all the time going on and on. These habitation units, platoons, companies, regiments, taken all together, did they not hint at some radiant distant prospect, veiled for the present in mist? But in time, when the mists cleared and the distant prospect was revealed. . . . . And what was this distant prospect? What did it hold?

'Barracks!' came the clear reply of the heroically-fired imagination.

'Barracks!' echoed the punishment-orderly in turn and, at the same time, he vowed a vow of such monstrous extravagance that his superiors felt they had been seared by some mysterious fire. . . .

Having dealt with Grustilov and dispersed the mad assembly, Ugryum-Burcheev at once applied himself to the fulfilment of his plan.

But Glupov, as he found it, far from corresponded to his ideal. It was more a disorderly jumble of huts than a town; there was no definite centre; the streets ran in all directions; the houses clustered together without a hint of symmetry, here crowding on top of each other, there standing apart with huge waste spaces between. And so the task was not to improve, but to create afresh. But what can the word 'create' mean to a man who from his youth up has been tempered in the functions of a punishment- orderly? 'To create' means to imagine yourself in a virgin forest; it means to take an axe in your hand and advance resolutely in whichever direction you happen to face, brandishing this instrument of creation right and left as you go. This was precisely what Ugryum-Burcheev did.

The very first day after his arrival he walked right round the town. Nothing caused him to stop – neither the crookedness of the streets, nor the multitude of narrow lanes, nor the untidy sprawl of the inhabitants' houses. One thing alone was clear to him: that before him lay a virgin forest, and that this forest would have to be dealt with. Whenever he came upon some irregularity, Ugryum-Burcheev fixed it for a moment with an uncomprehending look, but then immediately recovered and motioned silently ahead with his hand, as though projecting a straight line. He continued in this way for a long time, constantly stretching out his hand projecting lines, and it was only when confronted with the river that he sensed that something out of the ordinary had happened to him.

This he had overlooked . . . nothing like this had he anticipated . . . . Up to now his imagination had all the time been pressing straight ahead, all the time over even ground; it had been brushing aside, hewing down, and erecting afresh in the space of a moment, knowing no obstacles, feeding solely on itself. And suddenly . . . there was this twisting band of liquid steel sparkling in his eyes; it sparkled, and not only failed to vanish, but did not even wilt before the gaze of this administrative basilisk. It went on moving and rippling, making odd, but undoubtedly living sounds. It was alive.

'Who's there?' he asked in horror.

But the river murmured on, and in its murmuring there was something teasing, almost ominous. The sounds seemed to be saying: 'It's a good one, this crazy scheme of yours, but there's another, you know, which will perhaps be even better.' Yes, that was it – this was another such fantasy as his. Two fantasies had come face to face – one, the creation of Ugryum-Burcheev, the other, this intruder which declared its complete independence from Ugryum-Burcheev's scheme.

'Why?' he said to the police inspectors, after his initial bewilderment had passed, motioning towards the river with his eyes.

The police inspectors did not understand, but there was something in the town-governor's look which so clearly excluded all possibility of their not answering that they decided to reply, even though they had not understood his question.

'The river, sir . . . Dung, sir . . .', they murmured, saying whatever came into their heads.

'Why?' he repeated fearfully, and suddenly, as though afraid of going further into the matter, he turned sharply on heel and went back.

With fitful steps he returned home, muttering to himself as he went:

'I'll stop it, I'll stop it!'

Once home, he decided the crux of the matter in the space of a minute. Before him there were two equally great tasks to perform: one, the destruction of the town, the other, the elimination of the river. The means for achieving the first of these aims had already been worked out; the means to achieve the second were still vague and indistinct in his mind. But as there was no force in nature capable of convincing Ugryum-Burcheev that there was anything he did not know, his ignorance in the present instance was not only as good as knowledge, it was even in a certain sense better.

He had no technical or engineering skill – but he was a strong-willed punishment-orderly, and that is also a kind of strength, possessed of which one can conquer the earth. He knew nothing of the formation of rivers, or of the laws by which they flow down and not up; he was convinced that he had only to say: 'From here to here!' and dry land would doubtless appear in the area indicated, and the river would continue to flow as before, but now on either side.

Having fixed on this idea, he began to prepare.

He wandered through the streets in a state of wild contemplation, hands behind his back, muttering incoherently to himself. He passed some of the inhabitants on his way. They were dressed in the most varied assortment of rags, and bowed low before him. Before some he stopped and, eyeing their rags with his uncomprehending gaze, said:

'Why?'

Then, lapsing into thought once more, he continued on his way.

These periods of contemplation were the hardest of all for the Glupovites to bear. Like people in a trance, they stood petrified before him, lacking the strength to tear their eyes from his steely gaze. In this gaze lay some inscrutable secret, and this secret hung over the whole town like a heavy leaden canopy.

The town's spirits fell. There was an oppressive closeness in the air.

He had still taken no steps, had expressed no thoughts, had communicated nothing of his plans, but everyone knew that the *end* had come. They were convinced of it by the way in which this idiot with his inner secret kept flitting through the town; they were convinced of it by the low grumbling which came from his innards. A vague feeling of terror crept unseen into the midst of the inhabitants and took them in its grip. All their powers of thought concentrated on the enigmatic idiot, and in a torment of anxiety they moved round and round in the magic circle of which he was the centre. People forgot the past and gave no thought to the future. They performed their essential daily tasks with indifference, and with the same indifference they met each other and lived from one day to the next. For what? – that was the only question that presented itself clearly, when they saw the idiot approaching in the distance. What was the point of living, if life was for ever poisoned by the thought of the idiot? What was the point of living, if one could not shield one's eyes from the horror of his universal presence? The Glupovites even forgot their mutual discords, and hid themselves in corners to wait in dejected anticipation....

He also seemed to know that the end had come. He did not attend to any current business, and never as much as looked into the council offices. He had decided once and for all that the old life had passed beyond recall, and that consequently there was no cause for disturbing this lumber-pile, which bore no relation to the future. The police inspectors were in a state of mental and physical torment. Standing to attention, holding their breath, they lined the path along which *he* passed, and waited for orders – but no orders came. He passed by in silence, not deigning even to glance at them. In Glupov there ceased to be any administration of justice, mild or harsh, summary or slow. At first, the Glupovites thought to follow their old custom and brought their complaints and claims to him, but he did not even understand.

'Why?' he would say to a plaintiff, looking him up and down in wild amazement.

In dismay, the Glupovites looked back and saw to their horror that there was nothing there.

At last the terrible moment came. After some brief hesitation he had made his decision, first, to destroy the town, and then to tackle the river. Evidently, he still had hopes that the river would of itself come to see reason.

A week before St. Peter's Day he issued an order requiring everyone to fast in preparation for the feast. Although the Glupovites had always readily fasted on such occasions, they were troubled by the sudden command of Ugryum-Burcheev. Some decisive moment must indeed be imminent if such preparations were needed to help them meet it. Their hearts filled with a gnawing anguish. At first they thought that it was shooting that *he* had in mind, but when they looked into the governor's courtyard, where the artillery usually employed for bombarding the inhabitants stood, they saw that the cannons were not loaded. They then decided there would be a general 'confiscation', and they prepared to meet it, hiding books, letters, scraps of paper, money, even icons – in short, anything that might be regarded as 'evidence'.

'How do we know what religion he is?' the Glupovites whispered among themselves. 'He might even be a freemason.'

But *he* still went on marching in a straight line, hands behind his back, revealing his secret to no one.

On St. Peter's Day everyone took communion, and there were many even who had received extreme unction the day before. When the communion hymn started, sobbing broke out in the church; 'louder than the weeping of the others was the weeping of the Chairman of the Council and the Marshal of Nobility, fearful for their great possessions'. Then, as they left after the service and passed the town-governor, everyone bowed and gave him good wishes on the feast-day, but he stood there brazenly, never as much as nodding his head to anyone. All day it was unimaginably quiet. People began to break their fast, but no one could swallow a morsel, and they all wept again. But whenever the governor went by (that day he marched at forced-march pace), they hurriedly wiped their tears and tried to put a carefree, trusting look on their faces. Hope had still not altogether died. They still thought their superiors might see their innocence and pardon them . . . .

But Ugryum-Burcheev saw nothing and pardoned nothing.

'On the thirtieth of June', says the chronicler, 'on the day following the Feast of the Holy and Glorious Apostles St. Peter and St. Paul, the first steps to the destruction of the town were taken.' The town-governor led the way. Axe in hand, he rushed from his house and like a man possessed set to on the building of the Town Council. The inhabitants followed suit. They had been divided into detachments (with special sergeants and spies appointed to each the day before), and now set about the work of destruction at different points simultaneously. Axes thudded, saws screamed; the air was filled with the shouts of men as they worked and the crashing of beams as they fell to the ground; dust hung in a dense cloud over the town, blotting out the sun. Everyone was there, every last man of them: those who were fully grown and strong hewed and smashed; the young and weakly raked the rubble and carted it to the river. From dawn to dusk the people went tirelessly on destroying their own homes, and sheltered for the night in temporary shacks on the town common, where all their possessions had been brought. They did not understand themselves what they were doing, and never even asked one another if it were real and not a dream. They were conscious of only one thing: that the end had come, and that wherever they went, they were watched by the uncomprehending gaze of the grim idiot. Some of the old men hazily recalled similar instances in the past, particularly in the time of governor Borodavkin, who had introduced lead soldiers into the town, and once, in a moment of reckless valour, had commanded them to smash it to pieces. But that, after all, had been war, while now . . . for no reason . . . in the tranquillity of peacetime. . . .

Ugryum-Burcheev paced steadily about in the midst of the general ruin, and on his lips there flickered the self-same smile that had lit his face in the moment when, in his burst of devotion, he had cut off his right forefinger. He was satisfied. He even let his fancy wander. In his mind he was already going further, beyond the limits of simple destruction. He was sorting the inhabitants according to height and build, divorcing husbands from wives and matching them with the wives of others, allotting children to families according to their situation; he was appointing commanders of platoons, regiments, and other units, selecting spies, and so forth. The vow he had taken before his commanders was already half fulfilled. Everyone alert, active, ready to spring to arms. Only the details remained, but they too had long been foreseen and decided on. A sweet feeling of elation filled the whole being of the grim punishment-orderly and transported him to distant realms.

In the intoxication of his pride he would stare up at the sky and gaze at the heavenly bodies. He seemed perplexed by what he saw.

'Why?' he would mutter under his breath, and for a long time remain thinking, trying to work something out.

What exactly?

At the end of six or eight weeks not a stone was left standing on another. But as the work of demolition advanced towards the river, Ugryum-Burcheev's brow grew darker and darker. The last house, the one nearest the river, came crashing down; the thud of the axe sounded for the last time, yet still the river kept on. Just as before, it flowed and breathed and babbled and twisted; just as before, one bank was steep and the other low, with water-meadows which flooded far and wide in spring. This other fantasy continued.

Huge piles of rubbish, dung, and straw were stacked ready along the banks and only waited the signal to vanish into the depths of the river. The brooding idiot wandered among these piles and counted them, as though afraid that some of the precious material might have been made away with. Now and again he muttered confidently:

'I'll stop it! I'll stop it!'

At last, the cherished moment came. One fine morning he summoned the constables and took them to the river. He paced out an area and, motioning towards the river, pronounced in a clear voice:

'From here – to here!'

However oppressed the inhabitants were, even they were roused by this. So far it had been only the works of men's hands that had been destroyed, but now it was something permanent, not man-made. Many opened their mouths to protest, but Ugryum-Burcheev paid no attention to their hesitation, and seemed only surprised to find them lingering.

'To work!' he commanded the constables, with a glance at the milling crowd.

The battle with nature commenced.

The people who, with hidden sighs, had broken down their homes, now, with the same hidden sighs, thronged in the water. It seemed that the labour force of Glupov had become inexhaustible, and that the more brazen the demands, the more expandable became the resources to fulfil them.

Many there were who had come to Glupov and destroyed it – some as a joke, others in moments of sadness, temper or abandon, but Ugryum-Burcheev was the first to think of destroying it in all seriousness. From daybreak people crowded in the water, driving piles into the river bed and tipping rubbish and dung into the river's seemingly bottomless depths. But the water jokingly swept aside and scattered all this lumber that had cost so much super-human effort to assemble, and every time it channelled its course still deeper. Sticks, manure, straw, rubbish were all carried off into the unknown by the swiftness of the current, and Ugryum-Burcheev looked on 'with uncomprehending eye', as he watched in surprise and awe this almost miraculous disappearance of his hopes and plans.

Finally, people became exhausted and fell sick. Ugryum-Burcheev listened sternly to the section-leaders' daily reports of the number who had fallen out, and, not twitching a muscle, ordered:

'To work!'

New workers appeared, who had grown up somewhere in secret like the fern-flower, only to vanish at once in the swirling depths of the river. In the end, they even brought along the Marshal of Nobility, who was the only person in the town to consider himself exempt from work. They pushed him towards the river, but the Marshal would not go at once and protested, referring to some rights or other.

'To work!' ordered Ugryum-Burcheev.

The crowd roared with laughter. At the sight of the Marshal, blushing and abashed, tucking up his trousers, they felt cheered and redoubled their efforts.

But now there was a new difficulty. The piles of rubbish were fast disappearing and soon there would be nothing left to tip into the river. A start was made on the last pile, on which Ugryum-Burcheev was resting all his hopes. The river paused in thought, there was a bubbling in the depths, but in a moment it was flowing again more gaily than before.

For once, however, fortune smiled on him. With the whole store of rubbish exhausted, the inhabitants summoned up the remains of their strength and began on the building material. At one go they shifted a huge pile of it into the river, then with a whoop hurled themselves into the water and pushed it to the bottom. The whole force of the water streamed against this new obstacle, then suddenly the river started to twist around. There was a cracking and whistling, and some almighty bubbling noise as though millions of unknown reptiles were hissing together in the watery depths. All was silent. For a moment the river stopped, and then, very slowly, began to flood the meadow bank.

By evening the flood stretched as far as the eye could see and the water still kept rising. There was clamouring in the distance. Somewhere, apparently, whole villages were being destroyed, and the cries and groans and curses came from there. Haycocks, beams, rafts, and fragments of peasants' huts came floating downstream and, as they reached the dam, crashed together, sank, bobbed up again and gathered in a stagnant mass. Of course, Ugryum-Burcheev had foreseen none of all this, but still when he saw the huge mass of water, his delight was such that he was even moved to words and started boasting:

'May the people now behold!' he said, thinking to strike the pious tone of Photius and Arakcheev[78] which then prevailed, but remembering that he was, after all, only a mere punishment-orderly, he turned to the constables and told them to round up the priests: 'To work!'

There is nothing more dangerous than the imagination of a punishment-orderly when it is unchecked and not continually threatened by the prospect of a flogging. Once stirred, it loses all sight of reality and raises the most grandiose schemes in the mind of its owner. To extinguish the sun, to bore through the earth and make a peep-hole to Hell, – only such objects will a true punishment-orderly acknowledge worthy of his efforts. His head is like a wild desert, in every corner of which arise shapes known only in the most fantastic demonology. These surge and whistle and shout, and with a whirr of unseen wings head off into some dark and dawnless distance . . . .

The same thing happened to Ugryum-Burcheev. No sooner had he seen this mass of water, than he was struck by the idea of having his own sea. And since nobody threatened to flog him for such an idea, he enlarged on it further and further. If there were a sea, then that would mean fleets of ships, first, of course, warships, then merchant ships. The warships could carry out an occasional bombardment, and the merchant ships transport valuable cargoes. And since in Glupov there was an abundance of everything, and nothing at all was consumed except birch-rods and administrative measures, and since other territories, such as the villages of Shortcommons and Hungerton, were starving and anyway uncommonly greedy, it was natural that the balance of trade would always tend to be in favour of Glupov. There would be plenty of money in coin – which the Glupovites would, however, certainly scorn and toss on the dung-heaps, where it would be secretly dug out by Jews and used to obtain railway concessions.

And what was the result? The very next morning all these dreams collapsed. No matter how energetically the Glupovites trod down the newly-made dam, no matter how much they guarded it through the night, treason had managed to penetrate their ranks.

Ugryum-Burcheev had scarcely opened his eyes before he was hurrying off to admire the creation of his genius. But when he drew near to the river, he stopped in his tracks. A new fantasy had taken place. The meadows were clear of water, the remains of the monumental dam were floating untidily downstream, and the river babbled and flowed within its banks, just as it had the day before.

For a time Ugryum-Burcheev was speechless. With an odd curiosity he watched as wave followed wave, first one, then another, then another, and another . . . all rushing away somewhere, and somewhere disappearing. . . .

Suddenly, he let out a piercing roar and turned impulsively on heel.

'R-i-i-ght turn! Follow me!' came the command.

He had made up his mind. The river would not go away – then he would. The place where the old Glupov had stood was hateful to him. The elements were not obedient, at every step there were gullies and ravines which barred the way to speedy movement; magical things took place before your very eyes, none of which were mentioned in the regulations or individual instructions. One had to get out!

He set off from the town at a sharp pace, the inhabitants following with drooping heads, scarcely keeping up with him. At last, towards evening, he reached the spot. Before him lay a completely level plain, its surface unbroken by hillock or gully. Whichever way you looked it was everywhere smooth, like a level table-cloth, over which you could march to eternity. This was also a fantasy, but a fantasy which corresponded exactly to the fantasy that nestled in his head. . . .

'Here!' he shouted in his flat, toneless voice.

A new town was being built in a new location. But as this took place, something else made its appearance, something for which no name had then been thought of, and which only recently has become known by the fairly well-established name of 'unwholesome passions' and 'unreliable elements'.[79] It would be wrong, however, to assume that this 'something else' was appearing then for the first time. On the contrary, it already had a history. . . .

As long ago as in the time of Borodavkin the chronicler mentions a certain Ionka Kozyr, who, after prolonged wanderings in lands where the rivers flow with milk and honey, returned to his native town and brought with him a book he had written, entitled 'Letters to a Friend on the Establishment of Virtue upon Earth'. Seeing, however, that the biography of Ionka Kozyr offers very valuable material for the historian of Russian liberalism, the reader will surely not object if it is recounted here in some detail.

Ionka's father, Semen Kozyr, was just an ordinary scavenger, who had taken advantage of the troubled times to acquire for himself a considerable fortune. In the brief period of anarchy (see 'Tale of the Six Governesses'), when for seven days the six town-governesses were snatching from each other the helm of government, Kozyr had shown for a Glupovite astonishing adroitness in switching allegiance from one party to another and, at the same time, so skilfully covering his tracks that the lawful authorities never doubted that Kozyr had ever been anything but its best and most dependable supporter. He took advantage of this short-sightedness, first provisioning the troops of Iraidka, then those of Klemantinka, Amalka and Nelka, and finally providing peasant delicacies for Dunka-Tolstopyataya and Matrenka-Nozdrya. For all this he received 'market-prices' which he fixed himself, and since these were pressing times for Amalka, Nelka and the rest, there was no time for them to be counting money, and the accounts were settled by Ionka dipping his hand into their money-bags and carrying it off by the handful.

Neither the deputy governor nor the dauntless staff-officer knew anything of Kozyr's intrigues, so that when a real town-governor arrived in Glupov in the person of Dvoekurov, and the investigation of that 'absurd and risible confusion of the Glupovites' was begun, not only was Semen Kozyr found to be completely free from blame, he was also revealed to be a 'truly worthy citizen, most prompt in the suppression of revolution'.

Semen Kozyr found favour with Dvoekurov for several reasons: the first, because his wife Anna baked superlative pies; the second, because Semen, being a supporter of the governor's heroic acts of enlightenment, built a brewery in Glupov and gave a hundred roubles towards the foundation of an academy in the town; the third and last, because Kozyr never forgot the Feasts of Simeon and of Glyceria the Virgin (the name-days of the governor and his wife), and even celebrated them twice each year.

The order in which Dvoekurov announced to the inhabitants the opening of the brewery and expounded the evil of vodka and the benefits of beer was long remembered. 'Vodka', the order said, 'does not, as is commonly supposed, instil good cheer, and indeed, if taken in sufficient quantity, may turn a man away from cheerfulness and arouse in him a lust to do murder. Beer may be drunk in any quantity with perfect safety, for it inspires no gloomy thoughts, but only such thoughts as are wholesome and merry. We therefore urge and require that vodka be taken only before dinner, and then only in a small glass; at all other times it is safe to drink beer, now being produced, of excellent quality and at quite inexpensive prices, by the breweries of Semen Kozyr, Merchant of the First Guild.' This order had innumerable consequences for Kozyr. In a short time he prospered to such an extent that he began to find Glupov too small for him, and felt he should be off to St. Petersburg and present himself at court.

During Ferdyshchenko's governorship Kozyr enjoyed still greater good fortune, thanks to the influence of Alenka, the stage-driver's wife, who was his second cousin. At the beginning of 1766 he foresaw the famine and started buying up corn. At his suggestion Ferdyshchenko stationed policemen at all the entrances to the town, who stopped all the carts carrying corn and directed them straight to the factor's yard. There Kozyr announced that he was paying the official price for corn, and any sellers who had doubts on the subject he dispatched to the police-station.

But this fabulous wealth vanished in the air as suddenly as it had come. To start with, Kozyr did not get on with Domashka, the Musketeer woman who supplanted Alenka. In the second place, once he had been to St. Petersburg, he started boasting, referring to Prince Orlov[80] as Grisha, and saying of Mamonov and Ermolov[81] that they were men of small wit, and that he, Kozyr, 'had explained much to them concerning the politics of the nation, though it was but little they had understood'.

One fine morning Kozyr was unexpectedly summoned by Ferdyshchenko, who addressed him as follows:

'Is it true that you, Semen, referred to His Serene Highness Grigory Grigorevich Orlov, Prince of the Roman Empire, by the name of Grisha? And that you went about the taverns claiming before all conditions of men that he was your friend?'

Kozyr was struck with confusion.

'I have witnesses', continued Ferdyshchenko, in a tone which left no room for doubt that he really knew what he was saying.

Kozyr grew pale.

'This criminal act of yours I will forgive, out of the goodness of my heart', Ferdyshchenko went on, 'but such property as you have purloined will be made over to me. Now go and say your prayers.'

And so it happened in fact: the same day the Brigadier had all Kozyr's movable and immovable property made over into his own name, though he did give Kozyr a hut on the outskirts of the town, so that he would have somewhere to live and save his soul.

So Kozyr, sick, embittered, and forgotten by everyone, lived out his life; but as his end approached, he had a sudden access of 'unwholesome passions' and began preaching that property was an illusion, and that only the beggars and fasters would enter the Kingdom of Heaven, while the rich and the beer-swillers would lick red-hot frying-pans and be boiled in pitch. At the same time, turning to Ferdyshchenko (the custom in such matters was simple at that time: the town-governors plundered the inhabitants, but listened mildly to any truth addressed to him), he added:

'And you, you minion of the Devil, will feed on red-hot coals with Satan your brother, while I, Semen, will repose in the bosom of Abraham!'

Such was the first Glupovite demagogue.

Ionka Kozyr was not in Glupov at the time when his father suffered this terrible misfortune. When he returned home, everyone expected that he would at least be outraged by what Ferdyshchenko had done, but he took the news calmly, expressing neither grief nor even surprise. He was a man of some intelligence, but a complete visionary, who was absolutely indifferent to existing reality and backed this indifference by a large measure of utopianism. He had mental visions of some paradise where virtuous people lived and did virtuous deeds and achieved virtuous ends. But these were merely visions, which never took any specific form or found other expression than in simple – though not entirely lucid – aphorisms. Even his book 'On the Establishment of Virtue upon Earth' was no more than a compilation of such aphorisms, and gave no indication, and was not intended to give any indication, of their practical application. It was pleasant for Ionka to know that he was virtuous, and, of course, it would be even more pleasant if others too could share in this feeling of virtue. This was what his mild and visionary nature wanted; and it was also the aim of his propaganda. Virtuous people living together, freedom from envy, grief, and worry, friendly conversation, tranquillity and moderation – these were the ideals he preached, though not having the least idea how to attain them.

However, for all its vagueness, Kozyr's teaching gained so many disciples in Glupov that governor Borodavkin considered it a matter for concern. He first had the book 'On the Establishment of Virtue upon Earth' brought to him and examined it. Then he had the author brought, to examine him as well.

'I have read this book of yours', he said, 'and am disgusted by much of the villainy that is written in it.'

Ionka appeared astonished. Borodavkin continued:

'You think to make all people virtuous, but have you forgotten that it is not from you that virtue comes, but from God, and that it is also God who gives each man his proper place in life.'

Ionka was more and more astonished at this onslaught and waited, not so much in fear as in curiosity, to see how Borodavkin would end.

'If in the world there are slanderers, thieves, malefactors, and murderers (an accepted fact which is constantly stated in official decrees),' continued the governor, 'then how do you come to think that there should *not* be such people? And who gave you authority to take all these people away from their natural callings, and put them together with virtuous people in some ridiculous place which you have the gross effrontery to call "Paradise"?'

Ionka was about to open his mouth to answer, but Borodavkin cut him short:

'Wait. And if all the people in "Paradise" are to spend their time in singing and dancing, then who do you think is going to till the fields? And sow them, when they are tilled? And reap them, when they are sown? And gather the fruits to feed and sustain the gentry and men of other degrees?'

Ionka again opened his mouth, and again Borodavkin stopped him.

'Wait. And for these shameless statements of yours I have given you, Ionka, summary trial and passed the following sentence: your book shall be torn in pieces and trampled under foot' (saying which, Borodavkin tore it apart and trampled on it), 'and you yourself, as a corrupter of morals, will first be exposed to public scorn, and then be dealt with as I, the town-governor, think fit.'

Thus, with Ionka Kozyr, began the martyrology of Glupovite liberalism.

This conversation took place in the morning and at midday Ionka was led out on to the market-place. To make him appear the more abominable, he was dressed in a woman's smock (since there were many women among the followers of his teaching), and a tablet was hung on his chest, with the inscription: 'Womanizer and Adulterer'. To crown his disgrace, the police inspectors invited the stall-holders to spit on the criminal, and this they duly did. By evening Ionka was no more.

Such were the beginnings of Glupovite liberalism. But, despite this failure, the 'unwholesome passions' did not die out, but became a tradition which passed from one generation to the next under all the succeeding town-governors. Unfortunately, the chroniclers did not anticipate the terrible spread this evil was to have and consequently paid scant attention to the events they witnessed and recorded them with lamentable brevity. Thus, for instance, in Negodyaev's time there is mention of a certain Ivashka Farafontev, a nobleman's son, who was put in chains for uttering the infamous statement that 'the need of food is the same for all men, and he who has much should share with him who has little'. 'And in his chains Ivashka perished', the chronicler adds. There was another case in the time of Mikaladze, for though a liberal himself, Mikaladze, owing to his passionate temperament and the novelty of his situation, was not always able to restrain himself from slapping people's heads. During his administration thirty-three philosophers were scattered over the face of the earth, because they had said 'in unseemly wise: "Let him who labours eat, and let him who labours not taste of the fruit of his idleness"'. There was a third example in Benevolensky's time, when a nobleman's son called Aleshka Bespyatov was 'subjected to interrogation' for asserting in reproach to the governor, who was himself fond of legislation, that 'those laws which have to be written are bad, but excellent are those laws which need no writing, but are inscribed by God in every man's nature'. And he too 'died from the interrogation, of fear and anguish'. Pryshch and Ivanov were stupid; du Chariot was also stupid, and was anyway infected with liberalism himself. Grustilov, during the first half of his governorship, not only did not prevent, but even protected liberalism, since he confused it with libertinism, to which he was irresistibly inclined by nature. Only later, when the holy fools Paramosha and Aksinyushka took over the reins of government, did the liberal martyrology open once again with Linkin, the calligraphy-teacher, whose doctrine, as we know, was that 'men or beasts, we shall all die and go to the Devil'. Together with Linkin, Funich and Merzitsky,[82] two of the most noted philosophers of the time, also nearly landed in hot water, but they realized their position in time and began attending Grustilov's 'raptures' (see 'The Worship of Mammon. Repentance'). The change in Grustilov gave a new direction to liberalism, which might be called 'centripetal-centrifugal-inscrutable-nonsensical'. But it was liberalism just the same and bound, therefore, to fail, for the time had come when liberalism was simply not required. There was absolutely no need for it in any shape or form, not even in the form of an absurdity, not even in the form of rapture in the authorities.

Rapture in the authorities! What does rapture in the authorities signify? It signifies a rapture felt in them which at the same time concedes the possibility of *not* feeling such rapture. And from this to revolution is but a single step!

When Ugryum-Burcheev took office as town-governor, liberalism in Glupov ceased altogether, and the martyrology was not renewed. 'Overburdened with bodily exertions,' says the chronicler, 'the Glupovites, for very weariness, thought now of nothing but the straightening of their toil-bent bodies.' And so it was throughout the time that Ugryum-Burcheev was destroying the old town and battling with the river. But as the new town neared completion, the Glupovites' bodily exertions grew less, and as they had more time for leisure, so also the flame of treason flickered beneath the ashes. . . .

It so happened that the completion of the town was followed by a number of celebrations. Firstly, there was a celebration to mark the renaming of the town 'Resolution'; then there was a holiday to commemorate the victories of previous governors over the inhabitants; then, too, as autumn was beginning, the regular Feast of the Powers That Be came round. Although Ugryum-Burcheev's original plan was that holidays should differ from ordinary days only in the inhabitants being allowed extra marching instead of work, on this particular occasion the vigilant town-governor slipped up. His sleepless walking in straight lines had so devastated his iron nerves that, when the last blow of the axe was stilled, he scarcely managed to cry 'Break!' before he collapsed to the ground and began snoring his head off, without even arranging for the appointment of new spies.

Exhausted, abused and crushed, the Glupovites for the first time in ages breathed freely again. They looked at each other – and were filled with a sudden sense of shame. They could not precisely understand what it was that had taken place around them, but they felt that the air was full of vile abuse, and they could breathe this air no longer. Had they a history? Had there been moments in this history when they had been able to show their independence? They could not remember. All they could remember was that there had been a succession of Urus-Kugush-Kildibaevs, Negodyaevs, Borodavkins, and, to complete their humiliation, this terrible, ignominious punishment-orderly! And all these had beaten them, gnawed them, and torn them with their teeth – in the name of what? The blood surged in the Glupovites' breasts, their breath caught, their faces contorted in anger at the recollection of this ignominious idiot, who had come from nowhere, axe in hand, and had had the unspeakable effrontery to pronounce sentence of death on past, present and future. . . .

And he, meanwhile, lay motionless in the sun, snoring heavily. Now they could all see him, now they could examine him at liberty and see for themselves what he was – a genuine idiot, and nothing more.

When he had been destroying, battling with the elements and consigning to fire and sword, one could still conceive that he embodied something great, some all-conquering force, which, whatever its inner substance, could still capture the imagination. But now, as he lay prostrate and exhausted and no one wilted before his shameless gaze, it became clear that this 'great something', this 'all-conquering force' was nothing more than unbounded idiocy.

However intimidated they were in mind, so powerful was the Glupovites' need to free themselves from the obligation of trying to fathom the mysterious import of the words 'son of a bitch', that they actually came to see the significance of Ugryum-Burcheev in a new light. And this was a considerable boost to the fortunes of the 'unreliable elements'.

The punishment-orderly awoke, but his gaze did not create the same impression as before. It aroused anger, not fear. The conviction that this was not a villain, but simply an idiot who always marched in straight lines and saw nothing that happened on either side, grew daily more certain. And this increased their anger. The thought that this marching would go on for ever, that this idiot had some inner power to paralyse men's minds, became intolerable. No one had ever supposed that the idiot might calm down or change for the better, or that, given such a change, life would again be tolerable, even perhaps tranquil. But the idea of tranquillity, and even of happiness itself, seemed insulting and humiliating in sight of this punishment-orderly, who had personally destroyed such a multitude of thinking beings.

That *he* should give them happiness! That *he* should say to them: I have broken you and dazed you, I shall now permit you to be happy! And that they should calmly listen to *him* saying this! And with *his* permission be happy! Shame!!

But Ugryum-Burcheev marched on looking straight ahead, never in the least suspecting that 'unwholesome passions' were swarming under his very nose, or that 'unreliable elements' were surfacing almost before his eyes. As all zealous bestowers of order, he saw only one thing: that the idea which had matured so long in his calloused brain had at last been realized, and that he was now genuinely in possession of a straight line, along which he could march to his heart's content. Whether or not there was anything living in the path of this line, whether or not this living thing might be capable of feeling, thinking, experiencing joy or suffering, whether, finally, it might turn from being 'reliable' to 'unreliable' – such questions, as far as he was concerned, never even arose. . . .

The Glupovites' irritation increased the more, as they were still required to carry out all the confused rigmarole introduced by Ugryum-Burcheev. They cleaned themselves up, assembled, passed through the exercise halls, formed into squares, divided into groups for work, and so on. Every minute seemed right for liberation, yet every minute seemed also premature. There were continual meetings at night, and in some places isolated breaches of discipline, but it was all so uncoordinated, that in the end by its very slowness it aroused the suspicion even of such a confirmed idiot as Ugryum-Burcheev.

And, indeed, he had begun to suspect something. He was struck by the silence during the day and the rustling by night. He observed shadows straying through the town at dusk and disappearing somewhere, then at daybreak the same shadows would reappear in the town and scurry to their houses. This happened on several days in succession, and each time he was on the point of rushing from the house to investigate the cause of this nocturnal activity, but was held back by a superstitious fear. True to his station in life, he was terrified of devils and witches.

And then one day an order was circulated to all the habitation units announcing the appointment of spies. This was the last straw. . . .

But here I have to confess that the copy-books containing the details of this matter have been lost and I must therefore limit myself to giving only the dénouement of this history, and even that is only possible because a page describing it happens by chance to have survived.

'A week later' (than what?), writes the chronicler, 'the Glupovites were struck by an unprecedented sight. The northern sky grew dark and was covered with black clouds. Out of these clouds something came rushing towards the town, a cloudburst or whirlwind, one could not tell. Full of fury, *it* rushed along, churning up the earth, roaring, droning and moaning, occasionally belching hollow, croaking sounds. Although *it* was not yet near, the air in the town stirred, the bells dinned of their own accord, the trees were ruffled and the cattle went wild, rushing about the fields in vain attempts to find their way into the town. *It* came nearer, and as it approached the course of time gradually slowed down. At last the earth quaked, the sun grew dark . . . the Glupovites fell flat on the ground. An inexpressible terror appeared on their faces and seized the hearts of all.

It came . . .

At this solemn moment Ugryum-Burcheev suddenly turned bodily round to the dumbstruck crowd and pronounced in a clear voice:

"There will come . . ."

But before he could finish there was a resounding crack and the former punishment-orderly vanished in a moment as though he had melted in the air.

History had ceased its course.'

Supporting Documents

I *Thoughts concerning the Unanimity of Town-Governors, also concerning the Autocratic Authority of Town-Governors, etc. Composed by the Town-Governor of Glupov Basilisk Borodavkin**

It is essential that unanimity should reign among town-governors; that they should, as it were, speak with a single voice throughout the world. I shall enlarge briefly concerning the harmfulness of gubernatorial multanimity. What are the rights and duties of town-governors? Their rights are: that the evil-doer shall tremble, and that all others shall obey. Their duties: to employ mild measures, though keeping in mind the possibility of stern measures. Also, to encourage learning. In these brief points is contained the essence of the simple, though far from easy art of town-governorship. Let us consider in brief what may follow from the above.

'That the evil-doer shall tremble' – excellent! But who is this evil-doer? Obviously, if there be multanimity concerning this question, much confusion may result in practice. The evil-doer may be a thief, but a thief is, one might say, an evil-doer of the third degree; a murderer is an evil-doer, but even he is an evil-doer of only the second degree; and finally, the evil-doer may be a free-thinker, and he it is who is the real evil-doer, inveterate and unrepentant to boot. Of these three sorts of evil-doer each must, of course, tremble, but should they all tremble in equal measure? Indeed not. The thief should be made to tremble less than the

* This work consists of a child's copy-book in quarto. The manuscript is very difficult to read because of the quite barbarous spelling. For example, the word 'governor' is every time spelt 'guvenor' and even 'guvner'; the word 'duty' is spelt 'dooty', and so on. But it is on this feature that the value of the manuscript depends, for it is clear proof that it came straight from the pen of the sage town-governor, without revision by his secretary. It also shows that in former times what was required from a town-governor was not so much brilliance in spelling as profundity of mind and a natural bent for philosophical exercises.

murderer; the murderer less than the godless free-thinker. The latter must always see before him the piercing gaze of the town-governor and tremble unceasingly on account of it. Now, if in this matter multanimity among town-governors is to be allowed, then, clearly, the reverse may often result – namely, unbelievers will tremble in moderation, while thieves and murderers will tremble violently and unceasingly. And in this manner the sound principles of administrative science will be abandoned and the majestic order of administration destroyed.

But let us proceed further. It was said above: 'All others shall obey'. Who are these 'others'? Clearly, here are meant the inhabitants in general; but it is essential among this general category to distinguish the following: first, the noble gentry, secondly, the worthy merchantry, and thirdly, the husbandmen and other common folk. Though it is indisputable that each of these grades of inhabitants must obey, it must also be admitted that each may obey in its own particular manner. For instance, the gentleman obeys in noble fashion, adducing reasons as he does so; the merchant obeys with alacrity and begs you accept his hospitality; and the common people obey simply and, in awareness of their guilt, repent and beg forgiveness. What will result if the town-governor fails to enter into these niceties and, in particular, if he allows the common people to adduce reasons? I fear that in such matters multanimity among town-governors could have consequences not only injurious, but also irreparable.

The following tale is told. A preoccupied town-governor entered a coffee-house and ordered a glass of vodka; on receiving his order, together with a copper coin as change, he swallowed the coin and poured the vodka in his pocket. I find this entirely credible, for in the event of gubernatorial preoccupation such disastrous confusions are highly possible. And I take the opportunity to point out how careful town-governors must be in the consideration of their own actions!

Let us proceed further. I mentioned above that, in addition to rights, the town-governors have also duties. 'Duties'! – oh, how bitter a word is this for many town-governors! But let us not be too hasty, dear colleagues! If we give the matter due consideration we shall perhaps see that, judiciously employed, even bitter things may easily be sweetened! The duties of the town-governor, as has been said, consist in employing mild measures, while at the same time not neglecting the use of stern ones. In what do mild measures find expression? Such measures find expression principally in the giving of greetings and good wishes. The inhabitants, particularly the common people, are great lovers of this practice; but on such occasions it is essential that the town-governor should be in uniform and have an open countenance and benevolent look. It is also good for him to wear a smile on his face. I have many times had occasion to go out to assemblies of the inhabitants in this triumphal aspect, and when I cried in a voice melodious and pleasant: 'What cheer, my lads?' – then, on my honour, there were few who at the first sign of my favour would not readily have thrown themselves into the water and drowned, if only by so doing they could gain my approval. Of course, I never required this of them, but I admit that to see such readiness on every face was always a joy to me. Such are mild measures; as far as stern measures are concerned, they are sufficiently well known, even to those who have not been to a Cadet Corps school.[83] I shall, therefore, not enlarge upon them, but will come directly to a description of the means by which both sorts of measures should be applied.

First, I will point out that a town-governor must never act otherwise than by measures. Every action he performs is not an action, but a measure. An affable appearance, a benevolent look are just as much measures of internal policy as punishments are. The inhabitants are *always* guilty of something, and it is therefore *always* proper to bring some influence to bear upon their sinful wills. In this connection, the first measure for bringing such influence to bear should be a mild one. For, if a town-governor comes from his quarters and immediately starts shooting, then he will achieve nothing more than to shoot all the inhabitants and be left on the ruins, like Marius of old, alone with his clerk. So, having first employed a mild measure, the town-governor should carefully observe whether it has had proper effect, and then, if he sees that it has, he may return home; but if he sees that it has not been effective, then, he must without the least delay undertake the following measures. First, he must adopt a stern look, as a result of which the inhabitants should immediately fall on their knees. At the same time, his speech should become abrupt, his gait uneven and fitful, and his gaze give warning of further measures to come. But if, even then, the crowd continues to be refractory, the proper course is to rush on them at speed, seize from the crowd one or two persons to be designated ring-leaders and, withdrawing some distance from the rebels, flog them forthwith. And if this still does not suffice, then one must take from the crowd every tenth person, declare them ring-leaders, and flog them as the first. For the most part, these measures (especially if timely and swiftly applied) are sufficient. It may, however, happen that the crowd, as if set in their churlish and obdurate ways, will persist in their fury. Then it is necessary to shoot.

Such then is the variety of measures that exists, and such is the wisdom necessary for understanding all their subtleties. Let us now imagine what could result, if on this matter there existed disastrous multanimity among town-governors. The following might happen: in one town the governor would be content with judicious measures, while in the next town, given the same situation, the governor would have already started shooting. And since with us everything gets known, such lack of unanimity could inspire justifiable confusion, and even multanimity among the inhabitants themselves. Of course, the inhabitants must always be ready to endure measures of any kind, but they are not without certain rights in the respect that those measures should be gradually applied. In extreme cases they can even demand to be flogged first, and only then be shot at. For, as I have said, if a town-governor is going to shoot without proper consideration, then he will before long have no one left to flog. . . . And so once more the sound principles of administrative science will be abandoned and the majestic order of administration destroyed.

I further said that the town-governor is obliged to implant learning. That is so. But here too it is necessary to be clear as to what sciences to implant? There are different kinds of science: some, which are concerned with manuring the fields, with erecting dwellings for man and beast, or with military valour and insuperable firmness – these are beneficial sciences; conversely, there are others which are concerned with the noxious free-thinking of freemasons and Jacobins, with certain concepts and rights claimed to be natural to man, and which even touch on the structure of the world – and these are harmful sciences. What will happen if one town-governor implants the former kind, and another the latter? First, the second town-governor will be subject to prosecution and thus forfeit his pension rights; secondly, the inhabitants too will be harmed rather than benefited. For if inhabitants of different towns should meet on their boundary, one might ask a question about manuring, while the other would unheedingly reply concerning the natural structure of the world. And thus, their conversation ended, they would go their ways.

From this, the necessity and value of gubernatorial unanimity are obvious. Having dealt with this matter in requisite detail, let us now consider the means to its fulfilment.

For this purpose, I propose briefly as follows:

1. The establishment of a special training institute for town-governors. Town-governors, as men of special destiny, should also receive special education. Town-governors should be removed from their mother's breast and be fed not with ordinary milk, but with the milk of senate decrees and official orders. This is the true gubernatorial milk, and whoever is nourished on it will stand firm in unanimity and execute his governorship with severity and zeal. Other food meanwhile should be given in moderation, wine should be absolutely forbidden, and in matters of morality it should be hourly instilled into the child that the prime duty and obligation of a town-governor is the collection of tax arrears. To stimulate the child's imagination, pictures may be permitted. For example, a picture might be shown of a Minister of Finance sitting on an empty chest and wailing aloud. Or of a faithful cadet, with the inscription: 'A Future Town-Governor, or I Shall Die in Loyal Affection'. Instruction should be given in three sciences: (a) arithmetic, as an essential aid in the collection of tax arrears; (b) that concerned with the clearing of dung from the streets; and (c) that concerned with the gradual application of measures. For recreation the child should read official orders and stories from the lives of famous administrators. With such a system, it can be predicted: (i) that town-governors will be strong, and (ii) that they will not flinch.

2. The publication of the requisite manuals. This is essential for the purpose of removing certain abominable weaknesses. A town-governor, though raised on the rigorous fare of gubernatorial milk, is still constituted like ordinary men, and thus has certain natural requirements. One of these requirements, and that the most important, is the fair female sex. It is impossible to explain adequately how pressing this need is, or what losses are suffered on its account by the exchequer. There are town-governors whose every minute is spent in concupiscence and, in this pitiful state, they leave the decrees of the Town Council unsigned for months on end. It is necessary that the manuals above mentioned should preserve town-governors from this pernicious need, and keep their marital bed in a proper state of order. The second most pernicious weakness is the addiction of town-governors to dainty food and fine wines. There are town-governors who eat so fully of the sterlets which the merchants provide that they soon grow fat and become extremely indifferent to official orders. In such cases it is necessary to reinvigorate the town-governor with sections from the manuals and, in extreme

cases, threaten him with the rigours of gubernatorial milk. Finally, the third and most abominable weak . . .

(Here there is a gap of several lines in the manuscript, due to the fact that the author, wishing to sprinkle sand on what he had written, poured ink on by mistake. There is a note in the margin: 'Ink spilled here by mistake'.)

3. The organization of occasional secret congresses of town-governors in the provincial capitals. Those attending these congresses would read the manuals of town-governorship and refresh their memories in the disciplines of gubernatorial science. They should be exhorted to be firm and unheeding.

4. The introduction of the principle of equality in gubernatorial rewards. But this is such a large matter that I hope to speak about it separately.

Once thus centrally established, gubernatorial unanimity will infallibly lead to universal unanimity. Every inhabitant will see (a) that town-governors are unanimous on the subject of flogging the inhabitants, and (b) that they are unanimous on the subject of shooting, and the inhabitant and his fellows will likewise in unanimity prepare themselves to accept these measures. For from this gubernatorial unanimity he will find no escape. In consequence, there will be no disputing or wrangling, but universal flogging and universal shooting.

In conclusion, I will say a few words on the singleness of gubernatorial authority and other matters. Singleness of gubernatorial authority is essential, since without it there can be no unanimity among town-governors. But opinions differ on this question. Some say, for example, that the object of gubernatorial authority is the subjugation of the elements. One town-governor said to me personally: 'What kind of governors are we, my friend? Every day in my town the sun rises in the east, and no measures I can take will make it rise in the west!' Although these words were spoken by a truly exemplary town-governor, yet I cannot applaud them. For one should desire only that which is capable of attainment, and if one seeks the unattainable (for example, the subjugation of the elements, the cessation of the course of time, and such things), one will thereby not only not increase the authority of town-governors, but rather discomfit it the more. Therefore, one should treat of the gubernatorial authority not in respect of the sunrise or other hostile elements, but rather in respect of members, councillors, and secretaries of the various departments, courts, and councils. In my opinion, all these individuals are harmful, for they do nothing but raise obstacles before the town-governor in his unceasing, as it were, administrative course...

At this point this remarkable work breaks off. There is nothing more, apart from some short notes, such as: 'This is my new pen', 'The old priest is a fool', 'Report', 'Report', etc.

II *Concerning the Agreeable Outward Aspect of all Town-Governors. Composed by the Town-Governor Prince Ksavery Georgievich Mikaladze**

It is essential that the town-governor should be agreeable in his outward aspect; that he should be neither too fat, nor too lean, neither excessively large in stature, nor too small; that he should be rightly proportioned in all the parts of his body; that he should possess a pure countenance, free from disfiguring warts and (Heaven preserve us!) malignant pustules. His eyes should be grey, capable, according to need, of expressing clemency and severity. His nose should be fitting. In addition, the town-governor must have a uniform.

Excessive fatness, just as excessive leanness, may have unhappy consequences. One town-governor I knew, for all his excellent knowledge of the laws, was not a success owing to the fact that he was always short of breath from the quantity of fat accumulated within him. I knew another town-governor who was very lean and he was also not a success, for almost as soon as he arrived in the town, the inhabitants nicknamed him 'the lean kine of Pharoah', after which it was impossible for any of his measures to be properly effective. Conversely, a governor who is neither fat nor lean will always succeed, even if he is not an expert in the law. For he is brisk, fresh, quick, and always ready.

The above remarks on the subject of fatness and leanness apply equally to the height of town-governors. Their true height is between 5 feet 6 inches and 5 feet 8 inches. There are some striking examples of failure to conform to this at first sight insignificant requirement. I personally knew of three such cases. In

* This manuscript occupies a few small quarto pages; the writing is reasonably good, although it is only fair to say that the author wrote on ruled lines.

one of the Volga provinces the town-governor was 6 feet 11 inches tall, and what happened? A government-inspector came to his town who was short; the inspector was outraged, intrigued against the governor, and succeeded in having this otherwise worthy man brought to trial. In another province a similarly tall town-governor had an unusually large tapeworm. Finally, a third governor was so small that he was incapable of taking in laws of any length and died of strain. Thus, all three suffered through being other than the prescribed height.

Right proportions in the parts of the body are also of some importance, for harmony is the first law of Nature. Many town-governors have long arms, and in time they are deprived of office because of this; many are distinguished by the particular smallness of the same, and for this reason they become the object of ridicule or scorn. This must by all means be avoided, for nothing so undermines authority as prominent or noticeable abominations of this kind.

A pure countenance is an adornment not only of town-governors, but of all men. It fulfils, moreover, numerous useful functions, the first of which is to win the trust of one's superiors. A skin that is smooth without being tender, a look that is bold without being brazen, – all this wins the hearts of superiors, especially if the governor should stand with his body inclined forwards in an attitude of striving. Here the smallest wart is capable of destroying the harmony and lending the governor an appearance of extreme impertinence. The second useful function of a pure countenance is that it gains the affection of subordinates. When a countenance is pure and, moreover, freshened by ablutions, then the skin so shines that it can reflect the sun's rays. This appearance is most gratifying to subordinates.

The town-governor must have a voice that is clear and carries well; he must remember that gubernatorial lungs are created for the purpose of giving orders. I knew one town-governor who prepared himself for the office by specially taking up residence by the sea coast and there shouting imprecations at the top of his voice. This governor subsequently subdued eleven major rebellions, twenty-nine moderate uprisings, and more than fifty minor misunderstandings. And all this was achieved solely by the means of a voice which carried.

Now, on the subject of uniform. Of course, free-thinkers may suppose (though be it on their own heads) that, given the natural laws, it is all one whether a superior is clad in a coat of mail or a coachman's jacket, but in the view of experienced and serious-minded men the matter of uniform will always be of preeminent importance. Why is this so? Because, I declare to you free-thinkers, in the execution of official functions the uniform precedes, so to speak, the man, and not the reverse. Of course, in saying this I do not mean that a uniform can act and take measures independently of the man within it, but it can, I think, be boldly claimed that even the leanest town-governors may be tolerable in office, given a uniform of sufficient splendour. Finding that existing uniforms fulfil but poorly this important object, I would therefore consider it necessary to constitute a special commission on the matter, to be charged with the task of preparing a design for a town-governor's uniform. For my part, I can foresee the possibility of suggesting the following: a short jacket of silver brocade, ostrich feathers behind and a gold cuirass in front, pantaloons also of brocade, and the head-dress a golden helmet with a plume of feathers. I feel that thus attired any town-governor would order all matters in the shortest possible time.

All that we have said concerning the agreeable appearance of town-governors takes on still greater significance if we recall how often they are obliged to maintain clandestine relations with the female sex. The value which results from this is universally known, but the subject is by no means fully exhausted. If I say that by connections with the female sex an experienced administrator can at all times know the hidden tendencies of those he governs, then this will be quite sufficient to demonstrate the importance of this administrative device. By this means more than one diplomat has discovered the plans and intentions of the enemy and so brought them to nought; and more than one general has by the same means won a battle or made a timely retreat. And as one who has tried this expedient in practice, I can testify for my own part that as lately as in the last few days I was apprised by this means of the inadequate measures taken by a certain chief constable, whom I have consequently removed from office.

I feel it would not be out of place to say further, that a town-governor, in captivating the frail female sex, must seek to do so in solitude and not allow these activities to be made public or noised abroad. In such pleasant solitude he may, by affecting an attitude of tenderness or jocularity, learn much that is not always accessible to even the most efficient police investigator. Thus, for example, if the lady in question is the wife of a man of learning, it can be discovered what opinions her husband holds concerning the structure of the world, the authorities, etc. Generally, the unfailing consequence of such curiosity is that the town-governor soon acquires a reputation as a sounder of hearts. . . .

Having presented the above matter, I feel I have conscientiously fulfilled my duty. The parts of the gubernatorial nature are, of course, so numerous that they cannot all be covered by one man, and so I also do not claim to have covered and explained them all. But let others treat of gubernatorial severity, of gubernatorial unanimity, and of universal gubernatorial precedence. I, having related what I know of gubernatorial comeliness, console myself that 'Here my drop of honey too lies added to the common store. . .'.

III *Statute concerning the Benevolence proper to Town-Governors. Composed by the Town-Governor Benevolensky.*

1. All town-governors shall be benevolent.

2. All town-governors shall remember that severity alone, though it be a hundred times increased, can never satisfy the hunger or clothe the nakedness of man.

3. All town-governors shall give a hearing to inhabitants who come to them; a governor who starts to shout, or still more to beat the inhabitant without first hearing him, will shout and beat in vain.

4. All town-governors who see an inhabitant occupied about his business shall leave him to pursue it without hindrance.

5. All town-governors shall remember that if an inhabitant falls temporarily into transgression, then he may yet perform an even greater number of useful deeds.

6. In consequence, if an inhabitant sins, he should not at once be committed to be flogged, without diligent enquiry first being made to see whether or not the effect and protection of the laws of Russia extend to him.

7. The town-governor shall remember that the glory of the Russian Empire and the income of the exchequer have no other source than the inhabitants.

8. In consequence, the execution, scattering abroad or liquidation by other means of the inhabitants must be undertaken with due care, to ensure that no loss of advantage to the Russian Empire or of revenue to the exchequer will be incurred.

9. In the event of an inhabitant failing to bring gifts, all steps should be taken to discover the cause of this failure. If it prove for lack of means, he shall be forgiven, but if the cause be neglect or refractoriness, he shall be brought to remembrance and understanding until such time as he be reformed.

10. Every inhabitant shall labour and, having laboured, enjoy repose. In consequence, a man simply strolling or passing by shall not be seized and placed in gaol.

11. Laws shall be promulgated that are excellent and proper to the nature of man. Unnatural laws and, more particularly, laws that are incomprehensible or difficult of fulfilment shall not be promulgated.

12. At festivities and public gatherings the governor shall not oppress people; he shall, on the contrary, maintain on his face a benevolent smile, so that those making merry be not struck with fear.

13. No restrictions shall be imposed in matters of food and drink.

14. Enlightenment is to be instilled with moderation, wherever possible avoiding bloodshed.

15. All other matters are at the discretion of the town-governor.

Notes

1 Here and elsewhere in the *History* the 'tax-contractors' specifically in mind were those who secured the monopoly for the sale of vodka.

2 Ernst Johann Biron (1690-1772), Duke of Courland, the German favourite of Empress Anne. The period of his supremacy at court was one of crude tyranny.

3 Grigory Aleksandrovich Potemkin (1739-91), favourite of Catherine the Great; an energetic and successful soldier and statesman.

4 Aleksey Grigorevich Razumovsky (1709-71), favourite of Empress Elizabeth. He was of obscure Cossak origin.

5 1825 was the year of the unsuccessful 'Decembrist' rising (see Introduction, p.xiii, note), which was followed by the repressive reign of Nicholas I.

6 Pimen is the monkish chronicler in Pushkin's historical play *Boris Godunov*.

7 Contemporaries of Saltykov, authors variously of historical studies and novels on historical themes.

8 M. P. Pogodin (1800-75), a leading historian and contemporary of Saltykov.

9 A kind of weak beer made from rye.

10 P. I. Bartenev (1829-1912), founder and editor of *Russkii arkhiv* (*Russian Archives*), a journal which published documents of historical interest.

11 This chapter on the origin of the Glupovites is written as a parody of the style and content of the Russian chronicle account of the origin of the Russian state. The chronicle describes the lack of unity among the different tribes and their decision to summon Varangian princes (from Scandinavia) to impose order and rule over them. The ludicrous characteristics of the Glupovites' ancestors and the actions attributed to them are based on popular legends and sayings about the inhabitants of different Russian towns, drawn (as Saltykov indicated in his correspondence) from the collections of Sakharov and Dal (I. P. Sakharov, *Skazaniya russkogo naroda* [*Legends of the Russian People*]; V. I. Dal, *Poslovitsy russkogo naroda* [*Sayings of the Russian People*]). These allusions would have been understood by Saltykov's Russian contemporaries; the English reader will have no difficulty in understanding their general significance (or, indeed, their humour).

12-14 Saltykov's contemporaries: N. I. Kostomarov (1817-85) and S. M. Solovev (1820-79) were leading historians, A. N. Pypin (1833-1904) a historian and literary scholar.

15 The opening lines of *The Tale of Igor's Campaign*, a well-known work of medieval Russian literature, though of disputed authenticity.

16 Cf. the entry for 862 in the *Russian Primary Chronicle:* 'There was no law among them. Tribe rose up against tribe, and there was strife among them and they began to wage war one with another. And they said to themselves: "Let us seek for ourselves a prince who would rule over us and administer justice".'

17 Russian stringed instrument akin to the zither.

18 This song sung by the Glupovites is a well-known Russian folk-song, which tells of an outlaw facing trial and execution.

19 See note 2.

20 The Lopukhina in question here is evidently Natalya, an envied rival of Empress Elizabeth. In 1743, for alleged treason, she was subjected to exactly the punishment said here to have been suffered by Velikanov. The name Avdotya is suggested by an earlier member of the family – Evdokiya (Avdotya) Lopukhina, the first wife of Peter the Great, who died in 1731.

21 Count Kirill Grigorevich Razumovsky (1728-1803), brother of Elizabeth's favourite; field-marshal and hetman of the Ukraine.

22 Cf. Peter III, son of the Duke of Holstein and husband of Catherine the Great. His six-month reign as tsar ended in 1762 when he was murdered in the coup which brought Catherine to the throne.

23 Isler's Spa was a restaurant in St. Petersburg in Saltykov's own day.

24 See note 3.

25 Gatchina was the palace of Emperor Paul.

26 Leading members of the 'secret' committee set up by Alexander I at the beginning of his reign to consider the needs for reform. Hopes that the work of the committee would lead to constitutional changes were disappointed.

27 M. M. Speransky (1772-1839), a leading statesman in the reign of Alexander I. In the period 1809-12 he carried out a number of administrative reforms and prepared a draft plan for constitutional reform which was rejected as too radical. He was banished in 1812 and it was maliciously rumoured that he was in treasonable contact with French agents.

28 Elected organs of local government, introduced in 1864. The *zemstvo* and public court proceedings (introduced at the same time) were two major items in the reform programme of Alexander II.

29 N. M. Karamzin (1766-1826), a major figure in Russian literature and historiography. He was the leading representative of the Sentimental movement in Russia and was particularly well-known for his sentimental tales ('Poor Liza' and others).

30 In Bessarabia. The fortress of Khotin changed hands several times in the various Russo-Turkish wars of the eighteenth century. Here its capture by the Russians in 1739 seems to be in mind.

31 A pretender to the throne of Russia in the 'Time of Troubles' at the beginning of the seventeenth century. In 1608 he encamped his army at Tushino, a few miles from Moscow.

32 See note 2.

33 Winterhalter's was a well-known shop in St. Petersburg in the nineteenth century.

34 Russian political émigrés centred in London in the 1860s. Chief of these was Alexander Herzen, who published the influential revolutionary newspaper *The Bell*, which circulated illegally in Russia.

35 That is, the local commander of the Corps of Gendarmes, responsible for internal security – effectively, the local political police chief.

36 The Paleologues were the ruling dynasty during the last centuries of the Byzantine Empire. Russian rulers supported their claim to the imperial title by reference to the fact that Ivan III, the fifteenth-century grand-prince of Moscow, had married Zoë Paleologue, the niece of the last Byzantine emperor.

37 In the usage of Saltykov's day 'well-intentioned' meant 'loyal to the authorities'.

38 A reference to the suppression of the so-called 'potato riots' of peasants in the 1830s and 1840s. The peasants were protesting against the introduction of potatoes in place of their traditional crops.

39 A card game, the winner of which struck his opponent on the nose with his cards.

40 In times of famine Russian peasants used this plant for food.

41-42 The Musketeers (*streltsy*) were formed in the sixteenth century as a regular military force. Service was hereditary, and the Musketeers lived in special districts or suburbs. Their involvement in disputes over the succession brought about their suppression and disbandment by Peter the Great. The Cannoneers (*pushkari*) had a similar history.

43 An allusion to the notoriously extravagant tour of the new territories of Southern Russia on which Potemkin conducted Catherine the Great in 1787.

44 *Sevryuga* is a fish – the stellate sturgeon.

45 A well-known figure in Russian history. She played an important part in the affairs of Novgorod in the fifteenth century.

46 Borodavkin's Byzantine aspirations are associated particularly with the 'Greek project' of Potemkin in the 1780s, which aimed at expelling the Turks from Europe and establishing a kingdom of Dacia under Russian hegemony.

47 Lines from a poem by the Slavophile poet A.S. Khomyakov (1804-60) in which he dreams of pan-Slav unity. The Drava, Morava, and Sava are rivers in the Slavonic territories of central-southern Europe.

48 Saltykov wrote the *History of a Town* at the height of the railway boom in Russia. In his satires he makes frequent reference to the various commercial adventurers who sought government concessions to undertake the construction of new lines.

49 The reference is to Glinka's opera *Ruslan and Lyudmila*, based on the poem by Pushkin.

50 Prince of Kiev (d.972), noted for his military skill and many successful campaigns. He led a rigorous soldier's life and was killed in battle.

51 Baba Yaga is a witch in Russian folklore.

52 In Fourier's ideal scheme of social organization the co-operative community (phalanx) was to be based in a 'phalanstery'.

53 G. de Molinari (1819-1912), Belgian political economist and advocate of free trade; V. P. Bezobrazov (1828-89), Russian political economist.

54 See note 26.

55 In the figure of Negodyaev Saltykov hints at the harsh and capricious Emperor Paul, who was murdered in 1801 (cf. Negodyaev's 'fall' in 1802). Paul was a passionate militarist and his palace and estate at Gatchina were run on strict military lines. The irony of the 'democratic principles' of the place goes without saying.

56 Prince A. B. Kurakin, Russian ambassador in Paris in the period preceding Napoleon's invasion of Russia in 1812.

57 One of the early princes of Kiev. In 907 he besieged Constantinople, and two treaties he concluded with Byzantium fostered commerce between the two states.

58 Saltykov refers here to the so-called 'state' school of Russian historians. Representatives of this trend in Russian historiography, among the most notable of whom were B. I. Chicherin (1828-1904) and K. I. Kavelin (1818-85), considered that the exercise of monarchic and state power was the determining factor in shaping the course of national history.

59 Newspaper edited in Saltykov's time by the conservative M. N. Katkov (1818-87), one of Saltykov's most consistent political and journalistic opponents.

60 Prince Vladimir I of Kiev (d.1015), the christianizer of Russia.

61 Pagan deities of the Slavs. Perun was the god of thunder and rain; Volos the god of cattle.

62 D. V. Averkiev (1836-1905), a minor author and librettist.

63 French music-hall songs of Saltykov's own time.

64 A roisterous and unprintable Russian folk-song.

65 A French singer who appeared in St. Petersburg theatres in the 1860s.

66 An indirect hint at Alexander I's mistress, Marya Antonovna Naryshkina. The connection is made through the names Natalya Kirillovna, which were the forename and patronymic of an earlier well-known Princess Naryshkina (wife of Tsar Alexey Mikhailovich and mother of Peter the Great).

67 P. D. Boborykin (1836-1921) was a popular and prolific minor novelist. Saltykov wrote a hostile review of his novel *Evening Victim* (1868), criticizing its concern with 'nymphomania and priapism'.

68 Yarilo was the Slavonic god of the sun and fertility.

69 The term 'sounder of hearts' in Saltykov's usage commonly referred to police officials concerned with investigating the political reliability of individuals.

70 The whole episode of Grustilov and Pfeiffer's wife is clearly modelled on the relationship of Alexander I with the mystic Baroness Krüdener, whom he met at Heilbronn in 1815 and who for some time exercised a powerful influence on him, both personal and political.

71 A. F. Labzin (1766-1825), author and mystic. He was an important influence on Alexander I in the latter part of his reign.

72 Paramosha's appointment as inspector of schools can be linked with the appointment of the obscurantist officials Runich and Magnitsky (see note 82, below) as curators, respectively, of the St. Petersburg and Kazan educational districts.

73 Turkish fortress on the Black Sea, captured by the Russians in 1788.

74 N. N. Strakhov (1828-96), conservative publisher and critic; a political and journalistic opponent of Saltykov.

75 The Russian word *prokhvost*, translated here as 'punishment-orderly', has a semantic history which lends it a nice ambiguity. Its original meaning was 'master-at-arms' (on ships) or 'military policeman' (cf. its English cognate 'provost'), but later it came to mean 'sanitary orderly' and then to be used as a general term of vulgar abuse.

76 See note 50.

77 Cantonists were soldiers' sons, trained in military schools from which they passed on to service in the army.

78 Archimandrite Photius (1792-1838), a religious fanatic and intriguer who exerted considerable influence on Alexander I in the last two years of his reign. He was closely associated with Count A. A. Arakcheev (1769-1834), at one time minister of war, who was the dominant figure in Russian government circles after 1815. Arakcheev was notorious for his reactionary policies and brutal methods, and it was he who instituted the system of military colonies of which Ugryum-Burcheev's 'fantasy' is in part a parody.

79 'Unwholesome passions' and 'unreliable elements' were phrases commonly used in official and conservative publicistic parlance of the 1860s to refer to radical ideas and their proponents.

80 Count Grigory Grigorevich Orlov (1734-83), for several years favourite of Catherine the Great. Grisha is a familiar form of the name Grigory.

81 Count A. M. Mamonov (1758-1803) and A. P. Ermolov (1754-1836), for brief periods also favourites of Catherine.

82 A transparent reference to D. P. Runich (1778-1860) and M. L. Magnitsky (1778-1855), reactionary officials noted particularly for their purging of the universities of St. Petersburg and Kazan (around 1820) and prescribing an obscurantist religious and political line in teaching.

83 Schools for boys intending to become army officers, famed for their harsh discipline.